Tolley's
Corporate Killing
A Managers' Guide to Legal Compliance

Whilst every care has been taken to ensure the accuracy of the contents of this work, no responsibility for loss occasioned to any person acting or refraining from action as a result of any statement in it can be accepted by the author or publisher.

Tolley's
Corporate Killing
A Managers' Guide to Legal Compliance

Michael G Welham

Members of the LexisNexis Group worldwide

United Kingdom	LexisNexis Butterworths Tolley, a Division of Reed Elsevier (UK) Ltd, 2 Addiscombe Road, CROYDON CR9 5AF
Argentina	LexisNexis Argentina, BUENOS AIRES
Australia	LexisNexis Butterworths, CHATSWOOD, New South Wales
Austria	LexisNexis Verlag ARD Orac GmbH & Co KG, VIENNA
Canada	LexisNexis Butterworths, MARKHAM, Ontario
Chile	LexisNexis Chile Ltda, SANTIAGO DE CHILE
Czech Republic	Nakladatelství Orac sro, PRAGUE
France	Editions du Juris-Classeur SA, PARIS
Hong Kong	LexisNexis Butterworths, HONG KONG
Hungary	HVG-Orac, BUDAPEST
India	LexisNexis Butterworths, NEW DELHI
Ireland	Butterworths (Ireland) Ltd, DUBLIN
Italy	Giuffrè Editore, MILAN
Malaysia	Malayan Law Journal Sdn Bhd, KUALA LUMPUR
New Zealand	Butterworths of New Zealand, WELLINGTON
Poland	Wydawnictwo Prawnicze LexisNexis, WARSAW
Singapore	LexisNexis Butterworths, SINGAPORE
South Africa	Butterworths SA, DURBAN
Switzerland	Stämpfli Verlag AG, BERNE
USA	LexisNexis, DAYTON, Ohio

A CIP Catalogue record for this book is available from the British Library.

ISBN 0 75451 066-2

Typeset by YHT Ltd

Printed in Great Britain by The Cromwell Press, Trowbridge, Wiltshire

Visit Butterworths LexisNexis *direct* at www.butterworths.com

Contents

Contents

Contents

About the Author

Michael G Welham, MPhil, MSc, Dip OHSM, Dip Law, FIOSH, RSP, FIIRSM, is a health and safety professional, employed by the Health and Safety Executive. He has working experience of investigating and prosecuting individual and corporate manslaughter at work cases. He has undertaken academic research and presented papers on the subject of corporate killing representing the HSE at conferences and seminars. He is a magistrate and lectures on health and safety law at the Norwich Law School, University of East Anglia. He is reading for an LLM in Corporate Crime and Punishment at the University of East Anglia.

The views and opinions expressed within this book are as a result of continued independent research into manslaughter at work and do not reflect those of either the HSE or the Judiciary. While every care has been taken in the writing and editing of this book readers should be aware that only Acts of Parliament and Statutory Instruments have the force of law, and only the courts can authoritatively interpret the law.

The author wishes to thank Professor Ian Smith, Norwich Law School, University of East Anglia for his continued support.

Preface

The Government produced a draft bill in *Reforming the Law on Involuntary Manslaughter: The Governments Proposals May 2000* and this provides the basis of the books review of the proposed new laws. At the time of writing there is no parliamentary time identified for the new bill however, the government is committed to its introduction and both public and judiciary demands for the corporate and individual offences remains a high priority.

The proposed new law of corporate killing, reckless killing, killing by gross carelessness and killing where the intention is to cause less serious injury, is probably the most important development in health and safety criminal sanctions since the introduction of the *Health and Safety at Work etc Act 1974*. At this important time there will be many questions as to how the new law will affect organisations, those that manage them, those who work for them and those who are not employed but are affected by an organisation's activities. This book is intended for directors, executives, employers, company secretaries, managers, supervisors, safety officers, trade unionists, lawyers as well as the general public.

It is anticipated that the new law will encompass undertakings such as schools, hospitals, trusts, partnerships, the self employed as well as incorporated and unincorporated organisations. The objective of this book is to provide important information for the management of any undertaking that could be affected by the proposed new law. There is a need for management to understand the complexities of corporate and individual manslaughter and the dramatic change there will be with the new corporate killing and the individual offences.

Involuntary manslaughter is the unlawful killing of a human being without malice aforethought, where D did an act and A died as a result of the act but D did not intend to kill A. This meant that for there to be corporate gross negligence, an individual had to be identified as being a controlling mind of the organisation. The individual must have owed a duty of care and there needed to be evidence to show that the duty has been breached and as a result there was a death. This was the difficulty that the law faced when trying to fit all of the elements together to prove a manslaughter at work case.

The implications for management with corporate killing are far reaching because instead of the manslaughter element, it will be a case of management failure and, it will be the degree of that failure that will determine the corporate and individual charges that could be laid. This clearly shows that the proposed new offences will be encompassed in the failure of health and safety management, rather than gross negligence action of an individual. It is worth considering that prosecutions resulting from the well used *HSWA 1974, ss 2* and *3* are generally the outcome of some form of management failure.

There are no easy solutions to what is a complex subject but an insight and understanding is offered by reviewing the cases that were successful and those that failed when prosecuted for corporate manslaughter. It is necessary to examine the rationale between the successful small company prosecutions where there was considered to be hands on management, against the prosecution failures of large companies, where the management are deemed to be remote from an incident. The important common thread with the cases that are examined is that of management failure to a greater or lesser degree. That is what management at boardroom level or its equivalent in an undertaking will need to understand and focus on. This clearly promotes the fact that ownership of health and safety is at the highest level of management in every undertaking. Responsible management will not want to be placed in a situation of being prosecuted for either corporate or individual offences. Therefore, it is imperative that health and safety is adopted as an integral part of an organisations' day-to-day activities and culture and it is not an after thought, or considered an unnecessary expense.

The law on health and safety at work is evolving all the time with new regulations and codes of practice being introduced and updated, and it is not an acceptable defence to plead ignorance of the law. The management of every undertaking can take suitable and sufficient steps to manage health and safety in the same way that they manage other aspects of the business. To aid management there is a veritable mountain of books and documents, both official and unofficial relating to the management of health and safety. They range from technical academic editions to practical hands on material all providing information for a diverse range of industries and businesses.

Organisations differ in size, location, type and management structure, and they will involve a range of hazards from very low to very high, providing a wide range of risks that have to be managed. It follows that the law pertaining to health and safety can also be complex and may not be readily understood by management, after all it is but one tool in the management toolbox. The senior management of many undertakings will argue that it is not financially viable to employ a competent health and safety professional. However, that does not preclude utilising the services of a health and safety consultant, providing that person is competent. This means that the consultant will need to be member of a professional organisation and hold a position such as a corporate member of the Institution of Safety and Health (IOSH) and most importantly, is a Registered Safety Practitioner with IOSH, where competence can be established and verified.

No matter what the size of an undertaking, from multinational to self-employed person, the law of health and safety applies. It is a matter for those who create the risk to manage the risk, and failure to do so can result in criminal sanctions. It has been argued that health and safety crimes are not real crimes and do not receive appropriate sanctions from the courts, but there are charges for all health and safety prosecutions. The Magistrates' Association has issued guidelines to assist magistrates sitting on health and safety cases. The information includes guidance on determining the seriousness of the offence, the failure by management to control risks, the degree of negligence by the company and its officers or individuals. magistrates are directed to sentence realistically, with consideration given to sending the case to the Crown Court for sentencing where fines are unlimited and custodial sentences are an option for some health and safety offences.

While details of the proposed offences are described along with the sanctions that can be administered, there is in its most basic form information about the management of health and safety that all undertakings should adopt. While having systems in place is no guarantee that criminal sanctions will not be imposed, a judge and a jury will, when there have been deaths at or caused by work activities, take the level of positive health and safety management into consideration. The number of manslaughter at work cases progressed have been few, but there is evidence that there will be a substantial increase in corporate killing prosecutions.

M G Welham 2002

Foreword

Health and safety law is an area that most people in industry or business know exists, but detailed understanding has often been lacking, even among lawyers. A spate of disasters, starting with the Zeebrugge ferry case and progressing through high-profile events such as the Lyme Bay canoeing disaster to the series of rail crashes in recent years have put the issues squarely before the public, who have often expressed dismay at the reaction of the law. Small cogs (such as the bosun in the Zeebrugge case) may incur criminal liability for the deaths, but the machines themselves (in the sense of the operating companies) have largely escaped such liability, due to the limitations on UK manslaughter laws which have hitherto been premised on individual liability, not corporate. Even in the odd case of corporate liability, it has been confined to small enterprises where there is more individual responsibility on 'The Owner'. The big battalions have tended to escape.

All that is to change with proposals not only for an offence of corporate killing through management failure, but also for the wholesale (and long overdue) reform of our manslaughter laws generally. The government has committed itself to these changes. The question is what they will mean in practice to employing organisations and those running them.

To say that this book is timely must be a major understatement even by English standards. I have known and worked with Mike Welham for some time now. He is exceptionally well placed to review this new area of law from the standpoint of the detailed proposals and also their likely practical impact. The new laws are set against the background of the existing law and levels of workplace deaths, and also in the context of general principles of management of health and safety. I can certainly recommend the book to all who are potentially affected. That is a lot of people.

Ian Smith, Barrister,
Clifford Chance Professor of Employment Law,
Norwich Law School, University of East Anglia.

1 Deaths at Work Legislation 2002

This chapter considers the following:

- The need for reform.

- A review of current health and safety legislation.

- Enforcement policy.

- Identification of problems with the existing law.

- The *Homicide Act 1957* and manslaughter at work.

Introduction

1.1   It took a number of disasters within a four-year period from 1985 to 1989 to really focus public attention on the total lack of corporate liability for deaths, said to be caused by boardroom failures, to provide sufficient priority to health and safety.

The first case occurred in 1985 when 49 people died in the Bradford City football stadium fire. The wooden stand caught fire, possibly as result of a cigarette being discarded in rubbish accumulated under the stand over a long period of time.

In 1987 there were two major tragedies, but it was the *Herald of Free Enterprise* which was to be the catalyst to push the failings in corporate liability to the forefront of public attention. The *Herald of Free Enterprise* capsized outside Zeebrugge harbour having sailed with its bow doors open. This allowed the sea to swamp the car deck making the ship unstable with the outcome that it capsized. The result was 154 passengers and 38 crew being killed. The company P&O European Ferries (Dover) Ltd, was charged with corporate manslaughter, but the case was dismissed.

In the second tragedy in 1987, 31 people died and 60 were injured after fire engulfed Kings Cross underground station. The cause was attributed to a discarded cigarette igniting waste that had accumulated under the escalators.

The following year, there were again two major tragedies. The Clapham train crash, which killed 37 and injured 500 people, resulted from two trains colliding outside Clapham Junction. In the same year, an explosion destroyed the Piper Alpha oil platform causing the deaths of 165 crew members.

In 1989 there were three tragedies. The Purley train crash caused the deaths of five and injuries to 88 passengers when a train driver ignored a red light and crashed into the back of another train. The dredger *Bowbelle* collision with the River Thames pleasure craft the *Marchioness* caused the deaths of 51 and injures to 80 passengers. Finally in that year the Hillsborough football stadium disaster caused the deaths of 95 and injuries to hundreds of spectators after a large number of people were allowed to enter the stadium at one time, in an uncontrolled manner.

Since that four-year period of disasters there have been other incidents with loss of life including the Paddington rail crash involving Great Western Trains. The fact remains however, that only two large companies have faced manslaughter charges, those being P&O European Ferries (Dover) Ltd and Great Western Trains Ltd and neither of these prosecution cases were successful. It has been identified that it is necessary to raise the stakes in fatal accidents at work where there has been negligence or failure of management to ensure the health and safety of those at work and those affected by those activities. The objective of the new offence of corporate killing is to enhance health and safety at work and provide sanctions that will have far reaching consequences for all organisations particularly those in control of them.

Lobby and action groups

1.2   Manslaughter at work is a topic of increasing public interest and in the wake of some of the major disasters there has been the formation of a number of action groups such as Disaster Action, Herald Families Association, Marchioness Action Group and other established organisations such as Victim Support, the Royal Society for the Prevention of Accidents and the Trade Union Congress. These groups, along with others, are seeking redress against the controlling minds of companies, such as directors and senior management, and provide the power lobby for the proposed offence of corporate killing.

G Slapper identifies the issue of public unrest in the current failures in the law of corporate manslaughter in an article in which he states:

> 'In January, the Piper Alpha Families and Survivors association discontinued their attempt to execute a private prosecution of manslaughter against the oil company Occidental. They were ultimately thwarted by a number of legal obstacles stemming from the fact that since the disaster in 1998, when 167 people died, the company has been sold and changed its name and there have been several significant changes in key personnel. Ivor Glogg, who lost his wife in the *Marchioness* disaster in August 1989, is bringing a private prosecution against South Coast Shipping Company Ltd of Canute, Southampton, owners of the *Bowbelle* and the four senior managers. In February, committal proceedings were adjourned for the third time in this case pending judicial review being instituted by the defendants. This case could become only the third trial ever involving a charge of corporate manslaughter but Mr Glogg, who has already spent £20,000 on this matter, has a difficult battle ahead of him as he confronts a corporate defendant which is a subsidiary of the public company Ready Mix Concrete. When an engagement of this sort becomes a war of attrition those who face corporate defendants are plainly prejudiced.'

(The Legal Regulation for Safety, *Health and Safety at Work*, April 1992).

Further evidence of concern about the failing of corporate manslaughter is shown in an article in *Occupational Health* which states:

> 'In a recent letter to Phillip Oppenheim, minister for the Department of the Environment, Allan Black, the national officer for construction workers, commented on British Rail and Tilbury Douglas being fined only £25,000 for failing to meet safety standards which led to the death of two building workers ... The letter said:

> "This example is encouraging a lassez-faire attitude to the health and safety of workers. Non compliance with existing laws is allowing companies to get away with legalised manslaughter ...

Failure to force companies to comply with existing legislation ... petty fines on large corporations leaves employers with a greater freedom to kill."'

(A Funny Kind of Justice, *Hazards* 49, 1994/95, Hazards Publications).

G Howard reviews the subject of corporate manslaughter and poses the question 'why corporate liability?'

'There are some important arguments in favour of companies being prosecuted for corporate manslaughter. Fixing corporate liability is, in some cases, easier than prosecuting individual directors where there may be difficulty in determining which individuals are liable. Corporate liability ensures that the crime will not go unpunished and that a fine in proportion to the gravity of the offence may be imposed when it might be out of the means of the individuals concerned. Since the names of the officers will mean little to the general public, only a conviction of the corporation itself will serve to warn the public of the wrongful act which has been committed in its name.'

('Corporate Manslaughter – What Next?', *Occupational Health*, April 1992).

Lobby groups have evolved as a result of perceived failure of the enforcing and judicial systems to take to task those deemed responsible. They have progressed their causes through a variety of methods to obtain publicity such as that described by an article in the *South London Press* that describes the action of a London protest.

'A mass protest to remember those killed in accidents at work blocked traffic on Southwark Bridge ... Families of loved ones who had died and safety campaigners stood across the bridge ... Health and Safety Executive staff had to be evacuated from their headquarters ... Staff streamed out into Southwark Park street while irate motorists wanting to cross the river were diverted away by the police.'

('Memorial protest march to remember those killed in accidents at work', *South London Press*, 30 April 1999).

While some protest at a wide range of health and safety failings there are those who have specific concerns either with an individual or industry. The following involves a construction company,

4

which denied responsibility for the deaths of two employees who fell eight floors to their deaths. An article in the *South London Press* described support provided to the family:

'Their families were joined by dozens of members of lobby groups, the Construction Safety Campaign and the Joint Sites Committee ... the protesters picketed outside the court distributing leaflets demanding 'No More Workplace Deaths.'

('Company bosses deny safety rules failure', *South London Press*, 23 March 1999).

These are only two examples of action groups who seek more positive action for health and safety within companies and more accountability for the senior management when people die at or due to workplace failures.

Employers' legal obligations

1.3   Employers have an absolute duty under the *Health and Safety at Work etc Act 1974* (*HSWA 1974*) for the care of its employees and those not in its employment. Therefore, there is an obligation to provide a safe place and system of work.

HSWA 1974, s 2(1) states:

'It shall be the duty of every employer to ensure, so far as is reasonably practicable, the health, safety and welfare at work of all his employees.'

HSWA 1974, s 3(1) states:

'It shall be the duty of every employer to conduct his undertaking in such a way as to ensure, so far as reasonably practicable, that persons not in his employment who may be affected thereby are not thereby exposed to risks to their health and safety.'

This obligation is the responsibility of an employer and not connected to any liability that may arise in respect of injury caused to an employee by a fellow employee in the course of their employment. A breach of the employers obligation is not just negligence but is the employer's own negligence.

There are examples of case law which explain the general nature of the employer's obligation as in the civil law case *Wilson and Clyde Coal Co Ltd v English [1937] 3 All ER 628*, where Lord Wright said.

' ... a duty rests on the employer and which is personal to the employer, to take reasonable care for the safety of his workmen, whether the employer be an individual, a firm, or a company, and whether or not the employer takes any share in the conduct of the operations.'

On the question of duty and liability reference can be made to the case of *Donoghue v Stevenson [1932] AC 562* where Lord Atkin said:

'The duty which is common to all cases where liability is established must logically be based upon some element common to the cases where it is found to exist ... There must be, and is, some general conception of relations giving rise to a duty of care, of which the particular cases found in the books are but instances ... You must take reasonable care to avoid acts or omissions which you reasonably foresee would be likely to injure your neighbour. Who then, in law is my neighbour? The answer seems to be – persons who are so closely and directly affected by my act that I ought reasonably to have them in contemplation as being so affected when I am directing my mind to the acts or omissions which are called in question.'

J Munkman, *Employers' Liability at Common Law*, (11th edn), explains that this passage does not determine a finite or general rule of law, but provides a guide which, is followed in deciding whether a duty of care exists, unless there is good reason to the contrary.

It can be considered that there are three main areas encompassing a duty of care which are were the dictum of Scott in the case of *Vaughan v Ropner & Co Ltd (1947) 80 LL L Rep 119*, when he said:

'The three main duties [of the employer] are (1) to provide proper premises in which, and proper plant and appliances by means of which, the workman's duty is to be performed; (2) to maintain premises, plant and apparatus in a proper condition; (3) to establish and enforce a proper system of working.'

It follows that in order that a corporation can undertake its obligations of a *duty of care* there needs to be a corporate system for health and safety. This system is developed, adopted and driven by senior management and encompasses all aspects of the undertaking with the objective of providing safe methods of working. This topic is explored in detail in CHAPTER 10.

The Health and Safety Commission

1.4 The aims of the Health and Safety Commission (HSC) are to protect the health, safety and welfare of employees and to safeguard others, principally the public, who may be exposed to risks from work activity. This statement is the foundation which the HSC expects the enforcing authorities to follow, and it is the task of the authorities to secure compliance with the law. Health and Safety Inspectors of the Health and Safety Executive (HSE) and Local Authority Environmental Health Officers (EHO's) generally deal with those to whom the law applies, the employer, self-employed, employees and others. They also deal with members of the public who may seek information or wish to raise issues of concerns over safety. Inspectors offer information, advice and support and where necessary they have enforcement powers which include:

- Improvement Notices where a contravention needs to be remedied;

- Prohibition Notices where there is a risk of serious personal injury;

- withdrawal of approvals;

- variations of licences or condition, or exemptions; or

- ultimately prosecution.

Enforcement principles

1.5 The enforcement of health and safety law is structured upon the principles of proportionality in applying the law and securing compliance, consistency of approach, the targeting of enforcement action and transparency about how the regulator operates and what those who are regulated may expect.

Proportionality

1.6 Proportionality is described as the relating of enforcement action to the risks. The concept is that those the law protects and those to whom the duty applies, expect that action taken by the enforcing authorities to achieve compliance with the law should be proportionate to any risks to health and safety as well as the seriousness of any breach of those duties. In general, the concept of proportionality is built into the regulatory system through the principal of *so far as is reasonably practicable*. The decision on what is reasonably practicable to control risks involves those who create the risks, the employer and those who enforce the law. In situations where there is no agreement on what is reasonably practicable the final determination can be made by the courts.

Consistency

1.7   Consistency of approach is not a rigid structure but means that inspectors take a similar approach in similar circumstances to achieve similar ends. This derives from the expectation that those managing risks similar to others expect consistency from the enforcing authorities in their advice, Enforcement Notices and decisions on whether to prosecute. This is not a simple matter as inspectors are faced with numerous diverse situations, including the level of hazard, the attitude and competence of management, accident history and antecedence will vary between organisations. The decision on enforcement action is a matter of judgement and enforcers must exercise discretion.

Transparency

1.8   Transparency describes the means by which the enforcing authorities help those to whom the law applies understand what is expected of them and what they in turn should expect from the enforcing authorities. It also means making clear not only what has to be done but making it clear what they should not do. This means distinguishing between what the law requires to be done which is compulsory and advice or guidance about what is desirable but not compulsory.

Targeting

1.9   Targeting is the prioritising of enforcement officers' visits focusing on those whose activities give rise to the most serious risks or where hazards are not very well controlled. The focus is on those who are responsible for the risk and are best placed to control it. This applies to employers, manufacturers, suppliers and others.

Prosecution

1.10 The HSC expects that enforcing authorities will consider prosecution in the following situtations:

- It is appropriate in the circumstances as a way to draw attention to the need for compliance with the law and maintenance of standards required by law, especially where there would be a normal expectation that a prosecution would be taken or where, through the conviction of offenders, others may be deterred from similar failures to comply with the law.

- There is judged to have been potential for considerable harm arising from a breach.

- The gravity of the offence, taken together with the general record and approach of the offender warrants it, for example apparent reckless disregard for standards, repeated breaches, and persistently poor standards.

The decision to prosecute must also take account of the criteria set down in the Code for Crown Prosecutors, and in Scotland by the procurator fiscal as published in the *Crown Office and Procurator Fiscal Service's Annual Report 1992/93*, for example, evidence and public interest tests.

Death at work

1.11 Where there has been a breach of the law resulting in a work-related death, the enforcing authorities need to consider whether the circumstances surrounding the death might justify a manslaughter prosecution (culpable homicide in Scotland). Enforcing authorities will liase with the police, coroners and Crown Prosecution Service (CPS). If there is evidence suggesting manslaughter the police will take the lead and investigate in co operation with health and safety enforcement officers. If the police and CPS decide that there is insufficient evidence to proceed with a prosecution for manslaughter the health and safety enforcing authorities should prosecute or recommend prosecution if it is appropriate. In Scotland the responsibility for investigating sudden or suspicious deaths rests with the procurator fiscal.

Enforcement process

1.12   Inspectors of the HSE have to secure and maintain compliance with the law in situations where there is serious risk of injury. They also have to deal with the aftermath of an accident. In both situations the HSE have to make decisions about enforcement action and what level of action is required in a given circumstance. As part of the HSE's evolving quality assurance policy an Enforcement Management Model (EMM) has been developed which provides a framework to assist inspectors make informed enforcement decisions proportionate to the risks or seriousness of any breach and help ensure consistency. The EMM is designed to help meet the objectives of the HSC's enforcement policy. It is not a rigid system, as the circumstances of every investigation varies, but it is an aid that assists inspectors in determining enforcement action and in reaching a decision as to a course of action which includes the Issue of Notices or prosecution. In addition to the EMM inspectors have to take into account, if a prosecution is considered, whether the case is in the public interest and whether there is a reasonable chance of a successful conviction. In the latter case it may depend upon the situation whether there is sufficient evidence.

The majority of health and safety prosecution cases are heard in the magistrates court and generally involve a guilty plea. Fines are limited in the magistrates court (see CHAPTER 8) and if having heard the case the court decide that their powers are insufficient they can send the case to the Crown Court for sentencing, where fines are unlimited. Magistrates now have guidelines when dealing with health and safety cases. Prosecution of serious cases are transferred to the Crown Court for trial before a judge and jury. There does not have to be a fatality, but the case would be a serious breach of legislation and risk of harm to people. Crown Court fines are unlimited and the judge may be able to impose a custodial sentence on the defendant. All cases of manslaughter are heard in the Crown Court as the outcome of a guilty verdict should result in a custodial sentence and this will apply to cases brought under the offence of corporate killing.

Enforcement pyramid

1.13   The enforcement options available to HSE Inspectors and Local Authority Environmental Health Officers (EHO's) are portrayed in figure 1.1 below. The pyramid shape is used because it depicts the fact that the most common form of enforcement action used by inspectors are Improvement and Prohibition Notices and therefore form the base of the pyramid shape. As the shape narrows, so does the degree of prosecution activity, with manslaughter at the peak. The first level in the pyramid and the largest section in obtaining compliance with the law is through the Improvement Notice. These Notices are issued against a specific breach of health and safety law and require the failing to be rectified in a defined time period. The Improvement Notice is not seen as a punishment but as a legally binding agreement for companies to comply with legislation. The next level is the Prohibition Notice which is issued by an inspector where there is considered to be danger of serious injury or death to an employee, or those affected by the activities of the company or individual. There is a formal system for appealing against either an Improvement or Prohibition Notice by the recipient but failure to comply with the Notice can result in prosecution with the possibility of imprisonment. If the recipient of a Notice has future enforcement action taken and it

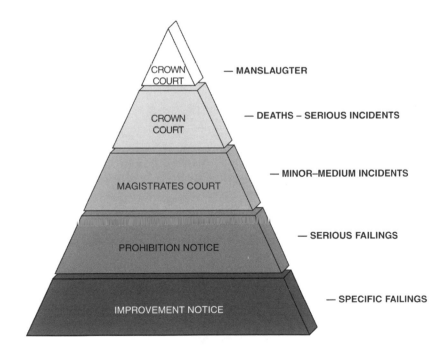

Figure 1.1: Enforcement Pyramid

results in a prosecution then the details of the Notice can be produced as the defendant's antecedence. The levels of action involve prosecutions both in the magistrates' and Crown Court and as the pyramid shape shows, the number of prosecutions reduce, the more serious the offence.

Cases referred to the CPS

1.14   All health and safety cases that are considered to be so serious that there could be charges of manslaughter are referred to the police, coroner and ultimately the CPS for review. The CPS has its own guidelines to follow and will need to have sufficient evidence available to make a judgement. Few cases are progressed, as there may be not be a realistic prospect of conviction, as the law of manslaughter requires that an individual is identified. With the offence of corporate killing proposed, research was undertaken by the HSE in 2000 to review the outcome of cases involving death at work that were submitted to the CPS for consideration to progress manslaughter prosecutions. These cases were considered under the then homicide law pertaining to manslaughter. The study identified 125 cases covering the period April 1992 to March 2000 which includes both companies and individuals. Of the 125 cases con-

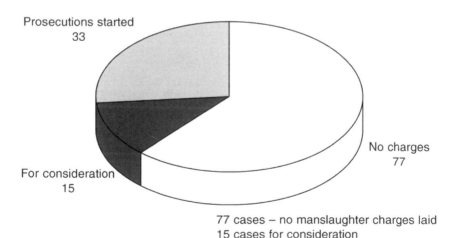

77 cases – no manslaughter charges laid
15 cases for consideration
33 cases – prosecutions started by CPS

Figure 1.2: Cases referred to the CPS to consider for possible manslaughter charges (April 1992 to March 2000)

sidered only 33 prosecutions were commenced while 15 cases were under consideration for the CPS to review the evidence and likelihood of success. There were 77 cases where the CPS declined to proceed to prosecution and the case would have been returned to the HSE or Local Authority for prosecution under health and safety legislation (see figure 1.2).

Prosecutions started by the CPS

1.15   Of the 33 prosecution cases commenced by the CPS, eight cases resulted in guilty verdicts, eight resulted in not guilty verdicts and the remaining 13 were either withdrawn or dismissed (see figure 1.3). This clearly shows the difficulties faced by the regulating and prosecuting authorities in taking manslaughter cases, when the vast majority of cases are unsuccessful. While prosecuting corporations for gross negligence manslaughter within the *Homicide Act 1957* has been virtually impossible, the proposed offence of corporate killing focuses not on what one individual does to another to cause death, but on management failure. Where an individual can be identified they can be charged with reckless killing, killing by gross carelessness or killing where the intention was to cause minor injury under the proposed legislation.

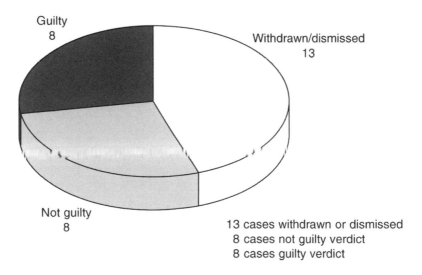

Guilty
8

Withdrawn/dismissed
13

Not guilty
8

13 cases withdrawn or dismissed
8 cases not guilty verdict
8 cases guilty verdict

Figure 1.3: 33 Prosecutions started by the CPS (April 1992 to March 2000)

HSE prosecutions – the new test

1.16 Currently the CPS has to evaluate potential cases based upon manslaughter within the *Homicide Act 1957* for an action of gross negligence that requires the identification of a 'guilty mind' and in the case of a corporation, a 'controlling mind'. Corporate killing is based upon management failure as being the fault element for cause of death. To evaluate the number of potential corporate killings cases the HSE reviewed 52 case in the period 1996 to 1998 that were prosecuted by the HSE under the *HSWA 1974*. Each case was evaluated against the draft *Corporate Killing Bill* – to determine, if in retrospect and based upon the investigation outcomes, the case would have been submitted for prosecution as a corporate killing case. Of the 52 cases, 21 cases would have been elevated from *HSWA 1974* charges to that of corporate killing while 29 were deemed not to meet the new standard and would remain as *HSWA 1974* charges. Two cases were examined where there was no decision either way, (see figure 1.4).

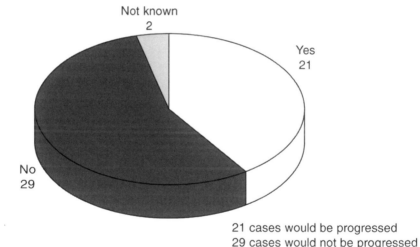

Not known
2

Yes
21

No
29

21 cases would be progressed
29 cases would not be progressed
2 cases were undecided

Figure 1.4: 52 prosecutions for deaths at work 1996 to 1998 reviewed under the new test

The outcome from this small but significant piece of research is that while currently few cases proceed to manslaughter, under the offence of corporate killing, almost half the cases would be upgraded to the serious offence. This would mean a potentially significant increase in deaths at work manslaughter prosecutions, albeit by another name. The most important aspect would be that an individual would not have to be identified as being negligent as it would be based upon a management failure. Every death at work examined under *HSWA 1974* is to some degree a failure of management, but it is the level of seriousness and degree of negligence that will be examined.

The *Homicide Act 1957*

1.17   It is proposed that corporate killing will be an offence in English criminal law involving deaths at or due to work and will be an offence of homicide. It is not the intention to describe in detail the criminal law of homicide which encompasses murder and manslaughter, but to provide an overview of the key elements and their status in the current criminal law. The constituents of homicide are described by J C Smith as follows:

'The *actus reus* of murder and manslaughter is generally the same. It is the unlawful killing of any person 'under the Queen's Peace', the death following within a year and a day. It must be proved that the defendant caused the death of the deceased person. At common law homicide was committed only if the death occurred within a year and a day of the act of causing death. That rule was abolished by the *Law Reform (Year and a Day Rule) Act 1996*. If an act can be shown to be the cause of death, it may now be murder, or any other homicide offence, or suicide, however much time has elapsed between the act and the death. The Act, however, requires the consent of the Attorney General to the prosecution of any person for murder, manslaughter, infanticide, or any other offence of which the element is causing a person's death, or aiding and abetting suicide, (i) where the injury alleged to have caused the death was sustained more than three years before the death occurred or (ii) where the accused has previously been convicted of an offence committed in circumstances alleged to be connected with the death.'

(Smith and Hogan, *Criminal Law*, (9th edn), 1999).

Manslaughter is described by Smith as a complex crime of no less than five varieties. It covers three cases where the defendant kills with the fault required for murder but, because of the presence of a particular extenuating circumstance recognised by law, the offence is reduced to manslaughter. These cases are traditionally known as *voluntary manslaughter*. The other cases are *involuntary manslaughter* and consist of homicides committed with a fault element less than that required for murder but recognised by the common law as sufficient to find liability for homicide. It should be emphasised that there is only one offence. Whether the defendant is convicted of the voluntary or involuntary variety, he is convicted simply of manslaughter. A life sentence is mandatory for murder but for manslaughter the maximum is life but there is no minimum. It is an offence which may be committed with a wide variety of culpability and sometimes may be properly dealt with by a fine or a conditional or absolute discharge. The law might be summarised as follows:

'A person is guilty of manslaughter where:

- He kills or is a party to the killing of another with the fault required for murder but he acted:

  - under diminished responsibility *(Homicide Act 1957, s 2)*

  - under provocation *(Homicide Act 1957, s 3)*;

  - in pursuance of a suicide pact *(Homicide Act 1957, s 4)*;

- he is not guilty of murder by reason only of the fact that, because of voluntary intoxication, he lacked the fault required; or

- he kills another:

  - by an unlawful and dangerous act; or

  - being (a) grossly negligent as to death or (b) reckless (in the Cunningham sense) as to the death or serious harm; or, possibly; (c) grossly negligent as to serious bodily harm or; (d) reckless as to any bodily harm.'

(Smith and Hogan, *Criminal Law*, (9th edn), 1999).

A person cannot ordinarily be found guilty of a serious criminal offence unless two elements are present: the *actus reus* or guilty act and the *mens rea* or guilty mind. A wrongful act on its own therefore cannot usually be criminal unless the wrongful state of mind required for that offence is also present. The *mens rea* for murder is malice aforethought, and that term has been made clearer through a House of Lords decision. The case of *R v Moloney [1985] AC 905* involved a soldier who became involved in a heated discussion with his stepfather about guns. The stepfather goaded him that he would not dare to fire a live bullet. At that point Moloney fired a loaded gun at him and killed him. The case focused on the definition of malice aforethought and the House of Lords determined that nothing less than the intention to kill or cause grievous bodily harm would constitute malice aforethought.

Where there has been a death, but the key element of intent is missing, the offence is reduced to that of manslaughter. There are two categories of manslaughter: voluntary and involuntary manslaughter. In the case of voluntary manslaughter the defendant has the *mens rea* and *actus reus* for murder but there were circumstances that offered some form of excuse for his conduct. On this basis, murder can be reduced to manslaughter on the grounds of provocation or diminished responsibility. These two manslaughter options are not offences in themselves but form a partial defence to murder. Involuntary manslaughter is unlawful homicide, but the *mens rea* for murder is not present. This is further divided into unlawful act manslaughter and manslaughter by gross negligence or recklessness. Unlawful act manslaughter is determined by an unlawful act (*R v Church [1965] 2 All ER 72*) which a reasonable person would realise creates a risk of injury, and death results. The defendant need not foresee the risk of death, nor need it be reasonably foreseeable.

Manslaughter by gross negligence occurs where there is an act or omission of negligence that goes beyond the civil law concept of negligence. The act or omission would be so extreme that criminal liability would be the outcome. The determination of the degree of negligence is a matter of legal process through the courts *R v Adomako [1994] 3 All ER 79*. It will be a matter for the jury to determine the degree of negligence to identify that there was gross negligence.

Gross negligence determined in *R v Bateman (1925) 19 Cr App R 8* based upon the existence of a duty of care owed by the defendant to the victim, breach of which has resulted in death, in circumstances of negligence that shows a disregard for the life and safety of others as to be deserving of a criminal sanction. In *R v Adomoko*, Mackay LC ruled that the test for gross negligence:

' ... will depend on the seriousness of the duty, in all the circumstances in which the defendant was placed when it occurred. The jury will have to consider whether the extent to which the defendants conduct departed from the proper standard of care incumbent upon him, involving as it must have done, a risk of death to the patient, was such that it should be judged criminal.'

The *actus reus* and *mens rea* of a corporation are raised by C M V Clarkson who states:

'The criminal law was developed as a mechanism for responding to individual wrongdoing. Individuals can be held responsible and blamed for their actions. Stigmatic punishment can be used to mark the appropriate degree of censure. Particularly when dealing with crimes involving *mens rea*, such individualistic notions of responsibility do not naturally encompass artificial organisations and could only be applied by humanising companies in the sense of breaking them down, metaphorically, into their underlying human components to see if there was an individual within the company who had committed the *actus reus* of a crime with the appropriate *mens rea*. This individual must be sufficiently important in the corporate structure to be said to represent the company's directing mind and will, and for his or her acts to be identified with the company itself; in such circumstances could be directly criminally liable (as well as the individual). This identification doctrine became established and the main route to the imposition of corporate liability, at least for crimes involving proof of *mens rea*.'

('Kicking Corporate Bodies and Damning Their Souls' (1996) 59 MLR 4).

There are reforms proposed in *Legislating the Criminal Code: Involuntary Manslaughter* (Law Com no 237), where there are recommendations to abolish the offence of unlawful act manslaughter. That would leave the offence of manslaughter by subjective recklessness, causing the death of another by being subjectively reckless as to whether death or serious injury occurred. The Law Commission leaves open the case for a separate category on manslaughter by gross negligence.

Manslaughter at work

1.18   There is no offence in law for corporate manslaughter and it is a term that has evolved where those at the highest level of the organisation are grossly negligent and while they are charged with manslaughter, they are considered to be the embodiment of the organisation and therefore constitute corporate manslaughter. This is described in the Law Commission Report, *Legislating the Criminal Code: Involuntary Manslaughter* (Law Com no 237) where there has to have been gross negligence on behalf of individual defendants who could be *identified* with the company and who are deemed to be the *controlling mind* who would themselves be guilty of manslaughter. In some cases it may be employees who are killed while in others it is members of the public. All have the common thread in that there have been serious failings in the management of health and safety. The *HSWA 1974* determines that it is the duty of the employer, in other words the board of directors of a company, to ensure the health and safety of those who are employed as well as those who are not employed but affected by their activities.

To meet these obligations, corporations must provide a health and safety policy outlining the companies standards and objectives with regard to health and safety. That policy must be adopted and signed by the most senior person of the company. Even if this has been done, the argument is made that directors do not have *hands on control* of the company and therefore cannot be reasonably liable for any failings within the company. For example it was argued that the managing director of P&O European Ferries, who at the time of the *Herald of Free Enterprise* disaster was not aboard the vessel and therefore, could not be liable for what went wrong. On the other hand in the case of Peter Kite and the Lyme Bay Canoe Tragedy (*R v Kite and OLL Ltd (1994) (Unreported)*) and the case of Alan Jackson, (*Jackson and Jackson Transport and English Brothers*) it was argued that, although they were directors, because they were operating in a *hands on manner* they, had first hand knowledge of the situation. It followed that they were reckless in that they did nothing to eliminate or reduce the risks to employees and those not employed, but affected by the activities of the business.

This means that small one-man type companies can be held accountable whilst, in large corporations, the controlling minds of the company can hide behind the remoteness of their positions. This is the case even though they may have had knowledge of failings of safety within their organisations. Therefore, because there is no specific offence of corporate manslaughter it has proved difficult, if not impossible, to identify an individual within a large corporation who had the direct responsibility for the management of health and safety.

The case for corporate culpability is made by C M V Clarkson who states:

'The Law Commission's proposed general test for the offence of killing by gross carelessness can easily be applied to companies The issue would be whether the risks would have been obvious to a reasonable corporation in that position and whether the corporation had the capacity to appreciate the risks. Of course, this latter requirement that the company have the capacity to appreciate risks will be of little significance in practice because a company, by definition, will necessarily have this capacity if the risks are obvious. However, it is important, if corporate killings are to be condemned appropriately, that liability be limited not only to those cases where the company's conduct fell far below what could reasonably be expected, but also to cases where the risks would have been obvious to other companies in the same situation. Application of the same test to both individuals and companies will serve to emphasise that corporate offences are not "poor cousins" of crimes committed by individuals ... The Council of Europe has proposed that whenever a company's activities or those of its employees lead to a prohibited harm, the company should be *prima facie* liable; the evidential burden would then switch to the company itself to prove that it had a safe system that could not be faulted.'

('Kicking Corporate Bodies and Damning Their Souls' (1996) 59 MLR 4).

The issues raised by C M V Clarkson show that the case for corporate culpability is not just a matter for domestic law but also of European law.

Manslaughter of individuals

1.19   Prosecutions of individuals for manslaughter at or due to work have been far more successful. The reason is simply that an individual can easily be identified. Although a number of cases of individuals prosecuted for manslaughter at or due to work are increasing, emphasis has been placed upon specific groups such as gas fitters and landlords, the latter cutting corners to get a cheap job particularly in low cost student accommodation. Prosecutions were brought against both parties and in some cases terms of imprisonment imposed on those found guilty. There are a number of cases discussed in the following chapters where individuals, albeit as directors were found guilty and received custodial sentences. It will be noted that in a number of cases the term of imprisonment was suspended for a defined period, generally two years. What this means is that the defendant does not get punished for the crime at the time sentence is passed however, if that defendant commits another offence of any description the original offence can be punished as well as any sanction for the new offence. The two offences do not have to be of a similar nature or connected.

Corporate manslaughter

in favour of no

1.20   Those campaigning for manslaughter at work prosecutions believe that it is not legal difficulties that result in failure to bring prosecutions but a lack of will by the HSE, Police, CPS and the judicial system to identify companies which endanger their employees. They also believe only the threat and use of prison sentences for company directors will offer an adequate deterrent. Fines for corporate manslaughter may not be significantly higher than fines for offences under Health and Safety at Work legislation, which are widely regarded as inadequate.

There are a number of elements that are considered to be the key ingredients of a corporate manslaughter case, which if not adopted, highlight failure within a corporation, but if they are adopted, offer a defence against the prosecution case or mitigation in the event of a successful prosecution. Within an organisation there has to be an individual who had direct involvement in the failure that caused the death and can be *identified* as having had involvement. The person who is identified must be a *controlling or directing mind* within the organisation in that they are of sufficient standing to control what happens or direct an activity. This would normally mean a director, executive or a person of similar standing.

Identification and controlling mind

1.21   The *identification* and *corporate culpability* aspects are issues that are more readily identifiable within a small company with a single director, where the blame can be squarely put on that individual. This is evidenced by the successful prosecutions for corporate and individual manslaughter in two such cases (examples of cases or they outlined above). However, that process has not been applied to larger corporations, where the culpability of directors is considered to be remote from the cause of death because nobody has been identified and therefore there is no case to answer. It is with the larger corporations that the failure to achieve a successful outcome arises and draws upon public disquiet, and the lack of blame being placed on directors when people die at or through work. The public see blame being placed upon employees when the *controlling minds* of the corporation have disregard for safety and health.

In 1987 the decision of a coroner (who had held that a corporation could not be indicted for manslaughter) was challenged in an application for judicial review. The issue was not fully argued, but Bingham J saw no reason in principle why such a charge could not be established and was tentatively of the opinion that an indictment would lie.

The same question was argued in depth in 1990 for the case against P&O European Ferries (Dover) Ltd. In that case Mr Turner J thoroughly reviewed the authorities (including some in other jurisdictions) and came to the conclusion that an indictment for manslaughter would lie today against a corporation.

Turner J noted that in the *R v Birmingham and Gloucester Railway Co (1842) 3 QB 223* and *R v Great North of England Railway Co (1846) 9 QB 315* cases, while it had been established that an indictment could lie against a corporation, it was said that a corporation could not be indicated for any offence involving personal violence. This was based on the grounds that a corporation had no social duties; it could not suffer from a *corrupt mind,* as natural persons could. This was identified in the case of *R v Cory Bros & Co [1927] 1 KB 810,* where C Wells quotes Finlay J who felt bound by the authorities to hold that:

> '... an indictment will not lie against a corporation either for a felony or a misdemeanour involving violence, on the ground that *mens rea* could not be present in the case of an artificial entity like a corporation.'

> (*Corporations and Criminal Responsibility,* (1st edn, 1993), Oxford University Press).

Turner J rejected the arguments that these understandings of the law demonstrated that a corporation could not be indicted for manslaughter. He considered in detail the subsequent authorities that had introduced and developed the principle of *identification.* It was this principal that had transformed corporate liability because it *identified* the corporation with the state of mind and actions of one of its controlling officers, and it became possible to impute *mens rea* to a corporation and so to convict it of an offence requiring a mental element.

Aggregation

1.22 The ruling by Turner J that an indictment for manslaughter could lie against P&O European Ferries (Dover) Ltd ultimately failed. The judge directed the jury that there was no evidence available that would allow them to properly convict six of the eight defendants, including the company of manslaughter. The principal basis of this decision was that to establish a manslaughter case against the company, one of the individual defendants who could meet the *identification* principle within the company would have himself to be guilty of manslaughter. There was no such evidence to convict any of the individuals, the case against the company had to fail. As part of the decision-making process, Turner J ruled against the adoption of the aggregation principle. Had aggregation been allowed it would have enabled the faults of a number of individual defendants to establish a mental element of manslaughter, so that when combined they created a sufficiently high level of fault that the company could have been convicted of manslaughter.

The aggregation principle is not new and was raised but not resolved in *R v H M Coroner for East Kent ex p Spooner (1989) 88 Cr App R 10* where Judge Bingham ruled:

> 'Whether the defendant is a corporation or a personal defendant, the ingredients of manslaughter must be established by proving the necessary *mens rea* and *actus reus* of manslaughter against it or him by evidence properly to be relied on against it or him. A case against a personal defendant cannot be fortified by evidence against another defendant. The case against a corporation can only be properly addressed to showing guilt of the corporation as such.'

However, Sir John Smith in *Smith and Hogan: Criminal Law*, (9th edn, 1999), Butterworths, draws attention to the fact that a company has a duty of care and if its operations fall far below the standard required then it is guilty of gross negligence. The review continues to determine that a series of minor failures by officers of the company might add up to a gross breach by the company of its duty of care. There is authority for such a doctrine in civil law and the concept of negligence is the same in the criminal law. He concludes that a corporation may possibly be liable for manslaughter on the aggregation principle, now that it is established that offences may be committed by gross negligence, and that may be established in the *P&O* case.

Summary

This chapter has examined the law that surrounded manslaughter at work and the role of the enforcing authorities in the process. It identifies the principal problems encountered and that to facilitate the need for an offence of manslaughter involving an undertaking, the law has to be changed. With the background explained, there have been a number of cases that involved gross negligence within corporations, but where no manslaughter prosecutions were forthcoming. A sample of cases are reviewed in the next chapter.

2 Workplace Accidents and Deaths

This chapter considers the following:

- High profile cases of deaths at work.

- Large companies versus small companies.

- Corporate manslaughter case failures.

- Workplace manslaughter cases against individuals.

- The case for and against an offence of corporate killing.

Introduction

2.1   The subject of deaths caused through work and the public demands for liability to be placed upon the directors is emphasised through the media in articles such as that by M Dewis when he states:

> 'The disasters which involved large numbers of the general public in the 1980's – Zeebrugge, Bradford City, Hillsborough, King's Cross – seemed to lead to a general consensus that criminal law should be able to reach up, identify and impose liability at a high corporate level. The obvious target is a board of directors, individual departmental directors with a safety brief and senior members of management.'
>
> ('Causing Death by Dangerous Management?' *Occupational Health*, July 1992).

Because there is no statutory offence of corporate manslaughter it has caused untold problems for the authorities that investigate and prosecute manslaughter at work cases. The problem has been well documented over a number of years with examples such as that recorded in the publication, *Hazards*:

'In October 1994, British Rail and Tilbury Douglas Construction were fined just £25,000 for breaches of criminal law including *serious mistakes by both defendants*. The case followed the deaths of two workers and hospitalisation of five others in the June 1992 collapse of St John's Bridge at a BR south London demolition site ... A year before British Rail and Tilbury Douglas Construction were fined following the accident which led to the deaths of (two) construction workers ... a jury at Southwark coroner's court had returned an *unlawful killing* verdict on both deaths .... After the inquest the case was referred to the Crown Prosecution Service (CPS) to see if manslaughter charges should be brought against the firms. The CPS would not recommend prosecution, saying there was insufficient evidence to secure a conviction ...'

('A Funny Kind of Justice', *Hazards* 49, 1994/5).

The article extends the problem further into the legal system when it identifies that:

'Judges are finding fault with a system that consistently lets employers off lightly. Judge George Bathurts-Norman, on sentencing Richard Baldwin, chairman and director of Baldwin Industrial Services Ltd of Slough, said, "If prison were an option open to me today you would be sent to prison". Baldwin was personally fined £20,000 and the company fined £70,000 after they pleaded guilty after failing to do safety tests on cranes and falsifying test certificates ...'

The prosecution of the Port Ramsgate case resulted in a record fine of £1.7 million, prompting P Dix to ask the question: 'What are the implications of such a fine for companies?' He provides his answer by stating:

'Unfortunately, the sentence is not designed to ensure that any faults within the companies' systems will be examined and rectified. The objective of sentencing a company found guilty of a breach of Health and Safety regulations should be to punish, to deter and perhaps most important of all, to rehabilitate. Under the present legislation, however, the only sentencing option for a judge is a monetary fine ... companies may very well be dismayed at the potential damage to their reputations, a fine does not have a rehabilitating effect ... the original charges brought against the companies do not reflect the seriousness of the crimes ... The companies could have been charged with the

26

same offences even if the walkway collapse had not caused any deaths or injuries. While we can accept that there was no intention to cause injury, a charge that reflects the level of harm done would be more appropriate.'

('Corporate Responsibility – the Victim's Perspective', *Safety and Health Practitioner*, June 1997).

The strength of the argument therefore, lies with the evidence that the current law places fatal and non fatal accidents under the same legislation with those considered to be more serious being submitted to the CPS for consideration for manslaughter. It is a requirement to prove gross negligence of an individual or individuals to obtain a conviction for manslaughter that causes the cases not to be progressed or to fail at court.

This is further clarified by J Gobert who stated:

'The problem with regulatory laws, as administered in practice, is not simply that they appear to undervalue the harm which has occurred. Sometimes that harm is the result of fortuitous circumstances, and prosecution would exaggerate the degree of the company's fault. The greater problem is that regulatory laws may not exert sufficient deterrent force to prevent violation. Most companies strive to maximise profits. The rational corporate brain trust might well reason that if the company violates the law and the violations are not discovered but all that is that the company comply in the future, nothing is lost. In the interim the company may have prospered, perhaps even to the point of eliminating a less unscrupulous rival; at worst it will have saved the costs of compliance for the period in which it was in violation of the law. If prosecuted, most commonly in a magistrates court, the company faces a maximum penalty of £5,000 [maximum penalty now £20,000], an amount which has been aptly compared to the equivalent of a parking fine for an individual. Thus there is little economic incentive for a company to obey the law, and as a rational profit maximises, it might seem economically foolish for it to do so.'

('Corporate Criminality: New Crimes for the Times', [1994] Crim LR, p 722).

Manslaughter cases resulting from deaths at or due to work pose a number of problems and M Wasik identifies the following points:

'When is it appropriate to proceed under health and safety regulations, and when to charge with manslaughter? ... The main problem in sentencing for manslaughter is the wide variety of factual situations in which the offence may be committed, across which the full range of penalties (from discharge to life imprisonment) is available ... In *Walker*, Lord Lane said that: Of all crimes in the calendar, the crime of manslaughter faces the sentencing judge with the greatest problem, because manslaughter ranges in its gravity from the borders of murder right down to those of accidental death.'

('Form and Function in the Law of Involuntary Manslaughter', [1994] Crim LR p 883).

While the courts have problems with sentencing, there is the situation of non-acceptance by management of the responsibility for health and safety within a corporation. Key issues are raised by M Allen who states:

'... the more diffuse the company structure, the more it devolves power to semi-autonomous managers, the easier it will be to avoid liability ... This is of particular importance given the increasing tendency of many organisations specifically to decentralise safety services. It is clearly in the interest of shrewd and unscrupulous management to do so ... If corporations perceive themselves to be at risk of prosecution for corporate manslaughter, an analogous process of decentralisation within the corporation might be developed to evade liability ... Priorities in hierarchical organisations like corporations are set predominantly from above. It is these priorities that determine the social context within the corporation's shop floor workers and the like made decisions about working practices. A climate of safety or unsafety may permeate the entire organisation but created at the highest level ... A key issue of the seriousness with which a corporation treats safety is the development of clearly delineated responsibilities for the scrutiny and revision of safety procedures.'

(Cases and Materials on Criminal Law, *Elliott and Wood*, Sweet and Maxwell, (7th edn), 1997).

Concerns about corporate manslaughter at work has permeated a wide range of areas, including the European Community, where C Oddy produced a written question:

'According to the UK Law Commission, there has been over 5,000 workplace deaths in the last ten years but only one criminal prosecution for manslaughter. Will the Commission consider an action programme under the White Paper on social policy to ensure that employers' liability for the deaths of employees is taken more seriously.'

An answer was provided by Mr Flynn replying on behalf of the Commission who stated:

'Penal law is within the competence of the member states. However, the Commission takes very seriously the need to ensure respect for Community law, and in particular health and safety legislation. Member States have to ensure that this is fully enforced through appropriate systems of control or sanctions which are effective in practice and have a deterrent value.'

(Official Journal of the European Communities No 179/23, *Written Question E – 447/95*, 22 February 1995).

There have been many high profile cases where there were deaths at or due to work involving negligence. A sample of those cases are examined below. The objective is to show the diverse types of work undertaken by the organisations as well as the type and level of negligence. Even though people died as a result of gross negligence none of the larger organisation have been convicted of corporate manslaughter. The successful prosecutions for manslaughter involved individuals and generally small organisations. This imbalance of culpability has been at the core of public disquiet and prompted the call for changes to the law.

The Marchioness case

2.2   A case that evoked much publicity for a corporate manslaughter prosecution was the sinking of the *Marchioness*, a Thames cruiser in August 1989 and raised the issue of public confidence as discussed in the Law Commission Report, *Legislating the Criminal Code: Involuntary Manslaughter* (Law Com no 237):

'The loss of 51 lives caused by the captain of the dredger *Bowbelle* not having a lookout. The vessel owners were not prosecuted. The captain was charged with the offence of failing to keep a proper lookout under the *Merchant Shipping Act, 1988, s 32*, but the case was dropped after two juries failed to agree. A private prosecution for manslaughter was then mounted against the owners; but the Divisional Court stated that the Director of Public Prosecutions might take over the proceedings and discontinue them or if it was too late to discontinue offer no evidence. It was thought that public confidence in industry and in enforcement bodies suffered if the perpetrator appeared to escape prosecution or conviction on a technicality rather than having his culpability tested in court by the same standards as that court would apply to a private individual on a charge of manslaughter.'

Neither the DPP or CPS progressed the case and it became the focus for the public of an example of the authorities failing to administer justice through the courts.

The report into the *Marchioness* tragedy was passed in March 2001 to the Director of Public Prosecution, David Calvert-Smith for review. The Deputy Prime Minister, John Prescott appointed the Right Hon Lord Justice Clarke to conduct the public enquiry into safety on the River Thames and the circumstances surrounding the sinking of the *Marchioness* pleasure cruiser. The report places responsibility on the skipper, the owners and the managers of the *Marchioness* and the Dredger *Bowbelle*.

There was criticism that there had not been a public enquiry earlier as it might have been possible to take disciplinary action against Captain Douglas Henderson, master of *Bowbelle*, under the *Merchant Shipping Act 1988*. It would be unfair to progress action now because Captain Henderson's civil rights determine that any action should take place within a *reasonable time*. The incident occurred in August 1989, and after eleven years there was little prospect of a successful prosecution.

David Holt Plastics Ltd case

2.3   The David Holt Plastics case did not involve corporate manslaughter but the prosecution for manslaughter of a director. A one-year term of imprisonment, suspended for two years was imposed upon Norman Holt, a company director of David Holt Plastics Ltd at Preston Crown Court on 1 December 1989. The prosecution followed an accident where George Kenyon, a 25-year old employee was killed in a plastics crumbling machine. In addition to the manslaughter prosecution, fines were imposed totalling £47,000. The company was fined £25,000 under the *Factories Act 1961, s 14* (FaA 1961) for failure to have the machine securely fenced. A further fine of £500 was imposed for failure to register the premises as a factory under the *FaA 1961, s 137*, and for breach of a Prohibition Notice a fine of £1,000 under *the HSWA, s 33*. David Holt, a director was charged under the *FaA 1961, s 14*, and fined £5,000 and for a second charge under *HSWA 1974, s 37*, there was a fine of £500. Norman Holt was charged under the *HSWA 1974, s 37* and fined £5,000.

The HSE investigated the accident and provided a report for the coroner who referred the matter to the CPS, who in turn asked the police in investigate the case as unlawful killing. The police investigation was based upon the HSE's investigation and resulted in the manslaughter charge and the charges under the *HSWA 1974*.

The *Pescado* case

2.4   Another case of management negligence involved the sinking of the trawler *Pescado* where Joseph O'Connor a director of the company Guideday, and Alan Ayres an investor in the company were charged with manslaughter and two charges of using forged instruments and documents knowing them to be false. However, the company was not charged with corporate manslaughter.

In an article, 'Crew of Novices Were Sent to their Deaths', *Daily Telegraph*, 17 January 1996, P Stokes stated that the basis of the case occurred when the fishing boat *Pescado* sailed from Falmouth on 25 February 1991 to fish for scallops. The boat carried an untrained, non-competent crew of five men and one woman. While in the course of its business the boat foundered with the loss of all six crew members and the boat operators Joseph O'Connor and Alan Ayres were charged with manslaughter. Joseph O'Connor, the managing operator was found guilty of manslaughter and jailed for three years while Alan Ayres was acquitted.

Guideday Limited owned the boat and the managing director Alan Ayres while the *controlling mind* of the company; he had no knowledge of vessel operations. Joseph O'Connor provided the fishing experience and was the managing agent and he knew what the safety regulations required but deliberately avoided complying with them. The defendants sent the *Pescado* and its inadequate crew to carry out a dangerous form of fishing in an unstable and unseaworthy sea vessel.

Key safety failings in the *Pescado* case were that the boat did not have a safety certificate, had inadequate equipment and means of alerting the rescue services. It was also claimed that the boat breached a number of safety regulations including only having one life raft instead of two. The life raft was provided by Joseph O'Connor from his garden having scraped the moss off it, before lashing it to the railings of the boat. There was no emergency positioning beacon, the compass did not work properly, nor did the autopilot and navigation lights and the boat had encountered engine problems on the previous voyage. The situation was so serious in respect to safety failings that a qualified skipper and two crew members had earlier refused to sail on the boat because it was dangerous, unstable and unseaworthy. The final statement went to the judge who in passing sentence said:

> 'That is, that by your gross negligence one member of the *Pescado* lost his or her life and it is on that basis that I sentence you.'

The *Pescado* clearly shows a deliberate failing in any form of safety management and while the outcome of the case was positive, it could be argued that there was a case for corporate manslaughter.

Port Ramsgate case

2.5   In 1995 six people were killed and seven others seriously injured when a ferry walkway at the Port of Ramsgate collapsed. This was not a manslaughter case, and the company was prosecuted under health and safety legislation. The outcome of the trial was a record fine of £1.7 million. Two Swedish companies responsible for the design and construction of the walkway were fined £1 million, Lloyd's Register of Shipping, £500,000 and Port Ramsgate Ltd, £200,000. Mr Justice Clarke determined that the companies had been guilty of gross negligence and that the level of fines were in part to deliver a message to the boardrooms of companies and the controlling minds of all organisations that the safety of the public is paramount. Port Ramsgate Ltd and the Swedish firms denied failing to ensure the safety of passengers, but were found guilty after a four-week trial. Lloyd's Register of Shipping, which issued a safety certificate had pleaded guilty. The Swedish companies were tried and sentenced in their absence, not guilty pleas having been entered on their behalf. Fartygsen-treprenader AB (FEAB) was fined £750,000 and Fartygskonstruk-tioner AB (FKAB) who designed the walkway was fined £250,000. In addition costs of £251,000 were awarded jointly against these two companies. Lloyds register was fined £500,000 plus costs and Port Ramsgate Ltd were fined a total of £100,000. As of this date the two Swedish companies have not paid either their fines or costs. This case raises the issue of liability with foreign companies operating in the UK who it appears can undertake work but not be liable for criminal offences.

The HSE reiterated the view given in court that the project had been described as a shambles from beginning to end. The walkway, which should have lasted a lifetime had been put into place in May and collapsed in September.

Simon Jones case

2.6   Simon Jones, a 25-year old student at Sussex University was killed on 24 April 1998 with two hours of commencing a job at Shoreham docks, West Sussex. He was employed by Euromin a Dutch owned stevedore company. Jones was sent as casual labour to a job at the docks by an employment agency. He was tasked with attaching bags of cobblestones to hooks, which had been welded to the inside of the open grab. The conventional method would have been to attach a hook to the crane but employees stated that the company was reluctant to change the crane from grab to hook and back again because it cost time and money. Jones received only a few minutes training and no health and safety briefing. As work progressed the crane driver pulled the wrong lever in the crane cab and the two-tonne grab closed, partially severing his head. The crane driver and Mr Martell, the manager of the company were arrested but released without charge. The Crown Prosecution Service decided that there was insufficient evidence to prosecute for manslaughter, which resulted in a campaign to have that decision reversed.

The Director of Public Prosecutions, David Calvert-Smith ordered a judicial review, which ruled that the CPS should reconsider its earlier decision not to prosecute. As a result of the review on the 19 December 2000 he announced that there was sufficient evidence to charge Martell with manslaughter through gross negligence. After nearly three years, summonses were issued against Richard Martell and Euromin.

The trial of Euromin Ltd and Richard Martell was held at the Old Bailey and on 29 November 2001 the company was found guilty of two breaches of the *HSWA 1974*. The company was ordered to pay fines of £50,000 and costs of £20,000. Richard Martell was cleared of manslaughter. The outcome increased calls for changes to the law in respect to manslaughter at work. David Calvert-Smith, QC, the Director of Public Prosecutions said:

> 'Employees like Simon Jones should be able to carry out their work in a safe environment free from the fear of death or serious injury.'

He confirmed the problems encountered with prosecuting companies with corporate manslaughter and called for immediate changes to the law.

Tony Baldry, MP for Banbury raised the Simon Jones case in Parliament expressing concerns as to the failure to obtain a suitable conviction:

> 'In 1998, a constituent of mine, Simon Jones, a student at Sussex University, was tragically and traumatically killed after just two hours on his first day working for the Dutch firm Euromin Ltd, at Shoreham docks. I believe that Simon's death and the subsequent acquittal of the company's general manager, James Martell, has made clear fundamental failures of the law when it comes to safety in the workplace. Regardless of the outcome of the court case, I have no doubt that there is a real need for the Government to examine closely the operations of the Crown Prosecution Service, the Health and Safety Executive and the police in cases of deaths at work. In Simon's case, we need simply to consider the gulf between the observations made by some of those authorities and the actions that they took. I understand that a now-departed ships agent and sales executive at Euromin wrote to the HSE to say that it would only be a matter of time before someone was killed, and that there was inadequate manning and safety at the docks. What did the HSE do? Nothing.
>
> Let us consider the activities of the CPS. I understand that it wrote to Simon Jones's family to say that there was no doubt Euromin employed an unsafe working environment. There is no doubt about the words of the CPS: Euromin employed an unsafe working environment. Despite there being no doubt as to the

severe lack of safety at Euromin, what did the CPS do after Simon's death? Nothing. It was not until the third time of asking – not until two High Court judges had told the CPS that it was *irrational* not to prosecute – that the CPS decided that it was in the public interest to prosecute.

I have no doubt that it is now in the public interest considerably to strengthen the law in relation to deaths at work. The death of Simon Jones at work demonstrates existing shortcomings both in the law and in the practices of the agencies that should be most concerned to ensure that everything that can be done to reduce the risk of workplace deaths is done. Sadly, other cases also demonstrate complacency and the slow and seemingly less than committed prosecution policies that currently exist. Although I intend to outline several problems, there is one overarching and urgent necessity: every work-related death should be treated as a manslaughter investigation from the outset – until manslaughter can be eliminated. Without that provision, it is clear that the hurdles will remain too high for those who want to prosecute.'

(House of Commons Hansard Debates for 19 March 2002 (pt 36)).

Roy Bowles Transport case

2.7   After the failure of the Great Western Trains corporate manslaughter case (SEE 3.9), the directors of Roy Bowles Transport were prosecuted for corporate manslaughter. While large organisations escape the legal process for manslaughter at work, smaller companies are not affected by the Scott Baker ruling (SEE 3.9) and continue to face corporate liability for deaths at work as in the Bowles Transport case. It was a small company with the directors having close control over the day-to-day operations. The incident involved when one of their employees, a driver of an articulated lorry fell asleep at the wheel allowing his vehicle to crash into the back of an empty skip lorry.

The outcome was for it to cross the central reservation landing on top of a Ford Mondeo. Seven vehicles were involved in the resulting pile up, and two people were killed. Stephen and Julie Bowles, directors of the company were accused of being grossly negligent in allowing their driver to spend more than 60 hours a week at the wheel and therefore breaking the law on driving hours. They were convicted of two charges of manslaughter in that they knew or should have known that the driver, Andrew Cox, was in a dangerously exhausted state. Sir Derek Spencer, QC for the prosecution told the court that Mr Cox was an accident waiting to happen and he often worked 60 hours or more without taking proper breaks. He earned a basic wage of £160, but when overtime was added that figure regularly rose to £500 a week.

On 19 November 1999 at the Old Bailey, Stephen and Julie Bowles as directors of the company were each given twelve-month prison sentences suspended for two years. Cox, the driver, was jailed for 30 months. This again shows that directors who have knowledge of the activities of their employees and know that by an individuals action there could be risk to others must shoulder responsibility when things go wrong. They were accused of being grossly negligent in allowing their driver to spend more than 60 hours a week behind the wheel and breaking the law on driving hours. A report in *The Times*, 20 November 1999 by A Leathley states:

> 'Stephen Bowles and his sister Julie were convicted of two charges of manslaughter, after the court was told that they knew, or should have known, that the driver, Andrew Cox, of Colnbrook, Buckinghamshire, was in a dangerously exhausted state.'

The report on the Bowles case identifies that only a company can be guilty of corporate manslaughter, with individuals guilty of manslaughter. With no other evidence available the conclusion is drawn that the company was found guilty of the corporate offence with the two individuals being identified as the controlling mind and found guilty of manslaughter as individuals and sentenced.

The Paul Browning case

2.8   Paul Browning, a lorry driver was undertaking deliveries when while driving his vehicle he killed a man while composing a text message on his mobile telephone. His concentration was on the message and not the road and he veered into a lay-by where his heavily laden lorry collided with a man. Paul Hammond was standing beside his mother car talking to her when the lorry struck and dragged him along the road killing him instantly. On 14 February 2001 at a special hearing at Southend Crown Court, Browning received a five-year prison sentence for killing the pedestrian. This is not an *at work* prosecution although Browning was at work at the time. He was sending the message to his girlfriend and not his employer, had that been the case then the company could have been implicated in the offence and faced potential manslaughter charges (see Roy Bowles transport case at 2.7). Every day drivers who are *at work* are using hand held mobile phones to undertake business communications, and with the growing use of text message phones and e-mail communications used by drivers while *at work* and probably whilst continuing to drive. Companies and their drivers could face corporate killing charges under the proposed offence in a similar case.

Easy Moss Products case

2.9 Following joint investigation by the HSE and the police Roger Jackson, trading as Easy Moss was charged with man-slaughter following the death of an employee. John Speight had learning difficulties and was employed under a scheme for the disabled. He was helping to transfer waste into a skip by being lifted in an unsecured former platform luggage trolley by a forklift truck. The trolley fell off the forks, crushing his abdomen beneath the steel cage. He died several days later. Jackson pleaded not guilty to the health and safety charges but changed his plea to guilty during the trial. On the 3 March 2000 Jackson was convicted of manslaughter and received a twelve-month prison sentence. The judge was in no doubt that he should impose the sentence but suspended it for two years for fear that the business might fail, putting 18 people out of work. He was fined £5,000 under *HSWA 1974, s 2* and £5,000 under *HSWA 1974, s 3* and ordered to pay £25,000 prosecution costs.

'Gas' manslaughter prosecutions

2.10 Many people have put their lives at risk when they live in privately rented shared houses and bedsits, so called *death trap housing* by the National Consumer Council. A vast number of those 1.5 million at risk from the lethal hazard of carbon monoxide poisoning are students. The HSE issued a statement stating that about 30 lives are claimed by the 'silent killer' every year. Responding to an increase in the number of deaths due to faulty gas appliances the HSE focused their enforcement activities on gas fitters, whose competency to undertake the work was in doubt. At the same time the landlords who opted to use unregistered workmen, so that could cut costs also faced investigation and prosecution. The National Union of Students (NUS) claim that 21 students died as a result of carbon monoxide poisoning in a six-year period.

In a landmark case a landlord and a gas fitter were imprisoned after a student died of carbon monoxide poisoning. Landlord Peter Owen and gas fitter Stuart Royale were found guilty of man-slaughter and jailed for two years and 15 months respectively in February 1998. This case was the first time that custodial sentences have been imposed in connection with failures to ensure safety in the maintenance of gas appliances. Sonya Hyams died from carbon monoxide poisoning at a house owned by Peter Owen in Basford, Stoke-on-Trent in November 1996. Owen hired Royale who installed an inappropriate type of boiler in the bathroom of the house. Royale was not competent to install the boiler and was not registered as a self employed fitter with the Council of Registered Gas Installers (CORGI) a legal requirement under the *Gas Safety (Installation and Use) Regulations 1994 (SI 1994/1886)*.

The death of Paul Foster in February 1996 was caused because gas fitter David Allison had installed a gas fire but failed to notice that the flue was capped with concrete and so would prevent the gas fumes from escaping. The landlord of the property Sucha Singh, and his son Curpal Singh who was acting on his father's behalf were found individually responsible for Fosters death. The two landlords were both sentenced to nine months in jail for man-slaughter. David Allison was sentenced to twelve months for manslaughter.

Landlord Thomas Beedie failed to service the gas fires in 18 bedsits and flats since they were installed nine years previously. Tracy Murphy, aged 19, was poisoned by carbon monoxide fumes from a gas fire in 1993. Beedie was given an 18-month suspended prison sentence. The flue behind the fire was completely blocked with rubble and the catchment space behind the fire was half the size that it should have been. The Court of Appeal quashed Beedie's conviction for manslaughter. It was found that because Thomas Beedie had pleaded guilty to an offence under the *HSWA 1974* he could not be charged later with manslaughter. He had been fined £1,500 for health and safety offences and ordered to pay £1,000 costs.

In 1994 an inquest jury returned a verdict of unlawful killing and the police notified the CPS. He was charged with manslaughter and received an 18-month suspended prison sentence. The trial judge rejected the plea that he had already faced a trial for the same incident. The appeal judges considered the trial judge to be wrong in finding special circumstances why the manslaughter charge should be heard.

The fact that it was in the public interest to bring a prosecution for manslaughter and the concern of the victim's family were good reasons for there to be a prosecution for manslaughter. However, the same evidence was used in both cases and a person cannot be prosecuted for the same offence twice. The case should have been referred to the CPS for review before considering prosecuting under the *HSWA 1974* and illustrates why the decision on prosecution in a death at or due to work should await the outcome of the inquest.

A tenant Christopher William Woffenden died on 21 February 1999 due to carbon monoxide poisoning. The landlord Mohammed Casim Ola was charged with manslaughter and after a five-day trial, was convicted by a majority verdict. The judge imposed a 15-month prison sentence.

The examples clearly show the liability that is placed not only on incompetent workers but also on landlords who look for cheap options. Because they cut corners with maintenance of safety critical appliances and through their gross negligence individuals who thought they were in a safe environment, died.

Railway accidents

2.11   The focus for greater corporate liability has been maintained by lobby groups and the general public by the number and seriousness of train crashes that have occurred and includes the following examples:

- December 1988 – the Clapham Junction disaster where 35 died and 500 were injured. There was a public enquiry and lax maintenance was blamed.

- March 1989 – a crash at Purley, South London resulted in five deaths and 90 injured. The driver, Robert Morgan was imprisoned for four months for causing the crash.

   In the same month two electric trains collided just outside Bellgrove station in east Glasgow. Two people died and 52 were injured. British Rail was blamed for introducing the single-track system, which confused the drivers.

- July 1990 – a train left Newton station near Glasgow on the new single-track system and collided with a train travelling in the opposite direction. One driver passed a red light.

- January 1991 – at Cannon Street station in London a commuter train ran into the buffers at the London terminus. Two passengers died and 240 were injured. The driver failed to break in time. No charges were brought.

- October 1994 – two trains collided on a single line at Cowden in Kent. Five people died and eleven were injured. The crash was caused by one driver passing a red signal.

- March 1996 – a Royal Mail sorting train ran into the back of a freight train at Stafford, Staffordshire. A fault on the freight train caused it to derail and in turn cause the accident.

- August 1996 – Watford Junction two trains collided leaving one dead and 69 injured. One driver passed a red signal, but was cleared of manslaughter.

- September 1997 – A Great Western train passed a red signal at Southall, West London and crashed into another train. Seven people died and 151 were injured as a result of the driver looking in his bag and passing a red signal. There was an unsuccessful corporate manslaughter prosecution (see 3.9 for details of the case). No charges were bought against the train driver.

- October 1999 – Ladbrook Grove, West London two trains collided leaving 31 dead and 150 injured.

Hatfield rail accident

2.12   In January 2001 the railways suffered another devastating blow when a train crashed at Hatfield in which four people were killed. The accident investigation found that a defect in the line had been discovered in November 1999 by Balfour Beatty and reported to Railtrack soon after. In contradiction to the rules no speed restrictions were imposed. A report identifies that work to replace the track should have been conducted but was not completed because a machine that would have speeded up the process did not arrive. Management should have closed the line or imposed a speed restriction, but this was not done.

The British Transport police believe that there is sufficient evidence to bring a prosecution for corporate manslaughter. In addition they believe that there is evidence to charge individuals with manslaughter. This includes three individuals from Railtrack and two from Balfour Beatty. For a prosecution to succeed the CPS will need to identify key executives who were negligent *and* controlling minds responsible for directing the will of the company. The police stated that they had such individuals. It is said that the evidence is in the form of documents which identify individuals in Railtrack and Balfour Beatty as having been warned about safety problems, but who failed to do anything. The CPS will have to examine the evidence and identify the individuals who are deemed to be the *controlling minds*, which has in the case of large companies been an impossible task.

In November 2000, Gerald Corbett, the former Railtrack chief executive, admitted that the track was in an appalling and totally unacceptable condition and that there should have been a speed restriction. He further stated that there were a multitude of other things that should have happened but did not. He told the Commons Transport Select Committee that Railtrack and Balfour Beatty had failed.

It is important to note that despite the admissions, Mr Corbett, who resigned after the tragedy, will not face prosecution. In fact it is proposed that no board director will face prosecution. This means that even with guilty knowledge, the controlling minds will not face trial for manslaughter or even lesser offences. Those to possibly face prosecution are further down the command chain, a situation that the reformers seek to remedy by having those in the boardroom held accountable.

The case for the offence of corporate killing

2.13   There is powerful evidence to support the requirement for an offence of corporate killing to be introduced into the current legal system. An interview 'Prescott acts on accident law' by D Harrison in the *Sunday Telegraph*, 22 August 1999, with John Prescott, the Deputy Prime Minister raised the profile of corporate killing yet further. Mr Prescott stated:

'New laws are to be brought in to punish companies responsible for fatal accidents such as the *Marchioness* riverboat disaster ...

41

Mr Prescott said that new laws would allow firms to be charged with corporate killing without the need to blame specific indi viduals ... the legislation would be brought in as soon as possible following the *fiasco* over the *Marchioness* ... The *Marchioness* case has brought home to everybody the urgent need for new legislation on corporate killing. We are working on it now and it will be brought in as soon as possible ... The victims relatives need to know that everything possible has been done to give them justice.'

Under current English law the *P&O European Ferries (Dover) Ltd* prosecution was a landmark case in corporate liability for corporate and/or individual manslaughter, but the process has been and still is a torturous and ad hoc system. A case proposed for manslaughter can be identified by the HSE, a coroner or the police, who submit details of the case to the CPS. The CPS then reviews the evidence and determine whether to proceed or not, and that decision is founded on the likelihood of a conviction and whether a prosecution is in public interest. An example of one such case is described by J Baleen:

'A coroner's court found that workers who were killed in the course of there employment had been unlawfully killed but a manslaughter prosecution appeared unlikely. The case has already been considered by the Crown Prosecution Service, (CPS) who, based upon their assessment that there was insufficient evidence, declined to prosecute. The coroner, as a matter of course referred the case back to the CPS but as the commentator identifies, history indicates that unless new evidence is produced the CPS will take no further action. The accident happened during the refurbishment of a shop, where the partial demolition of a wall on the first floor of a three storey premises was carried out as people worked in a shop below. It appears that a supporting wall was demolished without sufficient alternative support being in place. Two people were killed in the ensuing collapse. The two persons killed were not trained construction workers, but were working until something better came along.'

('Juries, the CPS and Unlawful Killing' *Safety and Health Practitioner*, December, 1995).

It is well established that under current English law it has to be proved that a company was reckless as to the risk of death or injury from its activities, for that company to be convicted of man-slaughter. A company does not posses a *mind*, the courts have required there to have been recklessness by one or more of the company's directors or senior managers. That person will have to be proved to have represented the *mind and will* of the company at the time of death. It is the requirement to identify an individual with control, within the company, who has shown recklessness that has been the stumbling block for corporate manslaughter cases. The exception to this has been *Kite, OLL,* and *Jackson Transport* (SEE 1.18), and that has provided some evidence that the size of the defendant company is a major factor. Both *OLL* and *Jackson Transport* were small companies and the directors were actively involved in the companies day-to-day operations. It was therefore easy for the prosecution to identify the *controlling mind* and prove recklessness.

In addition to the failure to obtain a successful prosecution for manslaughter against large corporations and the easier option with small company's often termed *one man bands*, there have been successful prosecutions of landlords and gas fitters for man-slaughter (SEE 2.10), which identifies individuals as causing death as a result of faulty work.

However, while the prosecutions of *OLL* and *Jackson Transport* were successful they did not open the way for the prosecution of larger company's where the directors or senior members of the organi-sation are removed from the day-to-day *shop floor* activities and systems of work. In an effort to redress what is considered by the Law Commission to be an imbalance in the justice system a new offence of corporate killing is proposed. For clarification, the management failure is focused upon the manner in which its activities are managed or organised in that they fail to ensure the health and safety of those employed or affected by those activities. Furthermore, the failure of the corporation can still be identified with the death even though there may be a failing by an individual.

The subject of corporate culpability is raised by C M V Clarkson who states:

> 'If it is the company that is culpable, then it is the company that deserves prosecution and punishment. When dealing with individuals, nobody would seriously argue that someone other than the culpable agent should be prosecuted on con-sequentialist grounds. If blameworthy individuals within the

company can be pinpointed, one might well wish to prosecute them additionally. However, prosecution of such individuals alone might be pointless and inappropriate as it ignores the corporate pressures that might have been placed upon them by the corporate structure. One might simply be punishing the "vice president responsible for going to jail", and the institutional practices and pressures will continue after the sacrifice. Even with small close-held companies there is a strong case for criminal liability and removing any illegal profits, as in such companies the directors will usually be the shareholders and so will be penalised by a loss of profit, and encouraged to correct the practices that led to the wrongdoing.'

('Kicking Corporate Bodies and Damning Their Souls', (1996) 59 MLR 4).

Clarkson continues to support corporate liability when there is a clear management failure and follows the doctrine that those who create the hazards and risks must control them and is argued that there should be no difference between individual and corporate liability, by stating:

'Companies should be liable for the same offences as individuals and subject to the same normal principles of criminal liability. With regard to the *actus reus* requirements, the first issue is whether it was the company's positive acts (for example, pumping effluent into a river) or omissions to act (for example, failing to implement a safety system that caused the prohibited harm). With regard to omissions it has been argued that it might be necessary to impose a general duty upon corporations to prevent their operations causing harm. However, such a measure seems unnecessary as such companies could almost inevitably be construed as having created a dangerous situation by operating in an unsafe manner, and therefore, would be under a common law duty to prevent the dangers materialising ... the problem of establishing corporate causation should be no greater than in cases of human causation ... what about the case where it is the actions or inaction's of an employee that directly lead to the prohibited result? Again, the solution seems clear. If the employee is acting within the scope of his or her employment and duties, the company cannot claim it did not cause the result. To emphasis this point, the Law Commission has proposed an express provision that a management failure can be a cause of a person's death, even if the immediate cause is the act or omission of an individual ... With regard to the culpability or *mens rea* requirements for more serious crimes, a company through its corporate policies and procedures can exhibit its own culpability. Manslaughter, for instance, can be committed by gross negligence. If a company blatantly fails to institute the necessary safety procedures, gross negligence can be attributed to the company itself.'

The case presented for the offence of corporate killing shows that there is a body of people who argue that the *HSWA 1974* has not provided the safeguards required and in many cases is not seen to be an effective sanction. It is therefore argued that a high level criminal offence that focuses on management failures as opposed to only individual culpability is required.

The case against the offence of corporate killing

2.14   The proposed offence of corporate killing has its opponents who raise the question as to the need for such an offence. They consider that the current health and safety offences are sufficient and provide an adequate deterrent.

'The Law on Corporate Killing could be on the Wrong Track' was the headline in the *Daily Telegraph*, 30 May 2000, where A Davidson stated:

> 'Creating the crime of corporate killing is just a political reaction to appease a public outcry and can have no benefit to society.'

He continues his argument and states:

> 'If the link and evidence are strong enough to show a director knew what was going on, he can be prosecuted now. If there is not enough evidence, so the company is prosecuted and the director suffers, there is a question of human rights ... the new process weakens the burden of proof for finding directors guilty, which cannot be right. The present law says if the person responsible for the death can be identified and the evidence can show "he actually acted in a way that resulted in the death", he can be taken to court. It hardly ever happens. The reason is the difficulty in allocating blame, or "showing they knew what was going on". Trying to remove the responsibility from the manager probably responsible to place it on someone remote who may

have known little about it, is not justice. Such an increased pressure is hardly likely to encourage people to incorporate or to become directors. That is especially true of non-executive directors who meet only monthly and are responsible to ensure that assets are looked after and procedures followed, but unlikely to know about detailed daily procedures though the law says they are equally responsible for the company's activities ... Fines are also a problem because they just hit the pockets of owners and shareholders though they are not to blame.'

Directors feel that they and their organisations could be exposed to a corporate killing offence or even an individual offence of reckless killing, or killing by gross negligence if the offence committed occurs outside of their direct knowledge or consent. There may be suitable company procedures and guidance and there may be a system to ensure that individuals employed are competent, but a deviation by an individual, particularly if working away from the organisations principal place of work, could expose the organisation and those who own or control it. There is also an argument that a responsible organisation employs safety professionals to manage health and safety issues, feeding the appropriate information in at boardroom level and that therefore the responsibility lies with the health and safety professional and not in the boardroom. There is further concern that if a director, or someone of similar status is appointed to be responsible for health and safety, they could be used as a scapegoat in the event of legal proceedings against an organisation. The proposition that directors could be disqualified from holding a management position is seen by some commentators as being a draconian measure.

Manslaughter is a serious offence and this point is raised by M Tyler who identifies in an article 'Corporate Manslaughter', *The Safety and Health Practitioner*, March 1999, that there is a maximum punishment of life imprisonment and therefore, charges of manslaughter should be reserved for only the most serious of offences. The CPS reviews cases for homicide offences and refers to the CPS code which determines that there has to be *a realistic prospect of conviction* and *be in the public interest*, which means that only the strongest cases proceed. Tyler provides an example with the sinking of the *Herald of Free Enterprise* and the prosecution for corporate manslaughter of P&O European Ferries (Dover) Ltd. The case which was examined at a public inquiry, was chaired by a High Court judge, and a corporate manslaughter prosecution failed with no case to answer.

It is identified by M Tyler, 'Corporate Killing Law Misses the Mark', *The Lawyer,* 12 June, 2000, that the intention was to include all *undertakings* not just corporations but charities, hospital trusts, small businesses, partnerships and local authorities. His concern is that these *undertakings* could be convicted more easily, with reduced evidential burden on the prosecution. He explains that the offence is committed where management failure is the cause, or one of the causes, of a person's death and that failure constitutes conduct that falls far below what can be reasonably be expected. His view then extends to consider that a failure would be treated as casual for these purposes even though the immediate cause of death was the act or omission of an individual. He also points out that companies and other organisations, unlike individuals, will not be tried by a jury of their peers, in other words, directors, partners or executives but by members of the public. While any management should aim to avoid killing its staff or customers, he concludes that juries will not need much persuading that an accident, especially one with multiple fatalities, could have been avoided.

In his article 'Corporate Manslaughter', *The Safety and Health Practitioner*, March 1999, M Tyler raises the question as to whether the proposed offence will be anything more than an aggravated form of contravention of the general duties under the *HSWA 1974, ss 2 and 3,* for which exactly the same penalty of unlimited fines was proposed for the offence of corporate killing. He states:

> '... let us be quite clear that when it comes to corporate crime in this area we are talking about accidents, not intentional, premeditated or malicious attempts to kill and injure.'

His case then focuses on providing a warning against identifying negligent companies and their management as violent criminals with the basis of his argument focusing on two main points.

> '... that work related deaths are in some sense tolerated within the existing legal systems; and that characterising management failings as traditional criminal offences of violence works as an effective deterrent.'

He further provides the argument that there is intent in insider dealing and fraud, but with incidents of workplace accidents they are not intended but are the consequence of unseen failures to identify and control risks. It therefore follows that it is difficult to determine how deterrence can be effective for individuals in often complex corporate structures. He extends the view that there is no evidence that the deterrence factor will have an impact in reducing workplace accidents.

Summary

This chapter has provided an overview of gross negligence manslaughter at or due to work and potential corporate manslaughter cases. The next chapter will review the success and failings within the homicide law of gross negligence manslaughter, which has an imbalance between a small one-man company and a large corporation.

3 Corporate Manslaughter and Key Elements of Manslaughter at Work

---

This chapter considers the following:

- Early cases of corporate manslaughter prosecutions.

- Manslaughter and small companies.

- The success of small company corporate manslaughter prosecutions.

- The failure of large company prosecutions for corporate manslaughter.

Introduction

3.1   There are demands from the public for the law to be used to charge corporations with manslaughter at work offences. There is also evidence that public opinion considers it wrong if all the blame is placed on a junior employee, if it is the directors who determine the operational philosophy as the *controlling minds,* and have the most to gain from the corporation.

For many years it had been thought that a corporation could not be guilty of manslaughter, because the law of homicide required the killing of a human being to be by an act of another human being. On this basis Justice Finlay in *R v Cory Bros Ltd [1927] 1 KB 810* made the decision, to quash an indictment against a company for manslaughter. It was clear that he found himself bound by earlier authorities, which he concluded, showed *quite clearly* that an indictment would not lie against a corporation for a case involving personal violence. The case of *R v Cory Bros* was, however, decided before the principle of *identification* was developed.

Cory Bros Ltd case

3.2   The case of *R v Cory Bros Ltd* was an interesting case in that it was a private prosecution brought by the deceased's brother through the South Wales Miner's Federation. The basis of the case involved the directors of a private mining company, who during the miner's strike of 1926, erected a fence around a power house belonging to the company. The thought process of the directors was that of protection against pilfering by strikers and their families, but to make the fence totally effective it was electrified.

The deceased, was an unemployed miner who was scavenging close to the fence, when he fell against it and was electrocuted. The South Wales Miner's Federation determined that the company and three of its engineers had set a premeditated mantrap and supported the private prosecution against them for manslaughter. Committal proceedings against the company and the engineers were successful but the outcome was to determine that the law did not allow an indictment to lie against a corporation. The charges against the three individual engineers remained and they were prosecuted but the outcome resulted in acquittals for those prosecuted.

Northern Strip Mining (Construction Co Ltd)

3.3   It was to be some 38 years before another case of corporate manslaughter reached the courts. During this time the attitudes of the courts changed and are highlighted in the case of *R v Northern Strip Mining Constructions Co Ltd (1965) (Unreported)*. The case involved a welder-burner that was drowned when a railway bridge which the company was demolishing collapsed. Employees had been instructed to burn down sections of the bridge, starting in the middle. At trial the defendant company was acquitted on the facts of the case, but neither counsel nor the presiding judge appeared to have any doubt about the validity of the indictment and the defence counsel seems to have concurred with those opinions.

It was reported in *The Times* 2, 4 and 5 February 1965, that the judge argued that it was the prosecution's task to show that the defendant company, in the person of the managing director, was guilty of such a degree of negligence that amounted to a reckless disregard, for the life and limbs of his workmen. There seems to be no report of the argument or of the judge's reasons. It is the identification principle that has been the key factor to corporate manslaughter offences and the reason for failure to obtain a conviction.

Lyme Bay Canoe Tragedy – Peter Kite case

3.4   The most important case in the development of a corporate offence for manslaughter is the case of *R v Kite and OLL Ltd (1994) (Unreported)*. The trial resulted in the first conviction in English legal history of a company for corporate manslaughter. The case more commonly known as the *Lyme Bay canoe tragedy* is an interesting case in that it identifies management failure to ensure a safe activity when evidence showed that warnings about safety had been given and led to gross negligence manslaughter.

3.5   The incident involved a group of sixth former students from the Southway Comprehensive school in Plymouth who were participants in an activity holiday at the St Albans Challenge Centre at Lyme Regis. Canoeing was among the range of activities that were available to the students and, as part of the introduction to the activity, the party was given a half-hour basic instruction with canoes in the swimming pool. The following day members of the party decided what activities they wanted to do and eight pupils and one teacher decided to go canoeing. Two instructors, one male and one female, neither of whom were qualified to teach canoeing, accompanied this group of novices. Each participant was provided with a wet suit and life jacket, but no foot or head wear. The days activity plan was basic and involved paddling from Lyme Regis to Charmouth and back, a journey to be undertaken at sea.

At about 10 am the party set off and soon encountered problems. One of the students' canoes capsized and it required the male instructor to right the craft and help the student back into it. The teacher then capsized and required the male instructor to assist in recovery of the canoe and help the teacher back into the canoe. During this incident, the female instructor directed the others to *raft up* in a line and so making a more controlled and stable group. However, the group was drifting out to sea and the wind had increased causing the waves to get bigger, all adding to the student's problems. They then became seasick which in turn caused distress, and added to the very evident concern as to their situation. While they did what they could to help one another, the problems developed rapidly with canoes capsizing and depositing the students in the cold water, clinging to the upturned craft.

The group was in serious trouble and because of a management failure, they had no method of raising the alarm. Nobody onshore was aware of any possible problems and so the hours passed with the youngsters in the water, cold, tired and distressed. In an act of desperation two students decided to swim to shore and as events unfolded were the last to be rescued. The male instructor and teacher were located some eight miles down the coast, having been in the sea for seven hours. The main group was rescued two and a half miles from the nearest coast. The final outcome was that four of the youngsters died as a result of the tragedy.

3.6   Mr Peter Kite, the managing director of Active Learning and Leisure Ltd, the operators of the centre, had failed to ensure the safety of the group. He had been notified in writing by previous employees of the failings in safety procedures and equipment. The ill-fated group had gone to sea, with very limited instruction, unqualified instructors, and no flares for alerting the Coast Guard, no emergency plan and no support boat. The students had not been taught how to work their lifejackets nor were they told to inflate them when they were in the water. The situation was compounded when the group failed to return, and the management delayed in alerting the rescue services.

The outcome was that on 8 December 1994 Peter Kite was found guilty of individual manslaughter and jailed for three years. The case against the Lyme Bay centre manager Joe Stoddart was dropped when the jury failed to reach a verdict. The company, OLL Limited, was convicted of corporate manslaughter and fined £60,000. It was a landmark case as it was the first corporate manslaughter conviction under English law. A crucial aspect to this case was the fact that Kite had personal knowledge of the safety failings. These were referred to in court by Mr Justice Ognall who identified the letters sent to Mr Kite months before the tragedy by two competent instructors, who had in fact left the centre, because they were concerned about safety. Mr Justice Ognall told Kite that it was obvious that what separates this case from others is the fact that warnings were given in cold clear terms as to the way he was operating and the potentially fatal consequences of failing to act. It was pointed out that those warnings became reality because of his complete failure to take action and that there was evidence that he was in part, more interested in sales than safety. He told Kite:

'... what clearly separates this case from others is the n[
were given in chillingly clear terms of the risk you were rure
and potentially fatal consequences ... Those dire forecasts
became reality because of your complete failure to heed it and to
act. I regret to say that to a degree you were more interested in
sales than safety.'

The key issues raised during the trial focused on the failings of Mr
Kite. A report by K Knight in *The Times*, 18 November 1994, carried
the headline 'Death Trip Canoe Instructors Had No Safety Training'. The report said:

'The instructor who led the canoeing expedition from Lyme Bay
in which four teenagers died admitted yesterday that he had no
information about local weather conditions, the tide or currents
on the day of the trip ... Mr Mann (instructor) said he had
received no instruction to carry his concern to Joseph Stoddart,
manager of Lyme Regis Challenge Centre. The students were not
issued with spray decks. It had caused me concern because of
the switch from double kayaks to single, with them sitting lower
in the water, there was obviously more chance of water enter-
ing.'

It is evident that the basics of managing known risks for an
adventure activity centre were ignored or dismissed and raised the
standard of negligence to a level that invoked manslaughter charges.

Peter Kite appeal

3.7   Peter Kite was convicted by a majority verdict on four counts
of manslaughter and sentenced to three years' imprisonment on
each count concurrently. He appealed against the convictions and
his appeal was referred to the Full Court. In the review, interesting
issues were raised by the defence in respect to mitigation in
manslaughter at work cases.

With regard to the management failure it is important to define the
charge that was laid which was one of manslaughter and that of
unlawful killing. Although there were nine people in the party,
excluding centre staff, the charge was bought against only one
person and were the same in each count. The charges were that on
22 March 1993 Peter Kite unlawfully killed the named person in
that:

'(a)   As the Managing Director of OLL Limited, owed a duty of care to those who took part in the outdoor leisure activities operated by OLL to take reasonable care for their safety;

(b)   In breach of that duty he failed to take reasonable care for the safety of [the deceased], by;

(i)   failing to devise, institute, enforce and maintain a safe system for the execution of an outdoor leisure activity, namely canoeing, by students attending the St Alban's Centre, Lyme Regis, Dorset;

. . .

(iv)   failing to heed, either or at all, the content of an undated letter sent to OLL by Pamela Joy Cawthorne and Richard Retallick in or about late June 1992;

(v)   failing to supervise the Manager of the Centre (namely Joseph Thomas Stoddart) so as to ensure that canoeing was being safely taught at the Centre;

(c)   His aforesaid breach of duty amounted to gross negligence on his part, and;

(d)   His aforesaid negligence was a substantial cause of the death of [the deceased]

In the case that was originally presented by the prosecution and submitted to the jury, were two additional allegations relating to a breach of duty;

(ii)   failing to procure the employment by OLL at the Centre of an adequate number of staff, suitably quali-fied to give safe instruction of canoeing . . .

(iii)   failing to procure the provision by OLL at the Centre of all equipment necessary for safe instruction of canoe-ing . . .'

The two additional allegations (ii and iii above) were, in the course of the trial, dropped by the prosecution and it was submitted that the abandonment of those two allegations were a significant factor in the case in that it provided evidence which showed that Mr Kite, had in fact complied, rather than failed to comply, in respect of those issues.

3.8   The details of the gross negligence case against Mr Kite were based on the absence of a safe system of operating at the centre, for failing to take notice of the letter from former employees, who made complaints about the absence of safety, and his failure to adequately supervise the manager. The evidence raised the point that Kite was not directly responsible for the canoeing activities that formed the fatal incident, which was the allegation made by the prosecution against Stoddart, the manager, who was jointly charged with Kite. However, the jury disagreed, and the prosecution decided not to continue the case against Stoddart.

The company known as Active Learning and Leisure Limited operated as a leisure centre at St Alban's Centre in Lyme Regis was charged with corporate manslaughter and as a result of the trial, convicted of that offence. The corporate structure was that Mr Kite was the managing director, and Mr Stoddart was the manager therefore the company was a one-man operation and so the *directing mind* was that of its managing director and the company's liability came from the *'directing mind'* having formed the *mens rea*. A company can only act and be criminally responsible through its officers or those in a position of real responsibility in conducting the company's affairs. In other words if it is proved that some person or persons who were the *controlling minds* of the company were themselves guilty of manslaughter then the company is likewise guilty.

The prosecution alleged that Kite, as the managing director of OLL Ltd had the primary responsibility for devising, instituting, enforcing and maintaining an appropriate safety policy and was therefore responsible for the safety standards at the centre which were found to be deficient. By way of industry standards it was said that the defendants had breached guidelines issued by the British Canoe Union.

Reliance during the case was placed on a brochure published by OLL Ltd and it was submitted that the judge did not give the jury the guidance that they could expect in relation to the relevance of the brochure. The prosecution also relied on the letter written by Miss Cawthorne and Mr Retallick, previous instructors with OLL Ltd, and the facts of that letter are quoted in part:

> 'At present we are walking a very fine line between *getting away with it* and having a very serious incident ... We would also like to know why we do not get supplied with a first-aid kit and tow-line ... It's unsafe and not organised ... having seen your 1993 brochure and planned expansion, we think you should have a

very careful look at your standards of safety, otherwise you might find yourselves trying to explain why someone's son or daughter, will not be coming home. Nobody wishes or wants that to happen, but it will sooner or later.'

Mr Kite's case, argued through his evidence that he took that letter seriously, and had acted upon the contents. The report identifies that the letter was written in 1992 and, consequently, it might not provide very useful evidence as to the situation as it was in March 1993. In fact it could be argued that the letter was good evidence because if notice had been taken and the concerns actioned, then a safe system of working would have been in place. It was identified in the evidence, that Mr Kite had made considerable efforts to comply with the complaints that were raised, and that substantial changes had taken place. It again could be argued that the changes were not suitable and sufficient, particularly based upon the evidence that convicted Mr Kite.

3.9   In addition to those matters the prosecution alleged that Mr Kite had failed to supervise Mr Stoddart which, because as the *controlling mind* of the company, he was expected to do. Expert evidence was called by the prosecution, and a number of criticisms were made including, in particular, the lack of experience and suitability of Mr Mann and Miss Gardner as instructors to lead the canoeing expedition.

Mr Kite gave evidence on his own behalf and he stated the he was responsible for overall policy and money matters, but left the actual day-to-day operational running of the centre to the manager, Mr Stoddart. He went on to state that he had absolutely no knowledge that novices were taking part in sea activities, and was horrified when he heard that they were and that this accident had occurred. He further stated that he had immediately taken steps in relation to the Cawthorne letter and had fulfilled his duties in so far as he could in relation to safety precautions. This evidence, and what is drawn from it, was central to the basis of his appeal. The appeal against conviction was dismissed.

The original sentence imposed on Mr Kite by the judge was one of three years' imprisonment. It was recognised that court proceedings involving health and safety failings generally cause great difficulties because the court has to make a balanced judgement between two extreme positions. There is the situation when people have been killed through a work place accident, and in particular when the lives of young people have been lost. It is therefore, very natural for the families of the deceased to take the view that no sentence can be too long in the light of what has happened. The opposite situation is where an individual who has been convicted of serious offences, but he had no *criminal intent*, will not readily understand why a prison sentence has been given.

There was never any suggestion that Mr Kite was directly responsible for what occurred on 22 March 1993 because he was not present, but it was his failure to provide a suitable health and safety system that rendered him guilty of the offence. When the judge had passed sentence on Mr Kite he stated that beyond doubt the matters were so serious that they demanded a sentence of immediate custody, and of some substance. While the fact that a term of imprisonment was imposed on Mr Kite as the *controlling mind* was not in question, what was in question, and the subject of the appeal, was whether in all the circumstances of the case, a sentence of three years' imprisonment was too long.

In the summing up of the appeal court it was recognised that Mr Kite aged 46 was a man of previously impeccable character. Any prison sentence imposed on a man in these circumstances is, of course, devastating to him. Nonetheless, the facts quite clearly demanded a substantial sentence. Taking those matters of a personal nature, together with the facts as proved, the appeal court were persuaded that the sentence imposed by the learned judge was too long. It was proposed to substitute for the sentence of three years' imprisonment one of two years' imprisonment on each count to run concurrently.

3.10 Criminal intent is an interesting issue in health and safety cases. The *HSWA 1974* requires every employer to ensure the health and safety of those in his employment and those not in his employment but who could be affected by his activities. The *Management of Health and Safety at Work Regulations 1992 (SI 1992/ 2051)* (now revoked by the *Management of Health and Safety at Work Regulations 1999 (SI 1999/3242)*) define more explicitly the requirements of managing health and safety. If an individual or corporation disregards the prescribed legislation and Approved Code of Practice (ACoP's), then it could be described as intentional and therefore a criminal act, albeit not in the normal publicly accepted criminal content. It is the task of the court and in particular the jury to determine whether a particular case is one of gross negligence and that is what is often the most difficult. In this case the jury came to the conclusion that Mr Kite's conduct was that of gross negligence and found that he was criminally liable, and he was convicted on the basis of his negligence.

Jackson Transport

3.11   Following the success of the Lyme Bay case Jackson Transport (Ossett) Limited was convicted in 1996 of corporate manslaughter and fined £22,000. Its director Alan Jackson was convicted of individual manslaughter of one of his employees and jailed for twelve months and fined £1,500. The case centred on James Hodgson a 21-year old employee of the company who died less than an hour after being splashed with a deadly chemical while cleaning the inside of a chemical tanker at Jackson Transport's base in West Ossett, Yorkshire. Mr Hodgson was carrying out the dangerous cleaning job protected only by a pair of overalls and a baseball cap. Special suits for protection against chemical risks were only provided to the tanker drivers of the vehicles and the protective suits that were available on the company's premises were in poor condition and there were no hats, visors or goggles.

The trial judge, Mr Gerald Coles QC determined that if Alan Jackson did address the subject of safety clothing he failed to do so adequately. The fact that the deceased was not concerned to wear safety clothing made it all the more important that he should have made sure that he not only had it, but that he wore it. This is an important issue in that not only does the employer have a duty to provide adequate and suitable personal protective equipment, he has to ensure that it is used and used correctly. In this case the judge found that Jackson was totally indifferent to his statutory duties in that he failed to address the issue of a safe system of work. He also failed to take precautions against inevitable disasters, and that the failure to provide a safe system of work, was only the last in a long catalogue of deficiencies.

Reporting on the case G Jolliffe provides details of the summing up of the case where Judge Gerald Coles QC said:

> 'If you did address your mind to the subject of safety clothing you failed to do so adequately. The fact that the deceased was not concerned to wear safety clothing made it all the more important that you should have made sure that he not only had it, but that he wore it.'

He further stated:

> 'I'm afraid you were at most, totally indifferent to your statutory duties ... you failed to address your mind to any real system of safety and you failed to take precautions against inevitable disasters ... the failure to provide a safe system of work was only the last in a long catalogue of deficiencies.'

> ('Director jailed for indifference that killed 21-year old worker', *Safety Management*, December 1996).

Apart from the failings outlined by the judge regarding the lack of personal protective equipment (PPE), there were no trained first aiders nor was there first aid equipment provided by the company. There were no procedures to ensure safe entry to the tank or rescue equipment for use in an emergency. It was ironic that the failings were made worse as the company had drawn up a manual detailing safe methods of cleaning out tankers. That manual had been produced six years before Hodgson's death and had been put in a drawer and forgotten, however the management had identified the hazards and associated risks and failed to implement a safe system of work.

Herald of Free Enterprise case

3.12   The case of *R v P&O European Ferries (Dover) Ltd (1991) 93 Cr App R 72* was the first of a line of disasters that went to court for manslaughter prosecutions and failed. Here was a corporation prosecuted for its management failings, but where no conviction was obtained. It was a case of the corporate entity placing the blame on junior employees and because of the inability to identify a controlling mind the case was destined to fail. It was a case where the public saw a corporation fail to adopt safe practices and procedures and not be accountable at boardroom level. The public found that outcome unacceptable and through numerous lobby groups has placed pressure on successive governments to change the law.

The corporate manslaughter case of the capsizing of the *M V Herald of Free Enterprise*, Report of Court No 8074, 29 July 1987, Department of Transport otherwise known as the *Sheen Report*, reviewed the facts of this important case. It looked at the failings of the corporate body because under the offence of corporate killing, these are the fundamental boardroom issues that will need to be addressed by all undertakings.

3.13 The *Herald of Free Enterprise* was built for the Dover to Calais run and had very powerful engines, capable of rapid acceleration, to enable the crossing to be made at high speed. The concept of the vessel and her sister vessels was to be able to disembark their passengers and vehicles rapidly and then without any delay embark passengers and vehicles for the return voyage. This is of course done to ensure efficiency and cost benefit. On the Dover to Calais run, these ships were manned by a complement of a master, two chief officers and a second officer. The officers were required to work a twelve-hour shift on duty and have not less than 24 hours off duty. In reality each crew was on board the vessel for 24 hours and then had 48 hours ashore.

When the vessel was transferred to the Dover to Zeebrugge route the passage took four and a half-hours, and because it is a longer journey than that of the Dover to Calais route, it gives the officers more time to relax. On this basis the company only employed a master and two deck officers which they were quite entitled to do, providing proper thought had been given to the organisation of the officers duties and the safety of all those onboard.

At Zeebrugge, the turn-round was different from the turn-round at Calais in four main respects. Only two deck officers were available, only one deck could be loaded at a time, it was frequently necessary to trim the ship by the head, and the bow doors could be closed at the berth. It was because of these differences that no real thought was given to the organisation of the duties of the officers, which meant that as soon as loading was complete the Chief Officer considered himself under pressure to leave the loading deck to go to his harbour station on the bridge.

The report identified that there were three crews and five sets of officers for the manning of the *Herald* on this route, and that meant that the officers did not always have the same crew. This is a failing in the operating system because a competent superintendent, applying his mind to the organisation of the officers and crew, would have issued corporate adopted instructions, known within the company as Company Standing Orders, which would have been uniform for all the ships of one class. They would have covered all aspects of organisation, not only for the Calais run but also for the Zeebrugge run when the ship carried only two deck officers in addition to the master. This approach in management is fundamental however, no company orders were issued. While there were no Company Orders issued there were Ship's Standing Orders, and these were in place in March 1987 but they highlight that there was a lack of proper organisation.

3.14 On the 6 March 1997 the *Herald* under the command of Captain David Lewry sailed from Number 12 berth in the inner harbour at Zeebrugge. The ship was manned by a crew of 80 hands and was laden with 81 cars, 47 freight vehicles and three other vehicles. Approximately 459 passengers had embarked for the voyage to Dover. There was prevailing good weather with a light easterly breeze and very little sea or swell. The *Herald* passed the outer mole at 18.24 hours and capsized about four minutes later. During the final moments the *Herald* turned rapidly to starboard and was prevented from sinking totally by reason that her port side rested on the bottom in shallow water. Water rapidly filled the ship below the surface level with the result that 150 passengers and 38 members of the crew lost their lives and many others were injured.

The immediate cause of the disaster occurred because the ship went to sea with her inner and outer bow doors open. The assistant bosun accepted that it was his duty to close the bow doors at the time of departure from Zeebrugge and that he failed to undertake this duty. He had opened the bow doors on arrival in Zeebrugge and was engaged in supervising members of the crew in maintenance and cleaning the ship until he was released from work by the bosun. He then went to his cabin, where he fell asleep and was not awakened by the call *Harbour Stations*, which was given over the tannoy address system. He remained asleep on his bunk until thrown out of it when the *Herald* began to capsize.

The captain or master of the *Herald* on the 6 March 1987 was responsible for the safety of his ship and every person on board and he took the *Herald* to sea with the bow doors fully open. The result was the tragic consequences and therefore he must accept personal responsibility for the loss of his ship. While the full burden of the duty falls to the master to ensure that his ship was in all respects ready for sea subsequent investigations highlight a number of points of mitigation that were made on his behalf, of which there were three principal ones. First, the master merely followed a system, which was operated by all the masters of the *Herald* and approved by the senior master. Second, the court was reminded that the orders entitled Ship's Standing Orders issued by the company make no reference, as they should have done, to opening and closing the bow and stern doors. Third, before this disaster there had been no less than five occasions when one of the company's ships had proceeded to sea with bow or stern doors open. The management, who had not drawn them to the attention of the other masters, knew about some of those incidents. The master told the court that if he had been made aware of any of those incidents, he would have instituted a new system under which he would have required that the doors were closed.

Failure in management systems

3.15 This is clear evidence of a failure in the management system, where senior management knew or should have known that there was a hazard with a high severity risk outcome that placed both crew and passengers in a potentially unsafe situation. This was exasperated by the fact that one of the five masters who took it in turn to command the *Herald* was the senior master. One of the functions of the senior master was to act as a co-ordinator between all the masters and officers of the ship, in order to achieve uniformity in the practices operated by the different crews.

From the brief facts surrounding the disaster it is seen that the errors or omissions on the part of the master, the chief officer the assistant bosun, and the failure of the senior master combined to be the root cause. However, a full investigation into all the circumstances of the disaster determined that serious faults lay higher up in the company in that for some unknown reason, the board of directors did not appreciate their responsibilities for the safe management of their ships. In fact, all concerned in management, from the members of the board of directors down to junior superintendents were guilty of fault in that they must be regarded as sharing responsibility for the failure of management. In the *Sheen Report* there is the now famous statement:

> 'from top to bottom the body corporate was infected with the disease of sloppiness ... The failure on the part of the shore management to give proper and clear directions was a contributory cause of the disaster ...'

Based upon the evidence of the case, the Director of Public Prosecutions (DPP) instituted a corporate manslaughter prosecution. It was also considered that while the company was charged with manslaughter, any legal actions should reach every person, whatever their employment status and so two representatives of senior management, the assistant bosun, the bosun, the chief officer, and the two captains were charged with manslaughter.

Management failure in a large company

3.16 Although the *Herald of Free Enterprise* case failed under the law of manslaughter at the time, it is a useful case to examine what might happen in the future. Under the offence of corporate killing, which is focused upon management failure, this is a case that could be expected to be charged with the corporate offence, but with the potential for charges of individual charges of killing by gross recklessness or carelessness. On that basis the key failings that were identified in the enquiry are examined, as they are in the main management failings.

In July 1984 the company had issued a general instruction that defined that it was the duty of the officer loading the main vehicle deck to ensure that the bow doors were *secure when leaving port*. Evidence was forthcoming that the instruction had been regularly disregarded and had been viewed as meaning that it was the task of the loading officer only to see that someone was at the controls and ready to close the doors. That was not the management's intention through the instruction, which was not worded clearly, and as a consequence it was not followed. If the instruction had been clear and followed the disaster would not have occurred.

The focus here is that although instructions were issued they were not suitable for those who had to work to them and there is no evidence that there had been any training as to the need to adopt the procedures. It appears that while there were instructions, there was no system of review or audit to determine if the procedures were suitable and that staff abided by them. This is a fundamental foundation of the management of safety.

The operation of closing the doors could be completed in less than three minutes and it was not understood by the court as to why the loading officer could not remain on the car deck until the doors were closed, and secure before going to his harbour station on the bridge. The evidence showed that it was the culture of the officers that they always felt under pressure to leave the berth immediately after the completion of loading. This culture spread to the officer on the car deck who would call the bridge and tell the quartermaster to give the order *harbour stations* over the tannoy, often before loading had been completed.

3.17   There were further conflicts in that if the officer of the watch was the loading officer it caused a conflict in his duties. This problem was brought to the attention of management by a memorandum dated 21 August 1982 from the senior master of *Free Enterprise VIII* in which he said:

> 'Departure from Port:

> It is impractical for the OOW [Officer on Watch] (either the chief or second officer) to be on the bridge 15 minutes before sailing time. Both are fully committed to loading the ship. At sailing time, the chief officer stands by the bow or stern door to see the ramp out and assure papers are on board etc. The second officer proceeds to his after mooring station to assure that the propellers are clear and report to the bridge.'

This is further compounded by a damming internal memorandum dated 18 August 1986 sent to assistant managers by the operations manager at Zeebrugge:

> 'There seems to be a general tendency of satisfaction if the ship has sailed two or three minutes early. Where, a full load is present, then every effort has to be made to sail the ship 15 minutes earlier ... I expect to read from now onwards, especially where FE8 is concerned, that the ship left 15 minutes early ... put pressure on the first officer if you don't think he is moving fast enough. Have your load ready when the vessel is in and marshall your staff and machines to work efficiently. Let's put the record straight, sailing late out of Zeebrugge isn't on. It's 15 minutes early for us.'

The evidence that there was pressure on the deck officers was clear to the court even though the company stated, that the disaster could have been avoided if the chief officer had stayed on the car deck for another three minutes. The failure was that the company took no formal action to ensure that the chief officer remained on the car deck until the bow doors were closed. The Ship's Standing Orders issued by the company made no reference, as to the operating of the bow and stern doors. The court was told that before the disaster there had been other occasions when one of the company's ships had sailed with bow or stern doors open. A crucial element in this case is that the management knew about some of those incidents, and they had not done anything about it.

The chief officer relieved the second officer as loading officer of G deck shortly before he instructed the quartermaster to call the crew to harbour stations. Accordingly, it then became the duty of the chief officer to ensure that the bow doors were closed. He did not dispute the fact that this was his duty, but he interpreted the instruction laid down in July 1984 that it was the duty of the officer loading G deck to ensure that the assistant bosun was at the controls. Of all the many faults, which combined to lead directly or indirectly to this tragic disaster, that of chief officer was the most immediate. The corporations management system, which was in operation for all vessels, was fundamentally flawed, but it did not remove the personal responsibility of the captain for taking his ship to sea in an unsafe condition. By doing so he was seriously negligent in the carrying out of his duties and that negligence was one of the contributing causes of the accident.

An internal memorandum dated 22 November 1986, addressed to the chief superintendent stated:

> 'The existing system of deck officer manning for the *Blue Riband Class,* ship that relieves on the Zeebrugge run is unsatisfactory. When *Herald* took up the Zeebrugge service our deck officers were reduced from the usual complement of 15 to 10. The surplus five were distributed round the fleet. On *Heralds* return to the Calais service, instead of our own officers returning to the ship, we were and are being manned by officers from whichever ship is at refit. Due to this system, together with trainee master moves, *Herald* will have had a total of exactly 30 different deck officers on the books during the period 29 September to 5 January 1987 ... Many of the transient officers are only here for a few duties and in these circumstances, their main concern is to get the ship loaded and safely between Dover and Calais. Although they are generally good officers it is unrealistic to expect them to become involved in the checking of installations and equipment or the detailed organisation of this particular vessel which they do not regard as their own ...'

3.18   In a memorandum dated 28 January 1987 the captain stated:

> 'I wish to stress again that *Herald* badly needs a *permanent*

complement of good deck officers. Our problem was outlined in my memo of 22 November. Since then the throughput of officers has increased even further, partly because of sickness. During the period from 1 September 1986 to 28th January 1987 a total of 36 deck officers have been attached to the ship. We have also lost two masters (Hammond and Irving) and gained one (Robinson). To make matters worse the vessel has had unprecedented seven changes in sailing schedule. The result has been a serious loss in continuity. Shipboard maintenance, safety gear checks, crew training and the overall smooth running of the vessel have all suffered ...'

The faults already described lead to the disaster and involved the actions or lack of actions by the master, the chief officer, the assistant bosun, and the failure of the senior master to issue and enforce clear operating procedures or orders. A wider view into the events that led up to the disaster identifies that the underlying faults lay higher up in the company with the board of directors. It is alleged that they did not appreciate or understand their responsibilities for the safe management of their ships. Therefore, they did not apply their minds to the subject of what directions should have been given to all levels for the safety of their ships. Evidence showed that all concerned in management, from the members of the board of directors down to the junior super-intendents, failed in their obligations and duties and must be regarded as being party to the failures of management. If the culture of a company is such that safety is not an intrinsic part of the corporate management then it will be destined for failure.

Information such as the *Merchant Shipping Notice No M 1188*, July 1986 entitled *Good Ship Management* was available. The advice given in that Notice included the following points:

'The efficient and safe operation of ships requires the exercise of good management both at sea and ashore ... The overall responsibility of the shipping company requires the need for close involvement by management ashore. To this end it is recommended that every company operating ships should des-ignate a person ashore with responsibility for monitoring the technical and safety aspects of the operation of its ships and for providing appropriate shore based back-up ... Stress is placed upon the importance of providing the master with clear instructions to him and his officers. The instructions should include adequate Standing Orders. There should be close co-operation and regular and effective communication in both directions between ship and shore.'

This is very sound advice and it could be argued that in a well managed ship-owning Company such advice should not have been necessary to have ensured that its operational procedures complied with the information provided. While the *Sheen Report* only identifies one example of how the standard of management fell short of the recommendations contained in that Notice. It reveals a culture of complacency:

'On the 18 March 1986 there was a meeting of senior masters with management, at which Mr Devlin was in the chair. One of the topics raised for discussion concerned the recognition of the chief officer as head of the Department and the roles of the maintenance master and chief officer. Mr Devlin said, although he was still considering writing definitions of these different roles, he felt *it was more preferable not to define the roles but to allow them to evolve*. Mr Owen, described that attitude with justification, as an abject abdication of responsibility. It demonstrates an inability or unwillingness to give clear orders. Clear instructions are the foundation of a safe system of operation. It was the failure to give clear orders about the duties of the officers on the Zeebrugge run which contributed so greatly to the causes of the disaster. Mr Clarke, on behalf of the company, said that it was not the responsibility of Mr Devlin to see that the Company orders were properly drafted. In answer to the question, *who was responsible?* Mr Clarke said "Well in truth, nobody, though there ought to have been." The board of directors must accept a heavy responsibility for their lamentable lack of directions. Individually and collectively they lacked a sense of responsibility. This left, what Mr Owen so aptly described as, a vacuum at the centre.'

Note: Mr Devlin was the chief marine superintendent and in 1986 he became a director of the company. Mr Ayes was a director.

3.19 The investigation identified other failures on the part of the management, which emerged in the evidence and while they did not contribute to the disaster they are part of a poor culture that infected the company and they are matters of public concern. The culture was in part formed through the failures in the Standing Orders which made no reference to closing the bow and stern doors, and they appear to have led the captain to assume that his ship was ready for sea in all respects, merely because he had no report to the contrary. Most importantly was the failure to identify or accept responsibility at board level. This was identified in that Mr Devlin was prepared to accept that he was responsible for the safe operation of the company's ships and added that he thought that before he joined the board, the safety of the ships was a collective board responsibility. Mr Ayers another director told the court that no director was solely responsible for safety.

In examining the culture of the management, flaws were identified when Mr Devlin was asked who was responsible for considering matters relating to safety in the navigation of the company's ships. His answer was that it was ashore where the system would be to take a consensus of the senior masters. However, as the investigation developed, it became clear that the management onshore took virtually no notice of what they were told by their ships masters. This was highlighted when it was stated that there was one period of two and a half years during which there was no formal meeting between management and the senior masters. The *'marine department'* did not listen to the complaints or suggestions or wishes of their masters.

The *Sheen Report* identifies four specific areas in which the voice of the masters fell on deaf ears ashore:

(1)   A complaint that ships proceeded to sea carrying passengers in excess of the permitted number.

(2)   The wish to have lights fitted on the bridge to indicate whether the bow and stern doors were open or closed.

(3)   Draught marks could not be read. Ships were not provided with instruments for reading draughts. At times ships were required to arrive and sail from Zeebrugge trimmed by the head, without any relevant stability information.

(4)   The wish to have a high capacity ballast pump to deal with the Zeebrugge trimming ballast.

Mr A P Young who was the operations director was the recipient of the legitimate complaints from the Masters. These complaints were not well received by Mr Young and he made no proper or sincere effort to solve the problems. There was sufficient evidence to show that the shore staff of the company was well aware of the possibility that one of their ships would sail with the stern or bow doors open, but took no action. Furthermore, they were aware of the very sensible and basic device in the form of indicator lights that would indicate the status of the doors on the bridge, which had been suggested by responsible masters but ignored by management. Those charged with the management of the Company's Roll-on, Roll-off fleet were not qualified to deal with many nautical matters and were unwilling to listen to their masters, who were well qualified and so did not provide the confidence and backing of the management.

Outcome of the trial

3.20   The trial of *R v P&O European Ferries (Dover) Ltd (1991) 93 Cr App R 72* was terminated when the judge gave directions to the jury that, because of the law, there was no evidence available upon which they could convict six of the eight defendants, including the company, of manslaughter. The main reason for this direction in respect to the case against the company was that, in order to convict it of manslaughter, they would have to identify one of the individual defendants with the company and that individual would have to be guilty of manslaughter. Because there was insufficient evidence on which to convict any of those individual defendants, there was no prospect of a conviction against the company. The judge ruled against the introduction of the *principal of aggregation*. Had this principal been adopted it would have enabled the failings of a number of different individuals, none of whose failings would individually have amounted to the mental element of manslaughter, to be aggregated, so that in their totality they might have amounted to such a high degree of fault, that the company could have been convicted of manslaughter.

Another factor was that there was insufficient prosecution evidence to justify a finding that the risk of the vessel putting to sea with her bow doors open was *obvious* identifies that appropriate test of *obviousness* in this case was what the hypothetically prudent master or mariner or whosoever would have perceived as obvious and serious. This is further explained in that an ordinary person, with no experience of shipping, could not be expected to perceive this possibility as an obvious risk in an unfamiliar and complete system.

In terms of general safety and risk management the test balanced against the facts of the case are a cause for concern. It could be argued that even to a person with no marine experience, a ferry leaving port with its bow doors open, exposing a large open car deck is an obvious risk to the vessel. One could seriously doubt the competence of any mariner who did not perceive that risk whatever the system or pressure placed upon him. In the *Herald* case, the prosecution made the argument that the test should operate in a similar way to the test of *foreseeability* employed in cases of civil negligence. This would have allowed the jury to infer that the risk of the ship sailing with her bow doors open was obvious, and that the safety system in place was defective and that the defect had allowed that disaster to happen. Management engaged in the ferry business who evaluated the risks posed to their ships, need only look back into history to identify the incident of the Irish Sea car ferry, *Princess Victoria*, which sank on 31 January 1953 with a loss of 128 lives. At the inquest a member of the crew stated that the ferry had sailed with the cargo doors open. A wave hit the ship and water swept onto the car deck moving the cargo to the starboard side of the vessel causing it to list. Another dramatic incident occurred much closer in time and should have alerted ferry operators to risks and potential outcomes when the roll-on, roll-off ferry *European Gateway* capsized off Harwich in 1982. Six people were killed in the incident. In 1985 the Royal Institute of Naval Architects identified the need to change the design of the roll-on, roll-off vessels before there was a major incident with a large loss of life. None of the warnings were heeded and it was only two years later that the predetermined disaster occurred when the *Herald of Free Enterprise* capsized.

In the *Herald* case the judge stated:

> '... recklessness in manslaughter was intended to be more culpable than ordinary civil negligence: the criterion of reasonable foreseeability of the risk was not appropriate. Instead, it was necessary to show that the risk was *obvious* in the sense that it would actually have occurred to a reasonably prudent person in the position of the defendant. What was required was some evidence upon which the jury, being properly directed, can find that the particular defendant failed to observe that which was *obvious and serious*, which words themselves convey a meaning that the defendant's perception of the existence of risk was seriously deficient when compared to that of a reasonably prudent person engaged in the same kind of activity, as that of the defendant whose conduct is being called into question.'

The Law Commission Report, *Legislating the Criminal Code: Invo-*

luntary Manslaughter (Law Com no 237) states that the prosecution evidence did not go far enough on this issue. It consisted of the testimony of a number of ships' master who were, or had been, in the employment of the defendant company, who all said that it had not occurred to them that any risk existed, let alone that it was an obvious one.

This evidence must be considered to be of major concern, because as already stated, an ordinary person could accept the obviousness of the risk. The one aspect of this evidence that supported the prosecutions case against the company was the allegation that no-one in the company had given any thought to the risks. In addition the prosecution was not able to advance its case through the evidence of witnesses from other shipping companies that the risk was *obvious*.

Great Western Trains manslaughter failure ruling

3.21 The case of Great Western Trains Ltd (GWT) involved the 10.32 Swansea to London Paddington train, which was driven by Larry Harrison. The train, an Inter City 125 passed through a red signal at 125 mph and crashed into a freight train near Southall station in West London. The train was fitted with two safety devices, which could have prevented the incident, but neither was working. As a result the company was charged with corporate manslaughter and the train driver with individual manslaughter. It was anticipated that the managing director of GWT, Richard George, would be personally charged with manslaughter because of his responsibilities to ensure trains follow adequate safety procedures. The train driver had looked down to pack his bag and had therefore not seen the red signal. The case against him was dropped because it was said that the crash had left him psychologically unfit to face trial. That case for the Crown failed because it could not identify a senior figure within GWT who was the *directing mind and will* and who failed to ensure the safety of the passengers.

This was a landmark case and focused on the prosecution of a large corporation, GWT for corporate manslaughter. The trial was terminated by the Old Bailey judge, Mr Justice Scott Baker, as he threw out manslaughter charges against GWT accused over the deaths of seven passengers. The judge also launched a stinging attack on the government as noted by J Twomey who reported on the case:

'The Old Bailey judge rebuked ministers for failing to act on the recommendations of the Law Commission three years ago to introduce a new offence of corporate killing.'

('No one can be charged for this carnage', *The Express*, 3 July 1999).

The impact of this ruling for the future of corporate manslaughter prosecutions means that no large organisation can ever be prosecuted for manslaughter unless there is a radical change in the law. Twomey continued to state that:

'Attorney General John Morris is to appeal against the findings ... The case against the company foundered on an age-old principle ... For the prosecution to succeed, the Crown had to identify a senior figure within GWT who was the *directing mind and will*, and who failed to ensure the safety of the passengers.'

This again defines the basis of corporate manslaughter failings which was clarified by the judge who said:

'The only basis on which the prosecution may, in law, advance a case against Great Western Trains for manslaughter is by identifying some person within the company whose gross negligence was that of Great Western Trains itself. The only candidate would be managing director Richard George, who was responsible for all matters of safety. In the absence of Mr George having procured, authorised or directed any tortuous act, he cannot be guilty of manslaughter. Consequently, neither can Great Western Trains ... were the law otherwise, a conviction would mark public abhorrence of a slipshod safety system leading to seven deaths and many injured victims.'

In addition to the charge of corporate manslaughter against Great Western Trains being dropped, the train driver, Larry Harrison walked free after the prosecution stated that the crash had left him psychologically unfit to face trial. He took early retirement and will receive a pension. In reviewing the case it was accepted that the train was faulty because the automatic warning and protection systems were not working and there was no second driver in the cab. However, he was the driver and was under a duty undertake his work task correctly and he failed to do so. The case would have lasted several weeks and Mr Harrison would have been unable to pay a fine and would probably have been unfit to serve a prison sentence. It could be argued that he was the victim of a corporate culture of failure.

English Brothers

3.22 'Construction company guilty of corporate manslaughter', was the headline of HSE Press Notice E140: 01, 3 August 2001. English Brothers Ltd, a construction company was convicted as a result of a prosecution brought by the Crown Prosecution Service (CPS). The fatality involved Bill Larkman who was employed as a gang foreman for the erection of an onion store on a farm, The Crofts, Newton, near Wisbech in Cambridgeshire. Mr Larkman was working on the roof in June 1999 when the accident occurred. Although there were no witnesses to the actual incident it was thought that he lost his footing when roofing material slipped causing him to fall more than eight metres to his death. The seriousness of the incident was enhanced because a HSE inspector found Mr Larkman on another site working without the correct safety equipment. The matter was taken up with the company who agreed to remedy the problem, but they failed to take any action. This failure meant that the incident occurred not as an oversight but as a failure of management to take action. That failure amounted to gross negligence with the consequence of a manslaughter prosecution. Melvyn Hubbard, a director of the company was also charged with manslaughter, but after the company pleaded guilty to manslaughter, those charges were not proceeded with. The company was fined £25,000 for manslaughter. In addition there was a fine of £5,000 for an offence under *HSWA 1974, s 3* for failing to ensure the health and safety of people not in its employment. The company was also ordered to pay prosecution costs of £12,500. The financial penalty against the company was said to have amounted to one year's profits for the organisation.

Summary

The successes and failings of these cases highlight the fact that there are key elements that form the basis of establishing a manslaughter at work prosecution. Under the current homicide law it is doubtful if a successful case could be brought against a large corporation. The evidence shows that the directors of P&O European Ferries (Dover) Ltd had prior knowledge that the company fell short in its safety culture, and failed to do anything about it yet were not held liable under the present law. In the cases of GWT, Judge Scott Baker could not identify an individual *controlling mind* responsible for health and safety in the company.

4 Corporate Killing

This chapter considers the following:

- The proposed *Involuntary Homicide Bill*.

- The corporate killing offence.

- Management failure and responsibility.

- Competent employees and contractors.

- Small undertakings.

- Prosecution of new offence.

- Insolvency and dissolution of companies.

- Disqualification of individuals.

- Undertakings versus corporations.

- Penalties.

- Remedial requirements.

- Legal aid – criminal defence service.

- Directors and officers liability insurance.

- Meaning of injury.

- Application of proposed Bill.

Introduction

4.1   Although the new legislation has not been enacted, the draft *Involuntary Homicide Bill* provides a structure for a constructive review of what can be expected. Adopting the understanding that the new law will apply to a wide and diverse range of business, industries and organisations, the all-encompassing description of undertaking is used throughout the text. The offence of corporate killing is one of the offences proposed for the new *Involuntary Homicide Bill*. It will only apply to activities carried out within the

75

jurisdiction of the English and Welsh courts. Scotland is expected to make its own arrangements to align with the proposed offences.

The new offence far exceeds in terms of seriousness an offence under the *Health and Safety at Work etc Act 1974 (HSWA 1974)* and it is the degree of seriousness, resulting from a management failure that will have to be decided. It will be the outcome of an accident investigation that will determine whether an undertaking should be charged with the offence of corporate killing under the proposed *Involuntary Homicide Bill*. The title of the new offence is expected to have added impact in the public's perception of gravity whereby, it is clearly in the same league as the current law of manslaughter. The key element of the proposed offence is that the undertaking can be held liable and there does not have to be any individuals identified.

The offence will only be prosecuted in the Crown or High Court and the penalty for an undertaking is that of an unlimited fine. Prosecution costs would be claimed and awarded in addition to the fine. The court can also order remedial actions that could have serious implications for an undertaking, particularly if the organisation is not financially sound. Directors and senior officers could face disqualification from holding management positions. The courts may take the view that the management of an undertaking that failed to ensure safe practices and does not have the financial resources or management competencies available, should not be operating its business in any event. The implications for all undertakings and those who manage them are potentially serious with far reaching consequences.

The proposed Involuntary Homicide Bill

Clause 4

4.2   The proposed *Involuntary Homicide Bill, cl 4*, deals with the corporate offence for deaths at work. This is where there has been a management failure of such a serious nature that it warrants a charge of corporate killing. This offence is strictly for the undertaking and not individuals. If it is considered that there are individuals who can be identified as being at fault, they can be charged with separate offences of reckless killing (SEE CHAPTER 5), killing by gross carelessness (SEE CHAPTER 6) and possibly killing where the intention was to cause only minor injury (SEE CHAPTER 7). This differs

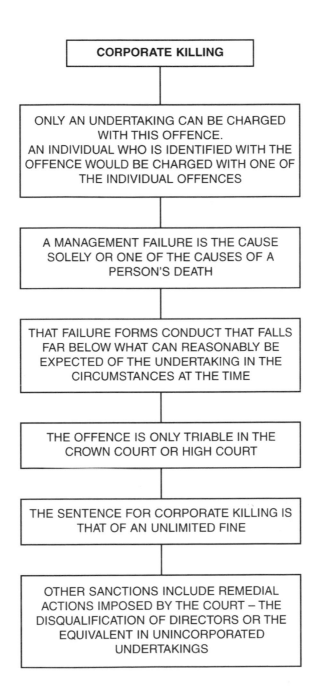

Figure 4.1: Key elements of the corporate killing offence

from the current law of manslaughter in that there is no need to identify a controlling or directing mind because the offence is one of management failures. It is anticipated that individual failures for the death at or due to work activities, will probably be from management but not exclusively, at boardroom level. There are a number of key elements that form the proposed offence described in figure 4.1.

Responsibility for the investigation and prosecution of the corporate offence is expected to lie with the Health and Safety Executive (HSE) and other enforcing authorities. However, there will need to be close co-operation with the police, as they will retain the authority to prosecute the individual offences. The proposed process is described in the flow chart below, figure 4.2, which gives an overview of the anticipated responsibilities. Clearly if there are corporate and individual prosecutions it will be expedient to progress all matters together, and that would involve a joint prosecution with the police and CPS in conjunction with the HSE or other regulatory bodies. As described in chapter 9 (SEE 9.29), there is already an established protocol for working cooperation between the appropriate authorities.

Clause 4(1)

4.3   This clause identifies the basis of the corporate offence which determines that a corporation is guilty of corporate killing if:

'(a) management failure by the corporation is the cause or one of the causes of a person's death; and

(b) that failure constitutes conducts falling far below what can reasonably be expected of the corporation in the circumstances.'

The key issue in (a) above is that of management failure. The onus will be on the prosecution is to prove, *beyond all reasonable doubt,* the test in criminal law, that there was a management failure and that failure caused or was a cause of the death of another.

In (b) above, the failure of the management in the corporation must be proven to be far below the standards that would be expected of the undertakings at the time of the fatality. The test would be based upon the law and accompanying approved codes of practice, accepted industry practices, codes of practice and guidance. Other

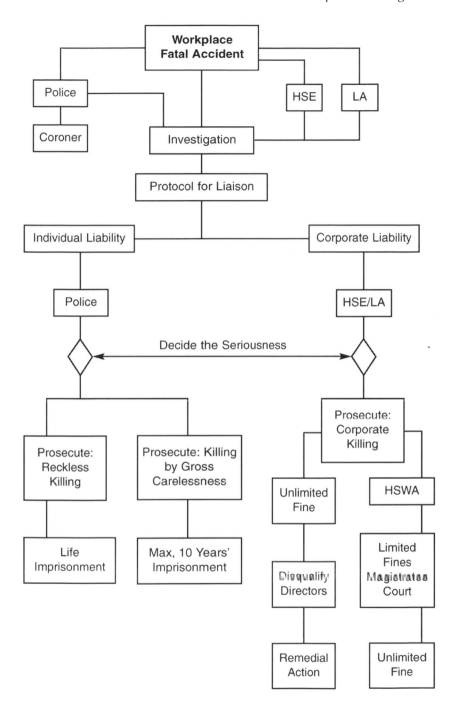

Figure 4.2: Key elements of the enforcement process

evidence could be in the form of safety management systems and methods of working from similar undertakings.

The prosecution would need to show that it was possible to manage the risks, by established example and in due course, case law and precedents, that the defendant management failed to adopt safe practices. Those unsafe acts led to a situation where serious injury or loss of life was probably inevitable. Therefore, management failed to identify the risks and control them, or that they knew of the risks and failed to provide safeguards.

Clause 4(2)

4.4   For the purposes of subclause (1) above cl 4(2) outlines:

'(a)   there is a management failure by a corporation if the way in which its activities are managed or organised fails to ensure the health and safety of persons employed in or affected by those activities; and

(b)   such a failure may be regarded as a cause of a person's death notwithstanding that the immediate cause is the act or omission of an individual.'

The key issues in (a) above focuses on management failure in the way it managed or failed to manage its activities. That failure was to ensure the health and safety, of its employees or persons not employed by the undertaking, but affected by the undertakings activities. This would include but would not be limited to, contractors, sub-contractors, peripatetic workers, self-employed and members of the public.

In (b) above, the management failure is deemed to be the cause of death even though an individual may have done something himself and that resulted in the death of another, but the individual was acting in an official capacity within the undertaking at the time of the offence.

Management failure

4.5   The basis of management control within an undertaking lies with the board of directors, particularly the chief executive, chairman, managing director or other superior officer. In unincorporated undertakings the titles of those persons will vary but they will be the management who control the affairs of the organisation. This means that no matter what the title or formation of the undertaking, the focus is on those who carry out the functions of management and speak and act as the organisation. The board of directors or equivalent may delegate some part of their functions of management giving to a delegated person, full discretion to act independently of instructions from them. However, this does not remove the fact that the ultimate control and directions evolve from the boardroom or equivalent status in an undertaking. Case law will evolve for the new offence, but it is of value to examine established case law involving the prosecution of corporations, particularly when examining management control and failure.

An example of existing case law is found in *Bolton (HL) Engineering Co v Graham (TJ) & Sons [1957] 1 QB 159* where Lord Denning said:

'A company may in many ways be likened to a human body. It has a brain and nerve centre, which controls what it, does. It also has hands that hold the tools and act in accordance with directions from the centre. Some of the people in the company are mere servants and agents who are nothing more than hands to do the work and cannot be said to represent the mind or will. Others are directors and managers who represent the directing mind and will of the company and control what it does. The state of mind of these managers is the state of mind of the company and is treated by the law as such.'

The directors of the company only met once a year. They left the management of the business to others, and it was the intention and actions of those managers, which was carried into the company. There have been attempts to apply Lord Denning's words to all servants of a company whose work is brainwork, or who exercises some managerial discretion under the direction of superior officers of the company. It is not thought that Lord Denning intended to refer to them as he only referred to those who 'represent the directing mind and will of the company, and control what it does'.

4.6 This was further explored in the case of *Tesco Supermarkets Ltd v Nattrass [1972] AC 153*. Tesco was charged with an offence under the *Trade Descriptions Act 1968 (TDA 1968)*. The company sought to raise a defence under *TDA 1968, s 24(1)* on the grounds that the commission of the offence was due to the act or default of another person. This was identified as the manager of the store at which the offence was committed, and that the company had exercised all due diligence to avoid the commission of the offence. The magistrates found that the company had set up a proper system, so it had exercised all due diligence; but the manager, who had failed to carry out his part under the system, was not *another person* and therefore, the company had not exercised all due diligence.

During the appeal it was found that although the majority in the House of Lords approved Lord Denning's *dictum* the speeches showed variations in the detailed application of the test. Lord Reid said that a company may be held criminally liable for the acts only of the board of directors, the managing director and perhaps other superior officers of a company (who) carry out the functions of management and speak and act as the company.

Viscount Dilhorne said:

' ... a company should only be identified with a person who is the actual control of the operations of a company, or of part of them. That person is not responsible to another person in the company for the manner in which he discharges his duties in the sense of being under his orders.'

Lord Diplock thought that the question was to be answered by:

' ... identifying those natural persons who by the memorandum and articles of association, or as a result of action taken by the directors or by the company in general meeting pursuant to the articles, are entrusted with the exercise of the powers of the company.'

Lord Pearson, too, thought that the constitution of the particular company should be taken into account. The tests outlined above would, if applied strictly, produce rather different results. Viscount Dilhorne's test would appear to be stricter than the others, since there are very few people in a company who are not responsible to others for the manner in which they undertake their duties. However, the general principle is clear: the courts must attempt to identify the *directing mind and will* of the corporation, the process of such identification being a matter of law.

It is noteworthy that under the principles coming from *Tesco Supermarkets Ltd v Nattrass*, a branch manager was not regarded as a controlling officer. Lord Pearson explained in that case:

'In the present case the company has some hundreds of retails shops, and it would be far from reasonable to say that every one of its shop managers is the same person as the company ... Supervision of the details of operations is not normally a function of higher management; it is normally carried out by employees at the level of foreman, chargehands, overlookers, floor managers and *shop* managers (in the factory sense of shop).'

Professor Glanville Williams suggests that the line was drawn too tightly in the Tesco case:

'There is no absolute right and wrong about this, but the practical effect of Tesco appears to be to confine the identification doctrine to the behaviour of a few men meeting, say, in London, when the activities of the corporation are countrywide or even worldwide. It would seem on the whole to have been more sensible to extend identification to cover the person or persons in control of local branches.'

(*Criminal Law*, (2nd edn, 1983)).

It is not clear whether the principle of identification can apply to a director or official whose appointment is invalid. Lord Diplock in the *Tesco Supermarkets Ltd v Nattrass* suggest that it would not. He emphasised that *the obvious and only place* to look in deciding whose acts are to be identified with the corporation is the constitution of the corporation, its articles and memorandum of association. This emphasis on the formal structure of the company would rule out anyone not validly appointed under the relevant *Companies Act*.

4.7 It can be seen that negligence by an employer is that of a failure by the management to identify risks and make provision to control them. It is the failure by management that is the focus of the new law of corporate killing. The concept of management failure is an attempt to define what, for the purpose of an undertaking equates to that of the individual offence, of killing by gross carelessness. It must of course be proved, as in the individual offence, that the defendant's conduct which, in the present context means an outcome of management failure, caused the death. To a large extent this will involve the application of the ordinary principles of causation, as in any other homicide offence. For example, the offence will not be proved if the jury is not satisfied *beyond reasonable doubt* that the death occurred because of *management failure*. Even if the death would not otherwise have occurred, it will be open to the jury to conclude that some unforeseeable act or event broke the chain of causation. In this situation it would be where the management failure was not itself a cause of the death, but merely part of the events leading up to it. An example could be where there was a failure to ensure that some potentially dangerous operation was properly supervised. The crucial question would be whether the conduct in question amounted to a failure to ensure safety in the management of the corporation's activities, and this would be a question of fact for the jury to determine.

It is recognised that there will be some cases in which the jury will have to determine the distinction between an employee's negligence and management failure. The main emphasis will be where the employer delegates the identifying and implementing of health and safety precautions to their employees and those not employed by them, which may be a failure to discharge their duty to ensure safe systems of work.

Management responsibility

4.8   There needs to be strong management and leadership from the most senior people in any undertaking who need to establish a culture of health and safety and are visibly seen to have ownership. There are basic requirements with regard to health and safety that apply to all undertakings, that are relevant to the proposed new offence which include:

- A corporate health and safety statement and policy, adopted and signed by the most senior officer in the undertaking.

- A culture that identifies health and safety as an integral part of the undertaking.

- A normal corporate operating and emergency procedures.

- Suitable and sufficiently competent staff.

- A management system for health and safety that is commensurate with the size and type of undertaking and associated risks.

- A method of monitoring and recording the working and effectiveness of the safety management systems.

- A monitoring and audit process to identify changes to the safety management system so far as to encompass change and new developments.

- A system of communication that feeds information up to the boardroom as well as cascading information down to all employees and those directly employed but affected by the undertakings activities.

These are key topics that the management of every undertaking should encompass within its corporate structure, but not be limited by them, as every undertaking is unique in its size, formation, risks, operations and management. The failure to employ any of the key issues or if there is a failure with any of the elements, means the management may well have failed, and the degree of that failure will be a matter for the courts. To make sound judgments the court will rely on the systems and process of other similar undertakings, which can be balanced against the degree of knowledge, understanding and failure by the defendant management.

If the undertaking does not have the appropriate systems including suitable, sufficient and up to date health and safety procedures then its management is leaving itself open to failure. Without the basic elements outlined above there may be a breach of statutory duties under the *HSWA 1974* and the *Management of Health and Safety at Work Regulations 1999 (SI 1999/3242)* and therefore the basis for management failure is already established with regard to health and safety.

Health and safety advice and support

4.9   Smaller undertakings are also exposed to the new law and while they may not be financially capable of maintaining in-house health and safety expertise, they will probably need to develop health and safety systems from external sources. No undertaking should purchase an off-the-shelf health and safety system because it may well not meet the requirements of the particular undertaking, and therefore, provide management with a false sense of security. It is critical that suitable and competent support should be sought.

With regard to external assistance there is a note of caution. There are health and safety consultants who have given wrong and poor advice and who are not competent. They have been prosecuted as well as the organisation that employed them. Management has the ultimate responsibility for health and safety because they know their business and it is the health and safety professional that can draw the elements of operating and control together, and highlight any shortfalls in the way in which the undertaking conducts its activities.

In summary:

- The senior management of the undertaking retains the sole responsibility for health and safety in the organisation and that responsibility cannot be devolved to others no matter what their competence or knowledge.

- If *external* health and safety advice and support is required the individual or organisation must have the verifiable professional knowledge and competence to provide the service.

- If *internal* health and safety advice and support is employed the individuals must have the verifiable professional knowledge and competence to carry out those duties.

- The professional status for either internal or external health and safety professionals should be the same.

In the event of an investigation to consider a prosecution for corporate killing the competency of health and safety professionals who are either employed or contracted in to the undertaking to provide advice and support will be subjected to scrutiny. Therefore the status of the health and safety professional is paramount and that person should be competent. In the UK that professional status can be identified as a Registered Safety Practitioner with the Institution of Occupational Safety and Health (RSP – IOSH). There are other organisations who identify health and safety professionals but only IOSH – RSP require Continuous Development Points (CDP) to maintain up-to-date professional status, which is audited, similar for example to the legal and accountancy professions.

Within the *HSWA 1974* an undertaking employing less than five persons does not have to have a written policy and the *Management of Health and Safety at Work Regulations* 1999 *(SI 1999/3242)* requires risk assessments to be carried out but only significant findings need be recorded. These two statements are factual and meet the obligations of an undertakings legal requirement. However, consider the situation that as a result of a fatal accident there is an investigation involving the HSE and the police. The investigation team will seek to establish how the undertaking has managed health and safety as well as identifying how the risks were controlled. Because the law does not require a policy and only very limited written evidence in the case of risk assessments it must be considered that a small undertaking could be at a disadvantage. With the proposed introduction of the new law of corporate killing and the individual offences it would be prudent for all undertakings, no matter what size, to go beyond the legal requirements. This would involve the development of a health and safety policy, written method statements and the carrying out and recording of risk assessments. This need not be prohibitive in terms of expense or be onerous. It is evidence and could influence the outcome of any potential investigation and enforcement action.

Prosecution of the proposed new offence

4.10 The corporate killing prosecution will be presented in court the same as a prosecution under the *HSWA 1974*, although the degree of seriousness is far greater. While a *HSWA 1974* prosecution may well involve management failure it is the level of that failure that will have to be determined and that will be a matter for the court. It is in the court room that it will be decided if the failure is such that only being guilty of corporate killing is appropriate. Initially it will be a matter for the enforcing authorities to investigate and determine the level of seriousness, and differentiate between the levels of management failure. There would be an option to lay *HSWA 1974* charges should the charge of corporate killing be unacceptable to the jury. As with all criminal prosecutions it will be for the enforcing authorities to prove *beyond all reasonable doubt* that the defendants failed to manage health and safety within their undertaking and that those failures resulted in a death. It follows that if the defendants have not met their legal obligations as described above then the stronger the prosecution case will be. Those undertakings that have adopted and encompassed the management of health and safety, and have the ability to provide substantive evidence that they have established safety systems and culture, will be better placed in any investigative and legal processes. It could be the difference between being charged with the proposed *Involuntary Homicide Bill,* corporate killing, or an offence under the *HSWA 1974*, and associated health and safety regulations. If an undertaking were found not guilty of corporate killing the court would be able to determine guilt on a lesser charge under the *HSWA 1974*. An important point is that having good health and safety management systems in place is in part a defence, but having systems and procedures and then not adopting them would have the opposite effect, as it shows that the undertaking had the knowledge but failed to act. An undertaking that does *not* have health and safety management systems does not have a defence.

It is proposed that individuals will have the option of taking a private prosecution against an undertaking. This means that if the authorities do not prosecute, there would be an option for individuals to bring charges through their own legal team.

Transmission of disease and corporate killing

4.11 It is proposed by the government that transmission of disease should be included where there is a management failure in an undertaking and a person dies as a result of contracting a disease, (see: *Reforming the Law on Involuntary Manslaughter: The Government's Proposals, May 2000*).

'(1) Management failure has been one of the causes of a persons death; and

(2) the management failure constitutes conduct falling far below what can reasonably be expected of the corporation in the circumstances.'

There needs to be liability where management failure leads to the transmission of a disease which in turn led to death. The liability could arise if a management failure was a cause, rather than the sole cause of death. Therefore, the inclusion of transmission of disease could have an impact on the number of cases of corporate killing that might be brought. It must be shown that the management's conduct has fallen far below what could be expected of an undertaking in the circumstances.

The transmission of disease is more complex than the general acceptance of the corporate killing offence. It will focus on those who recklessly or through gross carelessness pass on a disease that results in death. The undertaking should not be liable where the transmission of a disease occurs directly between one individual and another unless; the person who transmitted the disease to the person to whom it was passed on to owes a professional duty of care. This is an important aspect and there will be a need for a formulation of circumstances in which the transmission of disease could be covered by the new offences.

An example provided in *Reforming the Law on Involuntary Manslaughter: The Government's Proposals, May 2000*, describes situations where the offence may be used. One example is where a baker sells pies that he knew were infected and which might cause death. This could involve a corporate killing offence for the undertaking, but also an individual offence for the individual concerned. There needs to be included a requirement to draw into the potential offence anybody who contaminates food for blackmail purposes if a victim subsequently dies. Another example is where a patient is infected with a disease due to the obvious recklessness or gross negligence by a health care worker. In this situation there is a duty of care, and could encompass the undertaking as well as an individual.

It is imperative that those undertakings where some form of disease could be transmitted have effective safeguards in place. Staff must be aware of the potential risks, be competent and have sufficient knowledge and equipment to carry out their duties without risk to others.

Proposed Involuntary Homicide Bill, cl 4(3)

4.12   The proposed Involuntary Homicide Bill, cl 4(3) provides:

'A corporation guilty of an offence under this section is liable on conviction on indictment to a fine.'

The penalty for an undertaking upon conviction for corporate killing will be an unlimited fine. This is the same situation for an offence under the *HSWA 1974*, convicted in the Crown Court. The difference is that the offence of corporate killing is raised to that of homicide. The degree of seriousness of the offence will be a matter for the court once all of the evidence is heard and the facts deduced. The judge will examine the financial status of the undertaking and the potential costs of any remedial actions to be imposed. The defendant undertaking will be the subject of this examination and the judge will take into account any mitigation submitted based upon the *Friskies* judgment (*R v Friskies Petcare Ltd [2000] 2 Cr App R(S) 401*, SEE 8.76). This would include such details as a past good history with regard to health and safety and that there was a safety management system in place although it did not reach the required standard. Another factor would be that the failures identified as being a root cause of the incident had been addressed immediately after the fatal incident. If the management had co-operated fully with the investigating officers then this will also be taken into account. There will need to be a judgement made when balancing the fine, prosecution costs and remedial action costs if they impact on the sustainability of the business, as it may not be in the interest of justice to make an undertaking insolvent.

Insolvency and dissolution of companies

4.13   There will not be scope for avoidance measures by unscrupulous undertakings or directors, and any enforcement action will be applied to act as a real deterrent, even in large undertakings and within groups of undertakings. It will not be possible for holding undertakings to attempt to evade possible liability on a charge of corporate killing through the establishment of subsidiary undertakings carrying on the group's riskier business which could most readily give rise to charges of corporate killing. A subsidiary undertaking within a large corporate group might have insufficient assets to pay a large fine, and then, in such cases, liability cannot be transferred to its parent company. It is important that group structures cannot be used as a mechanism for evasion.

Directors of an undertaking, or of parent undertakings, will not be able to evade fines or compensation orders, or otherwise frustrate corporate killing proceedings, by dissolving the undertaking or by deliberately making it insolvent. The court will have the power to ensure that criminal proceedings in relation to corporate killing can continue to completion notwithstanding the formal insolvency of the undertaking.

It is proposed that the law should allow for the assets of undertakings to be frozen pending the outcome of the trial. These proceedings would be similar to the charging and restraint orders used under the drug trafficking offence legislation. In the case of a potential corporate killing prosecution, the prosecuting authority may be able to take some form of action to freeze certain company assets before criminal proceedings are started. This would prevent the directors or shadow directors of the undertaking transferring assets in the knowledge that it had been involved in a death that might give rise to a corporate killing charge. If this were allowed to occur then the directors could create a financial situation resulting in a much reduced fine.

A fundamental principle of English law, which is also contained in the *European Convention of Human Rights*, is that a person (which includes a legal person) is innocent until proven guilty. The court can more readily use such powers where a plea of guilty has been entered and where it is known what the likely penalty is and therefore that portion of the assets could be frozen. However, for the offence of corporate killing to be effective and encompass all undertakings, there must be no legal loopholes and senior management must be held culpable for any avoidance activities.

Disqualification of individuals

4.14 As part of the enforcement actions that can be taken in a corporate killing prosecution there are options for actions against individuals. It is proposed that there should be a sanction against any member of management who could be shown to have had some influence on, or responsibility for a situation where there was a management failure. That individual could be disqualified from acting in a management role, in any undertaking, within the jurisdiction of the English courts for a period to be determined by the courts. This would apply whether the individual is a manager in a partnership, a school governor or a manager or director in any type of undertaking.

The Company Directors Disqualification Act 1986 enables a court to make a disqualification order against a director convicted of an indictable offence connected with management and aimed at conduct which includes health and safety matters. This sanction is rarely used but one example is where the managing director of Waste Recycling Limited in Essex was disqualified in August 1999. He was prosecuted under *HSWA 1974, s 37* for breaching the *Provision and Use of Work Equipment Regulations 1992 (SI 1992/2932), Reg 11(1)*.

Enforcement procedures

4.15 Where a fatality occurs in an at work situation it has to be reported to the police who will attend and investigate the circumstances. Under current law, they will determine if there has been an unlawful act by an individual that could result in an investigation for manslaughter or some other offence such as perverting the course of justice. If there is no such evidence, the investigation will be transferred to the HSE or local authority officers to take any appropriate action.

It is anticipated that with the introduction of the proposed new law for corporate killing, the police will still attend the scene. They will be investigating for any evidence that could identify an individual who may have carried out a criminal act. The HSE or other regulating body will proceed to investigate for the corporate offence. If an individual is identified they will be questioned formally by the police, in conjunction with the other enforcing body, as the individual offences will probably be linked to a corporate offence. If there is sufficient evidence, an individual can be charged with reckless killing (SEE CHAPTER 5), killing by gross carelessness (SEE CHAPTER 6) or killing where the intention, was to cause minor injury (if adopted) (SEE CHAPTER 7). If charges for both corporate and individual offences were forthcoming, then all matters would proceed together, with the HSE, police, CPS and other parties co-operating in a joint prosecution.

Legal aid – Criminal Defence Service

4.16   What was previously known, as legal aid is now the Criminal Defence Service provided under the *Criminal Defence Service (Advice and Assistance) Act 2001*. Under the criminal legal aid system it was possible for advice and assistance to include, in certain circumstances, limited representation at a court hearing. It was always the intention that such limited representation would continue to be available in the same circumstances when the Criminal Defence Service sections of the *Access to Justice Act 1999* came into force on 2 April 2001, and replaced the legal aid scheme.

In criminal cases, and that includes those of corporate killing and the individual offences, where an individual is investigated and charged, the Criminal Defence Service will provide access to advice, assistance and representation as the interests of justice require. Funding will be provided for such advice and assistance that is considered appropriate during criminal investigations. It is intended that there should be some limited representation in the advocacy, similar to that provided under the *Legal Aid Act 1988*.

This service will not be available to undertakings that may be facing investigation and prosecution for corporate killing, but only to individuals who are investigated as part of the process.

Directors' and Officers' Liability Insurance

4.17 Directors and officers of a company can be held personally liable for any act that is negligent or outside of their authority or in breach of a duty of care. Those who could be potentially liable can obtain insurance cover under the Directors' and Officers' Liability insurance cover and the Commercial Legal Expenses insurance.

The insurance does not provide cover for any fines or costs incurred if the act for which they have been prosecuted has elements of wilful injury or they have been intentionally reckless. In this situation having been found guilty there will be no insurance and the individual will be liable for all fines, costs and legal expenses outside of any funds awarded by the Criminal Defence Service.

It will certainly be the situation if any individual is found personally culpable in a corporate killing prosecution and disqualified from holding office may not be covered by insurance. If an individual is found guilty of reckless killing, killing by gross carelessness, or killing where the intention was to cause minor injury (if adopted) there would not be insurance cover. It is anticipated that the insurance industry will review the situation in respect to potential cover if the new offences are introduced.

Proposed Involuntary Homicide Bill, cl 4(4)

4.18 This clause of the Bill states:

> 'No individual shall be convicted of aiding, abetting, counselling or procuring an offence under this section but without prejudice to an individual being guilty of any other offences in respect of the death in question.'

It is likely that this section will be withdrawn and therefore, no comment is made.

Proposed Involuntary Homicide Bill, cl 4(5)

4.19 This proposed clause states:

'This section does not preclude a corporation being guilty of an offence under section 1 or 2 above.'

The proposed *Involuntary Homicide Bill, cls 1 and 2* refers to reckless killing and killing by gross carelessness respectively. These are the individual offences for which separate charges would be laid. However, it may be the case that a corporation charged with the corporate offence finds that during the trial there is evidence of failings that open the conviction wider than the corporate charge. This may expose the need to identify with individual offences and would provide the option to the court. This situation could arise if evidence was produced during the trial that while an individual had not been charged, the court considered that there had been individual failure and should be identified in the trial with an impact on the verdict and subsequent penalties.

Proposed Involuntary Homicide Bill, cl 4(6)

4.20   This clause of the proposed legislation provides:

'This section applied if the injury resulting in death is sustained in England and Wales or –

(a)   within the seaward limits of the territorial sea adjacent to the United Kingdom;

(b)   on a British ship or Vessel;

(c)   on a British-controlled aircraft as defined in section 92 of the Civil Aviation Act 1982; or

(d)   in any place to which an Order in Council under section 22(1) of the Oil and Gas (Enterprise) Act 1982 applies (criminal jurisdiction in relation to offshore activities).'

Territorial Extent

4.21   English law generally determines that nothing done outside England and Wales is an offence under English criminal law. A statutory exception to this is that English courts have jurisdiction over its subjects for offences of homicide committed abroad. This applies to the proposed offences of reckless killing (CHAPTER 5); killing by gross carelessness (CHAPTER 6) and killing where the intention was only to cause some injury but the resulting death was unforeseeable (CHAPTER 7).

The jurisdiction for the offence of corporate killing is territorial based. This means that all undertakings including foreign registered companies are subjected to the jurisdiction of the English courts providing the injury that results in death occurs in a place where the English courts have jurisdiction. Undertakings which, are registered in England and Wales would not be charged with corporate killing if the offence were committed abroad. Investigation and enforcement against companies abroad is a matter for the country where the offence was committed.

Seaward limits of the territorial sea

4.22   This is generally defined as being within twelve miles out to sea from the low water mark on the English and Welsh shoreline, except where other definitions apply. This would include situations where offences were committed offshore on offshore oil and gas installations and offshore windfarms which are within the jurisdiction of the courts of England and Wales.

A British ship or vessel

4.23   This applies to ships and vessels that are registered in Great Britain. To avoid being subjected to British legislation, the majority of ships and vessels are registered overseas to operate under *flags of convenience* which means that activities onboard are subjected to the laws of the country where they are registered.

Civil Aviation Act 1982, s 92

4.24   The *Civil Aviation Act 1982, s 92* details the jurisdiction of UK authorities in respect of criminal offences committed on aircraft in flight. The aircraft covered are UK registered or controlled which, falls within UK Law. In 1996 the law was amended by the *Civil Aviation (Amendment) Act 1996* to include UK bound foreign aircraft which meant that police jurisdiction extended to not only UK registered aircraft but to foreign registered aircraft provided that the next landing of the aircraft is in the UK.

The Oil and Gas (Enterprise) Act 1982, s 22(1)

4.25   The *Criminal Jurisdiction (Offshore Activities) Order 1987 (SI 1987/2198)* applies to territorial waters of the United Kingdom and the waters in any area which at the time are designated under the *Continental Shelf Act 1964, s 1(7)*. Criminal law will apply to any act or omission, which takes place on, under or above an installation in waters where the Order applies or any waters within 500 metres of any such installation. If the offence took place in any part of the United Kingdom and is an offence within the criminal law, then it will apply offshore on or surrounding an installation.

Proposed Involuntary Homicide Bill, cl 4(7)

4.26 This clause of the proposed legislation states:

'For the purposes of subsection (6)(b) and (c) above an injury sustained on a ship, vessel or aircraft shall be treated as including an injury sustained by a person who is then no longer on board, and who sustains the injury, in consequence of the wrecking of, or of some other mishap affecting, the ship, vessel or aircraft.'

This section follows on from the *Involuntary Homicide Bill, cl 4(6)* to determine that in the event of an accident involving a British registered ship, vessel or aircraft, any person injured will have deemed to have been injured whilst onboard, or as a consequence of being onboard a ship, vessel or aircraft covered by the jurisdiction of the English and Welsh courts. A person who escapes a disastrous situation and is rescued will deem to have been injured whilst onboard the transport identified above. If a ship or vessel capsizes or has a fire onboard, those who are injured as a consequence of those incidents are included in this section.

Proposed Involuntary Homicide Bill, cl 4(8)

4.27 This clause of the proposed legislation provides:

'In this section "a corporation" does not include a corporation sole but includes any body corporate wherever incorporated.'

The offence of corporate killing applies to any body however formed and is encompassed in the all-embracing term 'undertaking'. This brings all limited liability and public liability companies as well as organisations such as local authorities, incorporated charities, trusts, educational institutes, incorporated clubs as well as all forms of partnerships, the self employed and other business formations.

The Home Office, police, CPS and HSE agreed with this concept which opens the offence of corporate killing to all undertakings.

Undertakings

4.28   It is proposed that the law of corporate killing should affect a diverse range of enterprises and it is intended to describe them as undertakings to conform with the *HSWA 1974, ss 2(1) and 3(1)*. This section refers to the duty of every employer to *conduct* his undertaking in such a way as to avoid exposure to risk. Although an undertaking is not specifically defined in the *HSWA 1974*, the HSE have relied on the definition provided in the *Local Employment Act 1960* where it is described as any *'trade or business or other activity providing employment'*. This definition avoids many of the inconsistencies that would have occurred if the offence were applied to corporations but not to other similar bodies. This means that at present there is no legal definition of what comprises an undertaking, but in a leading health and safety handbook, the following definition is provided:

> 'An undertaking includes one for the provision of services, and is *'conducted'* by the employer even when shut down for maintenance purposes *R v Mara [1987] 1 WLR 87 [1987] ICR 165*. In *Sterling-Windthrop Group Ltd v Allan [1987] SLT 652n 1987 SCCR 25*, it was stated that the conduct of the undertaking was not limited to the industrial process but would also cover trading and supplying or selling to customers.'

(Hendy and Ford, *Redgraves Health and Safety*, (1998, 3rd edn), Butterworths).

Further clarification was given when the phrase 'conduct his undertaking' was considered by the Court of Appeal in *R v Associated Octel Co Ltd [1994] 4 All ER 1051*.

> 'The court made it clear that the offence was concerned with a wider spectrum of activities than those under the company's control. All that the prosecution had to show, the court held was that the activity in question was part of the conduct of the employer's undertaking. It was then for the employer to show, if they could, that it was not *reasonably practicable* to prevent the accident.'

In the legal context further clarification was given in *R v Associated Octel Co Ltd* by Judge Stuart-Smith who said:

'The word undertaking means *enterprise or business*. The cleaning, repair and maintenance of plant, machinery and buildings necessary for carrying on business is part of the conduct of the undertaking, whether it is done by the employer's own employees or by independent contractors. If there is a risk of injury ... and, a fortiori, if there is actual injury as a result of the conduct of that operation, there is *prima facie* liability, subject to the defence of reasonable practicability.'

These statements provide a broad-based understanding of the meaning undertaking. Adopted in the proposed corporate offence it will encompass all aspects of an *at work* situation and place liabilities on those in *control* or *directing* an undertaking, whether they are a director, senior manager, partner, trustee or other person who could be construed to know or ought to have known but turned a wilfully blind eye.

Clearly, the use of the word undertaking greatly broadens the scope of the offence. It encompasses a range of bodies that have not been classified as corporations including schools, hospital trusts, partnerships and charities, as well as one or two person businesses such as self-employed gas fitters. In effect the offence of corporate killing applies to all employing organisations which means that they are potentially liable to the offence of corporate killing.

Proposed Involuntary Homicide Bill 1995, cl 5(1)

4.29 Clause 5(1) of the proposed *Involuntary Homicide Bill*, states

'A court before which a corporation is convicted of corporate killing may, subject to subsection (2) below, order the corporation to take such steps, within such time, as the order specifies for remedying the failure in question and any matter which appears to the court to have resulted from the failure and been the cause or one of the causes of the death.'

When an undertaking is found guilty of corporate killing, the court has the power to make remedial orders. The HSE and other enforcement bodies will use their powers to issue Enforcement Notices as part of, or following, their investigation and in advance of any hearing. However, the court has the power to order remedial action either where the HSE (or the other appropriate enforcement body) had not issued a Notice or where such a Notice had not been complied with.

The responsibility for drawing up the order should rest with whichever agency is prosecuting. All applications for orders in areas where an enforcement authority (such as the HSE) has responsibility should be made by or in consultation with that body to ensure that the terms of the order and any steps specified by the court are reasonable. Such orders should be in line with current enforcement policy and what the enforcement authority would regard as good practice. Both the prosecuting agency and the defence would have the opportunity to make representations or call evidence regarding the application. The enforcement authority will be given the task of checking compliance and referring matters back to the court where necessary.

Proposed Involuntary Homicide Bill, cl 5(2)

4.30 This clause of the proposed Bill provides:

'No such order shall be made except on an application by the prosecution specifying the terms of the proposed order; and the order, if any, made by the court shall be on such terms (whether those proposed or others) as the court considers appropriate having regard to any representations made, and any evidence adduced, in relation to that matter by the prosecution or on behalf of the corporation.'

It is a matter for the prosecution to apply to the court for an order to be made. This court will then hear representation from the prosecution as to what they consider is an appropriate course of action. This will be supported with evidence such as Approved Codes of Practice (ACOP's), industry guidance and any other information that is relevant to safe operations in the specific industry or operations. The defendants will have the opportunity to challenge the prosecution application if it is considered unreasonable, impracticable or impossible to comply with. Due consideration would be given to applications that could render an undertaking financially unable to meet the requirements. In this situation it would then be a matter for the court to decide the course of action to progress the matter.

Proposed Involuntary Homicide Bill, cl 5(3)

4.31 Clause 5(3) of the proposed legislation states:

'In subsection (2) above references to the prosecution include references to the Health and Safety Executive and to any other body or person designated for the purposes of that subsection by the Secretary of State either generally or in relation to the case in question.'

This section identifies that the prosecution can, when applying for remedial orders refer to the HSE or other competent bodies for recommendations of appropriate actions. Those bodies will be designated by the Secretary of State which means that the courts cannot call upon the services of an organisation that may have a vested interest in the outcome of defining such an order. This would preclude private organisations, such as consultancies or trade unions.

Proposed Involuntary Homicide Bill, cl 5(4)

4.32   This clause provides:

'The time specified by an order under subsection (1) above may be extended or further extended by order of the court on an application made before the end of that time or extended time, as the case may be.'

It may be that an order made by the court cannot be complied with because of circumstances beyond the defendant's control. This may include the unavailability of equipment or delays to progress through poor weather conditions. In such circumstances, and before the compliance date, the management of the undertaking will need to have sufficient and suitable evidence to convince the court that there is a genuine reason and that matters are beyond the undertaking's control. Successful applications will be provided with a new compliance date. It would be doubtful if the lack of finance would be considered acceptable.

Proposed Involuntary Homicide Bill, cl 5(5)

4.33   This clause provides:

'A corporation, which fails to comply with an order under this section, is guilty of an offence and liable –

(a)   on conviction on indictment, to a fine;

(b) on summary conviction, to a fine not exceeding £20,000.'

An undertaking that is found guilty of failing to comply with a court order to carry out remedial action will face a fine in the magistrates court to a maximum of £20,000. This does not then absolve the undertaking of complying with the original order. The magistrates may consider that there is an intentional disregard of the order and it should be an option to return the case to the Crown Court. In this situation the judge will have greater powers to deal with the matter.

Proposed Involuntary Homicide Bill, cl 5(6)

4.34   This clause provides:

> 'Where an order is made against a corporation under this section it shall not be liable under any of the provisions mentioned in subsection (7) below by reason of anything which the order requires it to remedy in so far as it continues during the time specified by the order or any further time allowed under sub-section (4) above.'

This clause determines that if an order is made against an under-taking and providing the remedial action is complied with in the time specified it will not be liable for specified actions identified in sub paragraph (7) below.

Proposed Involuntary Homicide Bill, cl 5(7)

4.35   Clause 5(7) provides:

> 'The provisions referred to in subsection (6) above are –
>
> (a) sections 1, 2 and 4 above;
>
> (b) the provisions of Part I of the Health and Safety at Work etc Act 1974,
>
> (c) the existing statutory provisions as defined in section 53(1) of that Act.'

HSWA 1974, Part 1, covers *ss 1 to 54* and encompasses the follow-ing:

- Securing the health, safety and welfare of persons at work.

- Protecting persons other than persons at work against risks to health or safety arising out of or in connection with the activities of persons at work.

- Controlling the keeping and use of explosives or highly flammable or otherwise dangerous substances, and generally preventing the unlawful acquisition, possession and use of such substances.

- Provides for the making of health and safety regulations and the preparation and approval of codes of practice and the replacement by the system of regulations and approved codes of practice.

- Risks arising out of or in connection with the activities of persons at work, including risks that can be attributed to the working of an undertaking.

HSWA 1974, s 15 enables the Secretary of State to have the power to make regulations, to be referred to as health and safety regulations. This section is the source of the mass of regulations, which now comprises the bulk of health and safety law. The regulations implementing the *European Directives* that came into effect on 1 January 1993 were made under this section.

HSWA 1974, s 53(1)(a) and *(b)* provides meanings for articles for use at work:

'(a) any plant designed for use or operation (whether exclusively or not) by persons at work, and

(b) any article designed for use as a component in any such plant;

...'

The meanings provide descriptions that apply throughout the *HSWA 1974*.

Proposed Involuntary Homicide Bill, cl 8(1)

4.36 This clause explains the meaning of injury

'In this Act "injury" means –

(a) physical injury, including pain, unconsciousness or other impairment of a person's physical condition; or

(b) impairment of a person's mental health.'

It can be seen to be very wide in its interpretation to include physical injury which, is self explanatory and more readily identifiable than pain and possibly unconsciousness. For there to be a prosecution for corporate killing a person or persons must be killed at or due to work activities. In the case of a fatal incident there may be others who are injured and as such may demonstrate the seriousness of an overall offence. An example can be identified with rail accidents where there are generally few killed but a considerable number are seriously injured. An injury outcome would require specialist medical involvement to determine the impairment of a person's mental health.

Proposed Involuntary Homicide Bill, cl 8(2)

4.37 This clause provides:

> 'This Act had effect subject to any enactment or rule of law providing a defence, or providing lawful authority, justification or excuse for an act or omission.'

The outcome of a criminal trial will leave available general and special defences. Those defences include:

* insanity before the trial

* insanity at the trial

* diminished responsibility

* mistake

* intoxication (certain offences only)

* duress and coercion

* necessity

* public and private defences

* superior orders

* impossibility

* non-compliance with Community Law.

It is not intended to describe the defences listed, as it is unlikely that they will apply to the corporate situation. However, they would be available in the appropriate circumstances.

Proposed Involuntary Homicide Bill, cl 8(3)

4.38   This clause states:

> 'This Act has effect subject to the rules relating to the effect of intoxication on criminal liability.'

Intoxication impairs a person's perception and judgement so he may fail to be aware of facts, or to foresee results of his conduct of which he would certainly have been aware, or have foreseen, if he had been sober. So, intoxication may be the reason why the defendant lacked the *mens rea* of the crime charged. Intoxication is not, and never has been, a defence in its own right. This means that it is never a defence for a person to declare, no matter how convincingly, that had he not had the drink, he would not have behaved the way he did. Alcohol and drugs weaken a persons restraints and inhibitions which generally control our conduct. A person may do things when drunk that they would never do when sober. In normal terms the mental element of being drunk and not knowing what they are doing, should lead to an acquittal. However, there are strong policy reasons against this that have led the courts to develop a way of dealing with cases which will normally lead to a conviction.

There are a number of elements covering intoxication and criminal liability:

- Voluntary and involuntary intoxication.
- Voluntary intoxication by alcohol and dangerous drugs.
- Intoxication otherwise than alcohol or dangerous drugs.
- Intoxication causing insanity or abnormal mind.
- Intoxication induced with intent to commit crime.

Any of the above could be submitted as a defence in criminal law if an individual is prosecuted and being intoxicated is a factor.

In a workplace environment any person who under the influence of alcohol does an act, the outcome of which leads to an incident that incurs serious injury or death, could be charged with reckless killing or killing by gross carelessness. It could be argued that the offender did not appreciate at the time that there was a risk of death or serious injury because he was intoxicated.

It is expected that undertakings would have an alcohol and drugs policy for at work situations. This should devolve awareness and responsibility from the boardroom through to the most junior member of the undertaking. Therefore, anybody who breaches the policy would not be able to use intoxication as a defence or mitigation.

Proposed Involuntary Homicide Bill, cl 10(1)

4.39   This clause provides:

'This Act comes into force at the end of the period of two months beginning with the day on which it is passed.'

When the Bill is agreed and accepted by Parliament it will be sent for Royal Assent. Once passed through this phase it will become effective as legislation two months after the date it is passed.

Proposed Involuntary Homicide Bill, cl 10(2)

4.40   This clause provides:

'This Act does not apply in relation to anything done or omitted before it comes into force.'

Any offence committed before the date that the Act comes into force cannot be charged with any of the new offences defined in this Act.

Proposed Involuntary Homicide Bill, cl 11(1)

4.41   This clause provides:

'This Act may be cited as the Involuntary Homicide Act.'

In any communication where any sections are quoted, they are done so under the enabling Act, and will be cited as a section within the Act.

Proposed Involuntary Homicide Bill, cl 11(2)

4.42   'The amendments in the Schedule to this Act have the same extent as the enactments to which they relate but, subject to that, this Act extends to England and Wales only.'

This Act will, once it receives Royal Assent only apply to criminal activities within the jurisdiction of English and Welsh courts. Scotland and Northern Ireland will establish the equivalent legal foundations for the corporate and individual offences if they are not already considered in existing law.

Summary

This chapter has examined the proposed *Involuntary Homicide Bill* for the offence of corporate killing. The principal elements of the offence have been identified, with important aspects such as the focus on management failure, and the adoption of the offence to undertakings. This offence does not need to identify an individual who has committed an offence. There are separate individual offences, the most serious being reckless killing which is the subject of the next chapter.

5 Reckless Killing

This chapter considers the following:

- Proposed *Involuntary Homicide Bill*.
- The proposed offence of reckless killing.
- The fault element.
- The reasonable man.
- Competent personnel.
- Prosecution of the new offence.
- Transmission of disease.
- Penalty.
- Health and safety advice.
- Legal Aid and Criminal Defence Service.
- Directors' and officers' liability insurance.
- Defences.
- Undertakings.
- Meaning of injury.
- Application of proposed Bill.

Introduction

5.1 The new law of reckless killing has not been enacted, but the draft *Involuntary Homicide Bill* (SEE APPENDIX) provides a structure for a review of what can be expected. Adopting the understanding that the new law will apply to an individual's conduct which, is the cause of the death of another at or in connection to a workplace activity. The offence of reckless killing is one of the new offences proposed in the *Involuntary Homicide Bill*. It will only apply to incidents that occur within the jurisdiction of the English and Welsh courts. Scotland is expected to make its own arrangements to align with the proposed offences.

107

The offence of reckless killing is one of homicide and is considered so serious that it falls just below that of murder. An individual found guilty of this offence could face life imprisonment. The key element of the proposed offence is that of continuing to act recklessly regardless of the outcome despite knowing that there is a risk of death to another.

Proposed Involuntary Homicide Bill

5.2 The proposed *Involuntary Homicide Bill, cl 1* deals with the individual offence of reckless killing that, in this situation involves deaths at work. This is where an individual has conducted themselves in such a way as to disregard risks that it warrants charges of reckless killing.

This means that the failure is that of an individual acting in some capacity either within an undertaking or self-employed. In an undertaking the individual will probably, but not exclusively, be at boardroom or senior management level. In either situation there will be a death at or due to work activities. There are a number of key elements that form the proposed offence described in figure 5.1.

Proposed Involuntary Homicide Bill, cl 1(1)

5.3 This clause identifies the basis for the individual offence of reckless killing:

'1. (1) A person who by his conduct causes the death of another is guilty of reckless killing if –

    (a) he is aware of a risk that his conduct will cause the death or serious injury; and

    (b) it is unreasonable for him to take that risk having regard to the circumstances as he knows or believes them to be.

(2) A person guilty of reckless killing is liable on conviction on indictment to imprisonment for life.'

The offence of reckless killing is one of the proposed new offences that will replace involuntary manslaughter. There are currently three ways of committing involuntary manslaughter:

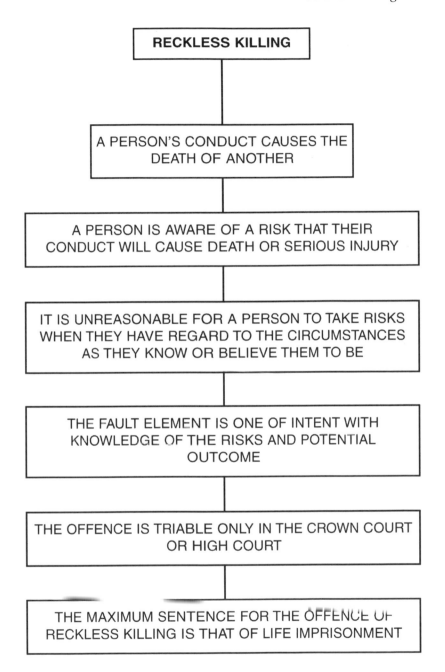

Figure 5.1: Key elements of the reckless killing offence

(1) Unlawful act manslaughter where the person who caused the death was engaged in a criminal act which carried with it the risk of some injury to another person.

(2) Gross negligence manslaughter where a person causes death through extreme carelessness or incompetence.

(3) Where a person is aware that their conduct involves a risk of causing death (or probably serious injury) and unreasonably takes that risk.

The offence of reckless killing proposed under the *Involuntary Homicide Bill* uses the same words as those in the *Offences Against the Person Bill*. As the offence is involuntary homicide it means that where an individual is investigated for reckless killing, it will be the responsibility of the police to lead on the investigation, and the responsibility of the Crown Prosecution Service (CPS) to review the evidence and bring the prosecution. An investigation into the actions of an individual will generally be linked to an investigation into the management activities in an undertaking where there had been an at work or through work fatality. There will need to be close co-operation with the police as defined in the protocol for liaison between HSE, police and CPS described in CHAPTER 9. The proposed process is described in the flow chart (see FIGURE 4.2 in chapter 4). which gives an overview of the responsibilities. Clearly if there are corporate and individual prosecutions it will be expedient to progress all the matters together.

It will be a matter for the prosecution to prove beyond all reasonable doubt that a person was aware of the risks, in other words that they had the knowledge and understanding of the potential outcome. It will be the conduct of that person that will be identified as being the cause of the death or serious injury. It is impossible to provide a definition of serious injury and it will be a matter for the jury to determine, having heard all of the facts and circumstances surrounding the incident causing the death.

Fault element

5.4   Unlike the offence of manslaughter where a person had to be identified as having undertaken a physical act that results in the death of another, an issue that has been examined in detail earlier in the book (SEE CHAPTER 1), reckless killing does not require the physical action by a person. This means that a director, executive, trustee, partner, self-employed person, manager, supervisor or any other person with responsibilities or connected to work activities, can be determined culpable. The main aim of this offence is to include senior management who by their conduct expose others to serious injury and death, but it does not exclude others. The prosecution will need to prove that the person was aware of the risks in a given situation, and that does not require the person to have direct contact or involvement. It will be the knowledge that an unsafe activity is being carried out and that by not stopping it, the result was that their conduct caused or was the cause of the death.

A broad example which focuses on a company but it would be the same for any undertaking is outlined below.

At a boardroom meeting the directors have on the agenda an issue that there are unsafe acts being done within the company. The acts are placing employees and others not employed at risk of serious injury and loss of life. A junior manager proposes a solution that is reasonable, achievable and financially viable. The board takes the decision not to adopt the solution. There is a serious incident with an outcome that there are numerous dead and injured. One of the causes of the incident is identified as the conduct of board members at the meeting. It will be a matter for the investigating authorities to determine if and who should be charged. In this situation it could be the chairman, managing director or senior management person attending the meeting who is charged as representing the board. Providing that the director responsible for health and safety was opposed to the board's action, and recorded that opposition then that person would not be culpable. It would be the most senior person present at the meeting or directing the meeting or with the controlling vote who would have the responsibility for the management's decision. The offence is that is was unreasonable for them to take the risk having regard to the circumstances as it is known or believed to be.

In the situation above it would need to be proven that the person was fully aware of the risk and potential outcome and with that information allowed the situation to continue. In addition to being aware of risk, it would be the element of conduct that was the cause. Following on from the awareness and conduct is the unreasonableness of the action.

5.5 Further points to consider with regard to the fault element are:

- A director or person of similar standing has not made adequate provision for health and safety within an undertaking that is a statutory duty. An outcome of this failure is the death of an employee or other who is not employed but affected by the undertaking's activities.

- A director or person of similar standing is aware that because they have not fulfilled the obligations of their statutory duties they are aware of a risk of causing death. It would not be a defence to say that they were not aware of health and safety legislation.

- That person having not made adequate provision to control health and safety within the undertaking and is aware that the risks of serious injury and death could be an outcome, continues to take the risk even though it is unreasonable for them to do so.

If a director, manager or appropriate person in control is reckless in their actions, either when they knew or should have known, that failure could result in an accident, then there is recklessness. The prosecution will base its case on the evidence they have resulting from an investigation and determine the degree of recklessness and lay the appropriate charges. However, the degree of the individual culpability is a matter for the court to determine when all of the evidence is heard. It may be that the evidence shows a lesser degree of recklessness than the charge requires, and the jury may consider that the less serious charge is deemed to be correct in the circumstances.

This would clearly place responsibility at the highest level of an undertaking, no matter its size. It should also remove situations where senior management have in the past, distanced themselves from serious incidents involving loss of life, occurring within their undertaking. In small undertakings and for the self-employed person the focus on responsibility is more readily identifiable. The change in law places liability on individuals in large and diverse undertakings and there is always evidence as to who is the most senior person in the undertaking. That person signs the undertaking's health and safety policy or can be identified through registration at Company's House, or certified revenue accounts.

5.6   When determining the sentence for the offence of reckless killing (see 5.13) the judge will take a number of factors into account. To date the judiciary has not always viewed health and safety manslaughter prosecutions in the same way that they view other criminal offenders. One problem is that juries have not been keen to convict an individual in a workplace fatality. This is because it has generally been a member of the workforce left to face the legal process, when there has clearly been management failure. This has been seen with train drivers, who having been charged with manslaughter for failing to abide by the rules, have had their trials stopped. The reason is that the drivers were exposed to poor corporate culture towards safe methods of work and were therefore considered to be scapegoats. As the directors were not prosecuted, juries were found to be sympathetic to the individual defendant who was seen to be following orders derived from those in senior positions. Under the new proposals it is the most senior person in an undertaking who could be identified and on trial.

5.7 An individual found guilty of reckless killing will, as with any criminal trial submit mitigation. If the individual pleads guilty at the earliest opportunity thus saving court time and money there will be a credit that could reduce the sentence. If the individual pleads not guilty and is subsequently found guilty, no discount will be made. The maximum sentence available to the court for reckless killing is life imprisonment. The actual period of sentence will be reached after the mitigation speech has been made. The individuals previous conduct, will be considered such as if they had been in a position of authority as a director, manager or other responsible status where an Enforcement Notice had been issued, or there had been a previous prosecution under health and safety legislation. Other factors will include the degree of negligence and culpability, but there will have been evidence to show that the actions were with full knowledge of the risks and potential outcomes.

It is anticipated that the management of every undertaking will endeavour to avoid prosecution for the offence of corporate killing and below are some of the issues which should be considered:

- An evaluation of the control elements as described in 4.0 in our to ensure that they are in place.

- Ensuring that the control elements are an integral part of the undertakings day-to-day operations.

- Understanding that failure to have elements of statutory duties in place is a failure of management.

- The assessment of risks created by the undertaking and the managing and controlling of those risks.

- Ensuring compliance with previous advice or enforcement actions by the regulating authorities.

- Employing competent safety professionals or contracting a competent health and safety consultant.

- Ensuring the status and ownership of health and safety at senior management level. This would involve minuted health and safety meetings and workforce involvement.

- Ensuring that senior management understands the risks created by their undertaking and the requirement for control measures.

- The need to have evidence of communication with employees and those not employed but affected by the undertaking on matters of health and safety.

The risks within an undertaking and the controls required must be assessed. A small undertaking could have high risks while a large undertaking could have low risks. It is matter for every undertaking no matter how large or small to be managed effectively. An undertaking must ensure that its employees are competent and suitable to carry out the task they are required to do. This applies to temporary staff, contractors, self employed, voluntary staff and in fact anybody who is employed in any capacity within the undertaking. It is important to note that this duty extends to those who participate in the activities but are not employed in the technical sense, such as voluntary workers.

Transmission of disease and reckless killing

5.8   There will need to be liability where individual failure leads to the transmission of a disease which in turn led to death. The liability could arise if an individual failure was a cause rather than sole cause of death. Therefore, the inclusion of transmission of disease could have an impact on the number of cases of reckless killing that might be brought. It must be shown that the conduct has fallen far below what could be expected of an individual in the circumstances.

The transmission of disease is more complex than the general acceptance of fault within the reckless killing offence. It will focus on those who recklessly transmit a disease that results in death. An individual should not be liable where the transmission of a disease occurs directly between one individual and another unless the person who transmitted the disease to the person to whom it was passed onto owes a professional duty of care. This is an important aspect as it involves workplace activities and there will be a need for a formulation of circumstances in which the transmission of disease where an individual could be culpable of the serious offence could be covered by the new offences. (SEE 4.11 for further discussion.)

Reasonable man

5.9   Lord Macmillan offers an explanation of what is a reasonable man in the context of reckless killing in *Corporation of Glasgow v Muir and Others [1943] 2 All ER 44*:

> 'The standard of foresight of the reasonable man is in one sense an impersonal test. It eliminates the personal equation and is independent of the idiosyncrasies of the particular person whose conduct is in question. Some persons are unduly timorous and imagine every path beset with lions; others, of more robust temperament, fail to foresee or nonchalantly disregard even the most obvious dangers. The reasonable man is presumed to be free both from over-apprehension and from over-confidence.'

The accepted definition of negligence is determined in the judgment by Alderson in the case of *Blyth v Birmingham Waterworks Co (1856) 11 Ex 781* who said:

> 'Negligence is the omission of something which a reasonable man, guided upon those considerations which ordinarily regulate the conduct of human affairs, would do, or something which a prudent and reasonable man would do.'

The management or anyone who requires special knowledge or skills in order to undertake or control their work are expected to have suitable knowledge of the risks and safety procedures that employees encounter in carrying out the work. This has been defined in part by John Munkman:

> 'In general, an employer is expected to keep reasonably abreast of current knowledge concerning dangers arising in trade processes, and should be aquatinted with pamphlets issued by the

Health and Safety Executive and other safety organisations drawing attention to risks which have come to light and means of avoiding them.'

(John Munkman, *Employers Liability at Common Law*, 1990)

These elements are borne out in the case of *Wilson v Tyneside Window Cleaning Co [1958] 2 QB 110* where Judge Parker said:

'The master's duty is general, to take all reasonable steps to avoid risk to his servants. For convenience it is often split up into different categories, such as tools, or safe system of work, but it always remains one general duty.'

Clearly, all reasonable individuals will ensure that health and safety and risk control is an integral part of their responsibilities to themselves and others.

Competent personnel

5.10 Those who are employed must be competent and able to carry out the task they are required to do. This applies to temporary staff, contractors, self employed, voluntary staff and in fact anybody who is employed or works in any capacity within the undertaking. It is important to note that this duty extends to those who participate in the activities but are not employed in the technical sense, such as voluntary workers.

In summary:

- The sole responsibility for personnel, their competencies and health and safety knowledge in the organisation remains with management. That responsibility cannot be devolved to others no matter their competence or knowledge and could expose individuals to charges of reckless killing.

- If internal or external health and safety advice and support is required, any individual must have the verifiable professional knowledge and competence to provide the service. A failure by management or the individual could in extreme circumstances, expose them to charges of reckless killing. The professional status for either internal or external health and safety professionals should be the same as the liability could be the same.

Health and safety advice and support

5.11 Individuals, whatever their title, in any undertaking should *not* purchase an off-the-shelf health and safety system as it may well not meet the requirements of the particular undertaking, and therefore, provide management with a false sense of security. It is critical that suitable and competent advice and support should be sought.

There is a need to ensure that there are competent health and safety professionals who are either employed or contracted into the undertaking to provide advice and support. The competence of these professionals will be subjected to scrutiny in the event of an investigation considering a prosecution for reckless killing. The status of the health and safety professional is paramount and that person must be competent (SEE 4.9). An important fact is those health and safety consultants who have given wrong and poor advice and not been competent, have been prosecuted as well as the organisation that employed them.

Prosecution of the proposed new offence

5.12 The prosecution for reckless killing will be presented in court in the same way as a prosecution is currently undertaken for the law of manslaughter. The failure of management will encompass the wider picture leaving the conduct of the individual to be determined. In the most serious of individual crimes it will be a matter for the jury to decide if it is a case of reckless killing. Initially it will be a matter for the enforcing authorities to investigate and evaluate the level of seriousness, and differentiate between overall management failure and individual culpability. There will be an option for the court, if the evidence determines it, to move to the lesser offence of killing by gross carelessness (see CHAPTER 6). As with all criminal prosecutions it will be for the enforcing authorities to prove *beyond all reasonable doubt* that the defendants conduct either:

- Caused the death of another as prescribed in the offence.

- That they were aware of a risk and that their conduct would cause death.

- Knowing the risk, they failed to take appropriate action and that their failure resulted in a death.

It will be for a jury to hear all of the evidence and then determine their decision and for the judge to pass judgment and sentence.

Penalty

5.13   The maximum penalty for an individual convicted of reckless killing will be life imprisonment. This reflects the seriousness of the offence which, means that the case can only be heard in the Crown Court. If a person is found guilty of reckless killing the judge will examine the mitigation submitted by the defence (SEE 5.7) in an effort to obtain the lowest possible custodial sentence.

It will not be possible for the management of holding companies to attempt to evade possible liability of a charge of reckless killing through the establishment of subsidiary companies. Such undertakings could be established to carry on riskier business which could most readily give rise to an individual being used as a scapegoat and left to face a charge of reckless killing.

Directors or those in control of an undertaking no matter how constituted, or of any parent undertaking will not be able to evade prosecution for reckless killing or otherwise frustrate legal proceedings, by dissolving the undertaking or by deliberately making it insolvent. The court will require the power to ensure that criminal proceedings in relation to reckless killing can continue to completion notwithstanding the formal insolvency of an undertaking.

Individuals such as self-employed persons will be subjected to the same procedures as individuals within an undertaking. The same level of culpability will be required for either situation. Past cases show that individual manslaughter for self-employed or individuals in small undertakings is more easily proven. The new offence should level that imbalance.

Other considerations

5.14   The following topics apply to this chapter but are examined in chapter 4:

- Management failure (SEE 4.5)

- Management responsibility (SEE 4.8)

- Legal Aid – Criminal Defence Service (SEE 4.16)
- Directors' and Officers' Liability Insurance (SEE 4.17)
- Proposed *Involuntary Homicide Bill*

cl 4(4) (SEE 4.18)

cl 4(5) (SEE 4.19)

cl 4(6) (SEE 4.20)

cl 4(7) (SEE 4.26)

cl 4(8) (SEE 4.27)

cl 5(1) (SEE 4.29)

cl 5(2) (SEE 4.30)

cl 5(3) (SEE 4.31)

cl 5(7) (SEE 4.35)

cl 8(1) (SEE 4.36)

cl 8(2) (SEE 4.37)

cl 8(3) (SEE 4.38)

cl 10(1) (SEE 4.39)

cl 10(2) (SEE 4.40)

cl 11(1) (SEE 4.41)

cl 11(2) (SEE 4.42)

Summary

This chapter has examined the most serious of the individual offences. The principal elements of the offence have been identified with the focus on the recklessness and intent aspect of the offence. The seriousness is identified in the maximum sentence of life imprisonment. For cases where the more serious aspects are not evident there is a secondary offence of killing by gross carelessness which is examined in the next chapter.

6 Killing by Gross Carelessness

Introduction

6.1   The new law of killing by gross carelessness has not been enacted, but the draft *Involuntary Homicide Bill* (SEE APPENDIX) provides a sound structure for a review of what can be expected. The offence of killing by gross carelessness is one of the new offences proposed in the *Involuntary Homicide Bill* that will only apply to incidents that occur within the jurisdiction of the English and Welsh courts. Scotland is expected to make its own arrangements to align with the proposed offences.

The offence is one of homicide and is considered so serious that an individual found guilty could face imprisonment. The key element of the proposed offence is that an individual knowing that there is a risk of death continues to act carelessly regardless of the outcome.

Proposed Involuntary Homicide Bill, cl 2

6.2 The proposed *Involuntary Homicide Bill, cl 2* deals with the individual offence of killing by gross carelessness that in this situation involves deaths at work. This is where an individual has conducted themselves in such a way as to disregard risks that it warrants charges of killing by gross carelessness.

This means that the failure is that of an individual acting in some capacity within an undertaking, or as a sole trader in whatever capacity results in a death at or due to work activities. There are a number of key elements that form the proposed offence described in FIGURE 6.1.

There will be close co-operation with the police as defined in the protocol for liaison (SEE CHAPTER 9). The proposed process is described in FIGURE 4.2 which gives an overview of the responsibilities. Clearly if there are corporate and individual prosecutions it will be expedient to progress all matters together. The proposed *cl 2* outlines:

'2. (1) A person who by his conduct causes the death of another is guilty of killing by gross carelessness if –

(a) a risk that his conduct will cause death or serious injury would be obvious to a reasonable person in his position;

(b) he is capable of appreciating that risk at the material time; and

(c) either–

(i) his conduct falls far below what can reasonably be expected of him in the circumstances;

(ii) or he intends by his conduct to cause some minor injury or is aware of, and unreasonably takes, the risk that it may do so.

(2) There shall be attributed to the person referred to in subsection (1)(a) above–

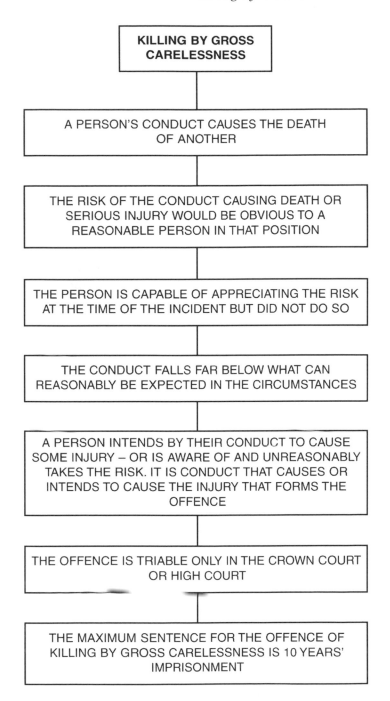

Figure 6.1: Key elements of killing by gross carelessness

(a) knowledge of any relevant facts which the accused is shown to have at the material time; and

(b) any skill or experience professed by him.

(3) In determining for the purposes of subsection (1)(c)(i) above what can reasonably be expected of the accused regard shall be had to the circumstances of which he can be expected to be aware, to any circumstances shown to be within his knowledge and to any other matter relevant for assessing his conduct at the material time.

(4) Subsection (1)(c)(i) above applies only if the conduct causing, or intended to cause, the injury constitutes an offence.

(5) A person guilty of killing by gross carelessness is liable on conviction on indictment to imprisonment for a term not exceeding 10 years.'

The offence of killing by gross carelessness is a serious crime but falls short of the most serious act of reckless killing (SEE CHAPTER 5). It is the degree of fault that distinguishes between the two offences. The basis of the fault is that with reckless killing there will be an act with full knowledge of the risk and failure to take action, while with killing by gross carelessness there will be a failure to appreciate the consequences of an action.

It must be proved beyond all reasonable doubt that a person's conduct causes the death of another. It could be the risk that the conduct of a person would cause the death and that it would be obvious to a reasonable person in the same position. The word 'obvious' in this context means immediately apparent, striking or glaring. A person cannot be blamed for failing to notice a risk if it would not have been obvious to a reasonable person in his place. The use of obvious as opposed to foreseeable is in the defendant's favour. It follows that the person must be capable of appreciating the risk at the time in question, and that the conduct of the person falls far below what can reasonably be expected in the circumstances. An objective of the definitions within the offence is to avoid reliance on the concepts of negligence and duty of care, which have caused much concern to the courts over the years.

The second part of the offence is that it was unreasonable for a person with knowledge of the facts to take the risk, having regard to the circumstances as it is known or believed to be. It would need to be proven that an individual was fully aware of the risks and potential outcome and with that information allowed the situation to continue. In addition to being aware of risk, it would be the element of conduct that was the cause. Following on from the awareness and conduct is the unreasonableness of the action and that the conduct intended to cause injury.

There may be an element of intention in the way a person conducts themselves in that injury was intended or may be caused. There will need to be awareness of the situation and that it may be unreasonable with regard to the risks taken and that the injury caused forms the basis of an offence.

Transmission of disease and killing by gross carelessness

6.3   There needs to be liability where individual failure leads to the transmission of a disease which in turn led to death. The liability could arise if an individual failure was a cause rather than sole cause of death. Therefore, the inclusion of transmission of disease could have an impact on the number of cases of killing by gross carelessness that might be brought. It must be shown that the conduct of an individual has fallen far below what could be expected of an individual in the circumstances.

The transmission of disease is a complex subject and no more so than in the offence of killing by gross carelessness. It will focus on individuals who carelessly transmit a disease that results in death. The rule applies that an individual should not be liable where the transmission of a disease occurs directly between one individual and another. This is unless the person who transmitted the disease to the person to whom it was passed owes a professional duty of care. This is an important aspect as it involves workplace activities. A death resulting from an incident would need to be examined to determine if there was some form of intent and if it was to a lesser standard. This would be a key factor in reducing culpability from reckless killing to that of killing by gross carelessness. There will be a need for a formulation of circumstances in which the transmission of disease where an individual could be culpable of a serious offence.

The offence of killing by gross carelessness uses the same words as those in the *Offences Against the Person Bill*. Because the offence is involuntary homicide it maintains elements of what has been recognised for many years as manslaughter.

Fault element

6.4 The current law of manslaughter requires a person to be identified as having undertaken a physical act that results in the death of another, an issue that has been examined in detail earlier (SEE CHAPTER 1). Killing by gross carelessness does not require physical action by a person. This means that a director, executive, trustee, partner, self-employed person, manager, supervisor or any other person with responsibilities or connected to work activities, can be determined culpable. It must be clear that the focus of this offence is to encompass senior management who by their conduct expose others to serious injury and death. The prosecution will need to prove that the person was aware of the risks in a given situation, and that does not require the person to have direct contact or involvement. It will be the knowledge that an unsafe activity is being undertaken and not taking action to stop the activity, with the result that it was their conduct that caused the death of another.

A broad example, which focuses on a company, but it, would be the same for any undertaking is given below.

6.5 At a boardroom meeting the directors have on the agenda an issue that there are risk activities being carried out within their company. They have knowledge that the activities are potentially placing employees and others not employed at risk of minor injury. The safety manager proposes a solution that is reasonable, achievable and financially viable. The chairman of the meeting, the managing director takes the overriding decision not to adopt the options. They understand that if there is an incident there may be very minor injury, but decide to proceed in the interest of the undertakings financial interests. There is a serious incident with an outcome that one employee and one person not employed are killed. Two other employees are injured. One of the causes of the incident is identified as the conduct of the managing director not having regard to the safety information provided to them at the meeting.

It will be a matter for the investigating authorities to determine if the managing directors actions alone were a cause of the incident. They will then determine the level of culpability and identify who should be charged and with what offence. The focus is that is was unreasonable for them to take the risk having regard to the circumstances as it is known or believed to be. In the situation above it would need to be proven that the person was fully aware of the risks and potential outcome and with that information they allowed the situation to continue. In addition to being aware of risk, it would be the element of conduct that was the cause. Following on from awareness and conduct is the unreasonableness of the action.

6.6 Further consideration should be given to the following points:

- That a director or person of similar standing has made adequate provision for health and safety within an undertaking as required by statutory duty, but failed to heed the safety advice provided which resulted in the death of an employee or other who is not employed but affected by the undertaking's activities.

- That a person who has knowledge of the facts is aware of their actions and is capable of appreciating a risk of causing death at the time of the incident.

- That person having made adequate provision to control health and safety within the undertaking is aware of the risks for causing serious injury and death, and, continues to take the risk even though it is unreasonable for them to do so.

If a director, manager or appropriate person in control is careless in their actions, either when they knew or should have known, that failure could result in an accident, then there is gross carelessness. The prosecution will base its case on the evidence they have resulting from an investigation and determine the degree of carelessness and lay the appropriate charge. However, the degree of the individual culpability is a matter for the court to determine when all of the evidence is heard. It may be that the evidence shows a lesser degree of gross carelessness than the charge requires, and the jury may consider that the less serious charge is deemed to be correct in the circumstances.

This would clearly place responsibility at the highest level of an undertaking, no matter what its size. It should also remove situations where senior management have in the past, distanced themselves from serious incidents involving loss of life, occurring within their undertaking. In small undertakings and for the self-employed person the focus on responsibility is more readily identifiable. The change in law places liability on individuals in large and diverse undertakings. There is always evidence as to who is the most senior person in the undertaking. That person signs the undertaking's health and safety policy or can be identified through registration at Companies House, or certified revenue accounts.

It is anticipated that the management of every undertaking will endeavour to avoid prosecution for the offence of corporate killing and some of the key factors include:

- An evaluation of the control elements as described above (SEE 4.8) to ensure that they are in place.

- Ensuring that the control elements are an integral part of the undertakings day-to-day operations.

- Understanding that failure to have elements of statutory duties in place is a failure of management.

- Assessing risks created by the undertaking, and the managing and controlling of those risks.

- Ensuring compliance with previous advice or enforcement actions by the regulating authorities.

- Only employing competent safety professionals or contracting a competent health and safety consultant.

- Providing evidence of the status and ownership of health and safety at senior management level. This would involve health and safety meetings and workforce involvement.

- Ensuring that senior management understands the risks created by their undertaking and the requirement for control measures.

- The need to have evidence of communication with employees and those not employed but affected by the undertaking on matters of health and safety.

The risks and controls required must be assessed. A small undertaking could have high risks while a large undertaking could have low risks. It is a matter for every undertaking no matter how large or small to be managed effectively. Management must ensure that those it employs are competent and suitable to carry out the task they are required to do. This applies to temporary staff, contractors, self employed, voluntary staff and in fact anybody who is employed in any capacity within the undertaking. It is important to note that this duty extends to those who participate in the activities but are not employed in the technical sense, such as voluntary workers.

Reasonable man

6.7   There is the question of what is a reasonable man in the context of killing by gross negligence and again it is useful to look at the explanation offered by Lord Macmillan in *Corporation of Glasgow v Muir and others [1943] 2 All ER 44* who said:

'The standard of foresight of the reasonable man is in one sense an impersonal test. It eliminates the personal equation and is independent of the idiosyncrasies of the particular person whose conduct is in question. Some persons are unduly timorous and imagine every path beset with lions; others, of more robust temperament, fail to foresee or nonchalantly disregard even the most obvious dangers. The reasonable man is presumed to be free both from over-apprehension and from over-confidence.'

The accepted definition of negligence is determined in the judgment by Alderson in the case *Blyth v Birmingham Waterworks Co (1856) 11 Ex 781* who said:

'Negligence is the omission of something which a reasonable man, guided upon those considerations which ordinarily regulate the conduct of human affairs, would do, or something which a prudent and reasonable man would do.'

The management or persons who require special knowledge or skills in order to undertake or control their work are expected to have suitable knowledge of the risks and safety procedures that employees encounter in carrying out the work. This has been defined in part by John Munkman:

'In general, an employer is expected to keep reasonably abreast of current knowledge concerning dangers arising in trade processes, and should be acquainted with pamphlets issued by the Health and Safety Executive and other safety organisations drawing attention to risks which have come to light and means of avoiding them.'

(John Munkman, *Employers Liability at Common Law*, 1990).

These elements are borne out in the case of *Wilson v Tyneside Window Cleaning Co [1958]* where Judge Parker said:

'The master's duty is general, to take all reasonable steps to avoid risk to his servants. For convenience it is often split up into different categories, such as tools, or safe system of work, but it always remains one general duty.'

This is further clarified in the case of *Wilsons and Clyde Coal v English [1937] 3 All ER 628* where Lord Wright said:

'The obligation is threefold, the provision of a competent staff of men, adequate material, and a proper system and effective supervision.'

Clearly, all reasonable employers and self-employed will ensure that health and safety is an integral part of their undertaking.

Competent personnel

6.8   Those who are employed must be competent and able to carry out the task they are employed to do. This applies to temporary staff, contractors, self-employed, voluntary staff and in fact anybody who is employed or works in any capacity within the undertaking. It is important to note that this duty extends to those who participate in the activities but are not employed in the technical sense, such as voluntary workers.

In summary:

- The management of the undertaking retains the sole responsibility for health and safety in the organisation. That responsibility cannot be devolved to others no matter what their competence or knowledge and could expose individuals to charges of killing by gross carelessness.

- External and internal health and safety advice and support requires any individual to have the verifiable professional knowledge and competence to provide the service. Failure means that they and the management who employed them could be exposed to charges of killing by gross carelessness. The professional status for either internal or external health and safety professionals should be the same as the liability could be the same.

Health and safety advice and support

6.9 Individuals, whatever their title, in any undertaking should *not* purchase an off-the-shelf health and safety system as it may well not meet the requirements of the particular undertaking, and therefore, provide management with a false sense of security. It is critical that suitable and competent advice and support is sought.

There is a need to ensure that there are competent health and safety professionals who are either employed or contracted into the undertaking to provide advice and support. The competence of these professionals will be subjected to scrutiny in the event of an investigation considering a prosecution for killing by gross carelessness. As described at chapter 4 (SEE 4.9) the status of the health and safety professional is paramount and that person should be competent. An important fact is those health and safety consultants who have given wrong and poor advice and not been competent, have been prosecuted as well as the organisation that employed them.

Prosecution of the new offence

6.10 Where an individual is investigated for killing by gross carelessness, it will be the responsibility of the police to lead on the investigation, and the responsibility of the Crown Prosecution Service (CPS) to review the evidence and bring the prosecution. An investigation into the actions of an individual where there had been a death will generally be linked to an investigation into the management activities in an undertaking. This means that the HSE or other enforcing authority will begin an investigation into the undertaking with the police investigating the individual. This will be the subject of operational procedures once the proposed Act is introduced and the new offence is enacted.

The prosecution for killing by gross carelessness will be presented in court in the same way as a prosecution is currently made relation for manslaughter. The failure of management will encompass the wider picture leaving the conduct of the individual to be determined. In the most serious of individual crimes it will be a matter for the jury if it is a case of killing by gross carelessness. Initially it will be a matter for the enforcing authorities to investigate and determine the level of seriousness, and differentiate between the levels of management failure and individual conduct. There will be an option for the court, if the evidence determines it, to move to the lesser offence. As with all criminal prosecutions it will be for the enforcing authorities to prove beyond all reasonable doubt that the defendants conduct either:

- Caused the death of another as prescribed in the offence.

- That they were capable of understanding what the risks were and that their conduct could cause injury or death.

- Having been provided with information that gave them the knowledge of the risk, they failed to take appropriate action and that their failure resulted in a death.

It will be for a jury to hear all of the evidence and then determine their decision and the consequence of the penalty.

It will be a matter for the prosecution to prove beyond all reasonable doubt that a person was aware of the risks, in other words that they had the knowledge and understanding of the potential outcome. It will be the conduct of that person that will be identified as being the cause of the death or serious injury. It is impossible to provide a definition of serious injury and it will be a matter for the jury to determine, having heard all of the facts and circumstances surrounding the incident causing the death.

When determining the sentence for the offence of killing by gross carelessness, the judge will take a number of factors into account. To date the judiciary has not always seen health and safety manslaughter prosecutions in the same way as they view normal criminal offenders. One problem is that juries have not been keen to convict an individual in a workplace fatality because it has generally been a member of the workforce left to face the legal process and be used as a scapegoat. Often, because the directors were not prosecuted, juries were found to be sympathetic to the individual defendant.

Penalty

6.11 An individual found guilty of killing by gross carelessness will as with any criminal trial submit mitigation. If the individual pleaded guilty at the earliest opportunity thus saving court time and money there will be a credit that could reduce the sentence. If the individual pleads not guilty and is subsequently found guilty, no discount will be made.

The maximum penalty for an individual upon conviction for killing by gross carelessness will be life imprisonment. This means that the case can only be heard in the Crown Court. For a person found guilty of killing by gross carelessness the judge will examine the mitigation submitted by the defence in an effort to obtain the lowest possible custodial sentence. This would include details such as the individual's previous conduct with particular regard to health and safety, and their management status within an undertaking. This should identify whether the individual had been in a position of authority and had been the recipient of the subject of formal Enforcement Notices, letters of condemnation, written or verbal warnings, any of which were focused on poor health and safety management or breaches of the appropriate legislation. Other factors would focus on whether there had been full co-operation by the individual with the investigating officers. The court will need to consider the failures that had been a root cause of the incident and balance them against any direct action or failure on the part of other senior managers.

It will not be possible for the management of holding companies to attempt to evade possible liability of a charge of killing by gross carelessness through the establishment of subsidiary companies. Such undertakings could be established to carry on riskier business which could most readily give rise to an individual being used as a scapegoat and left to face a charge of killing by gross carelessness.

Directors or those in control of an undertaking no matter how constituted, or of any parent undertaking will not be able to evade prosecution for killing by gross carelessness or otherwise frustrate legal proceedings, by dissolving the undertaking or by deliberately making it insolvent. The court will require the power to ensure that criminal proceedings in relation to killing by gross carelessness can continue to completion notwithstanding the formal insolvency of an undertaking.

Other considerations

6.12   The following topics apply to this chapter but are examined in CHAPTER 4:

* Management failure (SEE 4.5)

* Management responsibility (SEE 4.8)

* Legal Aid – Criminal Defence Service (SEE 4.16)

- Directors and officers liability Insurance (SEE 4.17)
- Proposed *Involuntary Homicide Bill*:

  cl 4(4) (SEE 4.18)

  cl 4(5) (SEE 4.19)

  cl 4(6) (SEE 4.20)

  cl 4(7) (SEE 4.26)

  cl 4(8) (SEE 4.27)

  cl 5(1) (SEE 4.29)

  cl 5(2) (SEE 4.30)

  cl 5(3) (SEE 4.31)

  cl 5(7) (SEE 4.35)

  cl 8(1) (SEE 4.36)

  cl 8(2) (SEE 4.37)

  cl 8(3) (SEE 4.38)

  cl 10(1) (SEE 4.39)

  cl 10(2) (SEE 4.40)

  cl 11(1) (SEE 4.41)

  cl 11(2) (SEE 4.42)

Summary

This chapter has examined the less serious of the individual offences. The principal elements of the offence have been identified with the focus on the carelessness and conduct aspect of the offence. The seriousness is identified in the maximum sentence of ten years' imprisonment. There is possibly a case for a third offence of killing where the intention is to cause less serious injury, which is examined in the next chapter.

7 Killing where the Intention was to Cause Only Minor Injury

This chapter considers the following:

- The proposed *Involuntary Homicide Bill*.
- Killing where the intention was to cause only minor injury.
- Transmission of disease.
- Fault element.
- Reasonable man.
- Competent personnel.
- Health and safety advice.
- Prosecution of the new offence.
- Penalty.
- Health and safety advice.
- Legal Aid and Criminal Defence Service.
- Directors' and officers' liability insurance.
- Defences.
- Undertakings.
- Meaning of injury.
- Application of Proposed Bill.

Introduction

7.1 The offence of killing where the intention was to cause minor injury and death was unforeseeable is a possible new offence being considered for the proposed *Involuntary Homicide Bill* that will only apply to activities undertaken within the jurisdiction of the English and Welsh courts. Scotland is expected to make its own arrangements to align with the proposed offences.

The offence of killing where the intention was to cause minor injury and death was unforeseeable is far more serious than an offence under the *Health and Safety at Work etc Act 1974 (HSWA 1974)*. The key element of the proposed offence is that an individual can be held liable and prosecuted for a death at work that was unforeseeable.

An important factor with this offence is that unlike the more serious offence of killing by gross carelessness, this offence requires a person to have intentionally or recklessly caused some injury to another. In some circumstances it may be seen that this offence is more blameworthy than the more serious offence. The factor that lowers its level of culpability is that a fatal outcome could not be foreseen.

Proposed Involuntary Homicide Bill

7.2   The *Involuntary Homicide Bill*, deals with a proposed additional individual offence of killing where the intention was to cause minor injury and death was unforeseeable for deaths caused at or due to work. This is where an individual carries out an act with the intention of causing minor injury which, is in itself a crime of assault. Any individual, who can be identified as being at fault, can be charged with the proposed offence. In this section there is an intention to cause a criminal act and involves a death at or due to work activities. There are a number of key elements that form the proposed offence described in FIGURE 7.1.

Responsibility for the investigation and prosecution for this offence will be within the jurisdiction of the police. There will need to be close co-operation between the police and the other authorities that may prosecute the undertaking. The proposed process is not shown in FIGURE 4.2 in chapter 4, as it is not known if the third offence will be included in the Act. Clearly if there are individual and corporate prosecutions it will be expedient to progress all matters together, and that would involve a joint prosecution with the police and CPS in conjunction with the HSE.

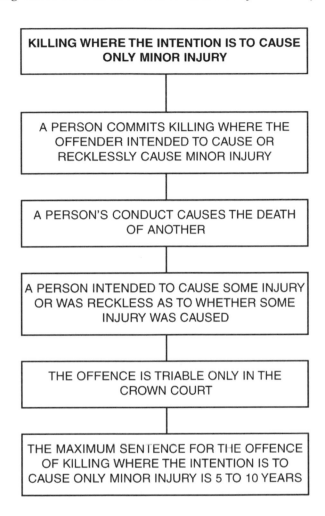

Figure 7.1: Key elements of the killing where the intention was to cause only minor injury offence

Proposed Involuntary Homicide Bill – The third offence

7.3   The question that is being reviewed is whether there should liability for involuntary homicide where the intention was only to cause some injury and the resulting death was unforeseeable. At present under the law on dangerous and unlawful act manslaughter, a person who intends or is reckless as to whether he commits what would otherwise be a relatively minor assault will be guilty of manslaughter if the victim dies as a result, even though death was quite unforeseeable. It is intended that with the intro-duction of the new Bill this offence should remain an option for the courts.

There is concern that the present law allows a person to be con-victed of an offence carrying a maximum penalty of life impri-sonment not because of his mental intention but because of what is termed an 'unlucky' event. Therefore, it may be considered wrong in principle for the law to hold a person responsible for causing a result that he did not intend or foresee, and which could not even have been foreseeable by a reasonable person observing his con-duct.

It is considered (see: *Reforming the Law on Involuntary Manslaughter: The Government's Proposals, May 2000*) that there is a need for an additional homicide offence to cover a situation where:

(a)   a person by his or her conduct causes the death of another;

(b)   he or she intended to or was reckless as to whether some injury was caused; and

(c)   the conduct causing, or intended to cause, the injury con-stitutes an offence.

This offence involves instances where an individual action causes the death of someone who, through gross carelessness, causes someone to be injured and, totally unforeseeably, death results.

Transmission of disease and the proposed third offence

7.4   There will need to be liability where individual failure leads to the transmission of a disease which in turn led to death. The liability could arise if an individual failure was a cause rather than sole cause of death. Therefore, the inclusion of transmission of disease could have an impact on the number of cases that might be brought for killing where the intention was only to cause minor injury and death was unforeseeable. It must be shown that the conduct has fallen far below what could be expected of an indi-vidual in the circumstances.

The transmission of disease is more complex than the general acceptance of fault because an individual could be liable. This could occur where the transmission of a disease occurs between one individual and another where there is a professional duty of care. This is an important aspect as it involves workplace activities and there will be a need for a formulation of circumstances, in which the transmission of disease where an individual could be culpable of the serious offence could be covered by the new offences.

Fault element

7.5   The third offence where the intention was only to cause some injury but a resulting death was unforeseeable is possibly the most difficult to accept and comprehend. The offence is unusual because it could be argued that it is more serious than killing by gross carelessness. This is because the offender must intentionally or recklessly cause some injury to another, but does not foresee death as an outcome. The law considers that anyone who embarks on a course of illegal violence has to accept the consequences of that action, even if the final consequences are unforeseeable, and minor injury was all that was intended. It is that person's action that is the cause or intended cause of injury that forms the offence.

Two examples of possible offences are provided where there was an act carried out by an individual at work, where minor injury was intended but death was not foreseen.

Current law manslaughter requires a person to be identified as having undertaken a physical act that resulted in the death of another. Killing where the intention was only to cause minor injury and death was unforeseeable does not require the physical action by one person against another. This means that a director, executive, trustee, partner, self-employed person, manager, supervisor or any other person with responsibilities or any person in workplace activities, can be determined culpable.

The focus of this offence is to cover senior management who by their conduct expose others to minor injury but death is a result. It is important to note that it does not exclude others who are not management. The prosecution will need to prove that the person was aware of the risks in a given situation, and that does not require the person to have direct physical contact. It will be their knowledge that an unsafe activity is being carried out and that by not stopping it, the result was that their conduct that caused or was a cause of the death.

7.6 The following are examples of what might constitute the proposed third offence:

Example 1: A person at work decided to set up a booby trap for another worker. It is to be a negligent act intended to cause minor injury to another. The scenario is that D fills a metal bucket with water and places it on the top of a part open door. The intention is that when V pushes open the door and walks through, the bucket with its contents of water, falls on him. In setting up a situation D's intention is for the bucket and water to fall on V who will suffer at worst only minor injury. In due course V enters the door and the bucket and contents fall onto him. The bucket hits him on his head and water soaks him. The prank has been carried out leaving V with a slight cut on his head and a severe headache. He reports the incident to his supervisor, who gets the nominated first aid person to check the cut and provide some painkillers. The pain does not go away and V complains of feeling unwell so the supervisor takes the decision to send V to hospital to have the injury checked. At hospital, V receives medical attention but his minor injury has caused serious medical complications with damage to his skull. The outcome is unforeseen in that the injury is a cause of V's death. This could be a case where skylarking exposed an individual to a situation where death was an unforeseen outcome but D could face prosecution for killing where the intention was only to cause V minor injury and death was unforeseeable.

In this example it was unreasonable for D to carry out an act of skylarking under any circumstances and particularly with the knowledge that there may be minor injury. It was unreasonable for D to take the risk having regard to the circumstances as he knew or believed them to be.

Example 2: A director sets up a system to deter or stop intruders. He obtains a large guard dog, which he knows will bite an intruder who may enter the premises. He allows the dog to run free when there are no employees at the workplace. He is advised that he needs to control the dog and to put up signs to warn potential intruders that a guard dog is on the premises. He ignores the advice. A group of boys pass the site kicking a football, which is accidentally kicked over the gate. One of the boys decides to climb over the gate with the sole purpose of retrieving the ball, totally unaware that a dog is loose on patrol. He gets the ball and throws it over the gate and proceeds to climb back over the gate. Suddenly the dog appears, barking and snarling at the boy and jumps at him delivering a bite. The boy is able to get free and manages to get over the gate but is aware of severe pain and that he is loosing a lot of blood. The other boys see the blood and panic. However, one goes for help. The dog's bite had severed an artery and by the time the emergency services arrived at the premises, the boy had died.

In this example it was unreasonable for the director to use a dog in this manner, in that it was uncontrolled. Further, he had failed to provide adequate warning that a dog was on guard. He had the knowledge that there may be minor injury caused by the dog. In this example it was unreasonable for the director take the risk having regard to the circumstances as he knew or believed them to be.

7.7   Further considerations as to the fault element are:

(1) The undertaking has a policy that excludes any acts of sky-larking with or without a risk of any injury, minor or not. An outcome of this failure is the death of an employee or other who is not employed but affected by the undertaking's activities. While the person conducting the act is responsible, the undertaking cannot absolve its obligations to its employees and others in respect to health and safety matters.

(2) Where no provision is made in the safety system to advise against such activities, a director or person of similar standing will not have fulfilled the obligations of their statutory duties. It would not be a defence to say that they were not aware of their legal obligations for health and safety.

(3) A person having not made adequate provision to control activities within the undertaking such as providing dogs that are uncontrolled dogs and being aware that the risks of injury could be an outcome of such activities could be held culpable.

A director, manager or appropriate person in a position of authority is reckless in their actions, either when they knew or should have known, that a failure to manage could result in an accident with minor injury. In the examples provided it is the individual who carried out the activity of skylarking and the director who deployed an uncontrolled guard dog who would be exposed to prosecution. However, the evidence that transpires from an investigation will determine the degree of recklessness and lay the appropriate charges against an individual and possibly a corporate offence, if there was knowledge of the activities on the part of management. Individual culpability is a matter for the court to determine when all of the evidence is heard. It may be that the evidence shows a lesser degree of recklessness than the charge requires, and the jury may consider that the less serious charge is deemed to be correct in the circumstances.

The management of an undertaking must ensure that those who it employs are competent and suitable to carry out the task they are required to do. This applies to temporary staff, contractors, self employed, voluntary staff and in fact anybody who is employed in any capacity within the undertaking. It is important to note that this duty extends to those who participate in the activities but are not employed in the technical sense, such as voluntary workers.

Reasonable man

7.8   There is the important question as to what is a reasonable man in the context of the proposed third offence and to that end an explanation is offered by Lord Macmillan in *Corporation of Glasgow v Muir and Others [1943] 2 All ER 44*:

'The standard of foresight of the reasonable man is in one sense an impersonal test. It eliminates the personal equation and is independent of the idiosyncrasies of the particular person whose conduct is in question. Some persons are unduly timorous and imagine every path beset with lions; others, of more robust temperament, fail to foresee or nonchalantly disregard even the most obvious dangers. The reasonable man is presumed to be free both from over-apprehension and from over-confidence.'

The accepted definition of negligence is determined in the judgment by Alderson in the case *Blyth v Birmingham Waterworks Co (1856) 11 Ex 781* who said:

'Negligence is the omission of something which a reasonable man, guided upon those considerations which ordinarily regulate the conduct of human affairs, would do, or something which a prudent and reasonable man would do.'

It will be a matter for the jury to determine if the actions of management or an individual equates to those of a reasonable man in the circumstances of the incident.

Competent personnel

7.9   Those who are employed must be competent and able to carry out the task they are required to do. This applies to temporary staff, contractors, self employed, voluntary staff and in fact anybody who is employed or works in any capacity within the undertaking. It is important to note that this duty extends to those who participate in the activities but who are not employed in the technical sense, such as voluntary workers.

Health and safety advice and support

7.10   Individuals, whatever their title, in any undertaking should *not* purchase an off-the-shelf health and safety system as it may well not meet the requirements of the particular undertaking, and therefore, provide management with a false sense of security. It is critical that suitable and competent advice and support should be sought, and balanced against the cost and practicality of carrying out the recommendations, the advice should be complied with.

There is a need to ensure that there are competent health and safety professionals who are either employed or contracted into the undertaking to provide advice and support. The competence of these professionals will be subjected to scrutiny in the event of an investigation considering a prosecution for reckless killing. As described in chapter 4 (SEE 4.9) the status of the health and safety professional is paramount and that person must be competent. An important fact is those health and safety consultants who have given wrong and poor advice and not been competent, have been prosecuted as well as the organisation that employed them.

Prosecution of proposed new offence

7.11   The prosecution for killing where the intention was to cause minor injury and death was unforeseeable will be presented in court in the same way as a prosecution is taken currently undertaken for manslaughter. The conduct of an individual will be determined and it will be a matter for the jury to decide if it is a case of killing where the intention was to cause minor injury and death was unforeseeable. As with all criminal prosecutions it will be for the enforcing authorities to prove *beyond all reasonable doubt* that the defendants conduct either:

143

- Caused the death of another as prescribed in the offence.

- That they were aware of a risk and that their conduct would cause death.

- Knowing the risk, they failed to take appropriate action and that their failure resulted in a death.

When determining the sentence for the offence of killing where the intention was to cause minor injury and death was unforeseeable, the judge will take a number of factors into account. To date the judiciary has not always seen health and safety manslaughter prosecutions in the same way that they view other criminal offenders. One problem is that juries have not been keen to convict an individual in a workplace fatality. This is because it has generally been to be a member of the workforce left to face the legal process, when there has clearly been management failure. Because the directors were not prosecuted, juries were found to be sympathetic to the individual defendant who was seen to be following orders derived from those in senior positions. In this situation it is the most senior person in an undertaking who could be identified and on trial. It will be for a jury to hear all of the evidence and then determine their decision and for the judge to pass judgment and sentence.

Penalty

7.12   An individual found guilty of killing where the intention was to cause minor injury and death was unforeseeable will as with any criminal trial submit mitigation. If the individual pleads guilty at the earliest opportunity thus saving the court time and money there will be a credit that could reduce the sentence. If the individual pleads not guilty and is subsequently found guilty, no discount will be made.

The maximum penalty for an individual upon conviction for killing where the intention was to cause minor injury and death was unforeseeable will be between five and ten years. This reflects the seriousness of the offence which, means that the case can only be heard in the Crown Court. The actual period of sentence will be reached after the mitigation speech has been made. There will be consideration of the individuals past conduct, such as if they had been in a position of authority as a director, manager or other responsible status where an Enforcement Notice had been issued, or there had been a previous prosecution under health and safety legislation. Other factors will include the degree of negligence and culpability, but there will have been evidence to show that the actions were with full knowledge of the risks and potential outcomes.

Individuals such as self-employed persons will be subjected to the same procedures as individuals within an undertaking. The same level of culpability will be required for either situation. Past cases show that individual manslaughter for self-employed or individuals in small undertakings is more easily proven. The new offence should level that imbalance.

It will not be possible for the management of holding companies to attempt to evade possible liability of a charge of killing where the intention was to cause only minor injury through the establishment of subsidiary companies. Such undertakings could be established to carry on riskier business which could most readily give rise to an individual being used as a scapegoat and left to face a charge of killing where the intention was to cause minor injury and death was unforeseeable.

Directors or those in control of an undertaking no matter how constituted, or of any parent undertaking will not be able to evade prosecution for killing where the intention was to cause only minor injury or otherwise frustrate legal proceedings, by dissolving the undertaking or by deliberately making it insolvent. The court will require the power to ensure that criminal proceedings in relation to killing where the intention was to cause minor injury and death was unforeseeable can continue to completion notwithstanding the formal insolvency of an undertaking.

Other considerations

7.13   The following topics apply to this chapter but are examined in CHAPTER 4:

- Management failure (SEE 4.5)

- Management responsibility (SEE 4.8)

- Legal Aid – Criminal Defence Service (SEE 4.16)

- Directors' and officers' Liability Insurance (SEE 4.17)

- Proposed *Involuntary Homicide Bill*:

cl 4(4) (SEE **4.18**)

cl 4(5) (SEE **4.19**)

cl 4(6) (SEE **4.20**)

cl 4(7) (SEE **4.26**)

cl 4(8) (SEE **4.27**)

cl 5(1) (SEE **4.29**)

cl 5(2) (SEE **4.30**)

cl 5(3) (SEE **4.31**)

cl 5(7) (SEE **4.35**)

cl 8(1) (SEE **4.36**)

cl 8(2) (SEE **4.37**)

cl 8(3) (SEE **4.38**)

cl 10(1) (SEE **4.39**)

cl 10(2) (SEE **4.40**)

cl 11(1) (SEE **4.41**)

cl 11(2) (SEE **4.42**)

Summary

This chapter has examined the proposed offence of killing where the intention was to cause only minor injury. The principal elements of the offence have been identified with the focus on the intention and conduct aspect of the offence. The seriousness is identified in the sentence of between five and ten years' imprisonment. This would be the third of the individual involuntary homicide offences.

8 Enforcement and Fines

This chapter considers the following:

- Fines for Heath and Safety at Work offences.

- Examples of cases receiving large fines.

- The *Howe* judgment.

- The *Friskies* judgment.

- Duties of directors – *HSWA 1974, ss 36 and 37.*

- Duties of employees – *HSWA 1974, s 7.*

Introduction

8.1   The level of fines for health and safety offences are directly related to the seriousness of the offence of corporate killing. They are an important indicator as to how serious the judicial system views such offences prior to the introduction of the manslaughter offence. Fines can be seen as a form of punishment but there are other considerations as identified by C M V Clarkson in his paper, 'Kicking Corporate Bodies and Damning Their Souls', (1996) 59 MLR 4, who describes a fine as being the punishment of innocent shareholders, creditors and employees. This means that shareholders may loose money, employees may loose their jobs and the public will ultimately have to bear the burden of the fine. The outcome is that the ones who really suffer will be those whom the law is aiming to protect.

The level of fines imposed for health and safety offences are deemed to be low and has for some time been an area of concern for both the Health and Safety Commission (HSC) and exponents who claim that there is a failing in the level of penalties, for all health and safety prosecutions. One reason for this is highlighted by Cellia Wells in *Corporations and Criminal Responsibility*, (1st edn, 1993) Oxford University Press, who writes that the word 'punishment' is dropped when corporations are the object of criminal

147

enforcement and is replaced by the altogether less emotive 'sanction'. This downgrades the whole status of a corporation being in court, which will be of concern in the event of an injury, but if there is a fatality then the status of that death is in effect downgraded further, albeit in a criminal court. Another interesting point is raised by Wells who puts forward the argument that both magistrates' and Crown Courts frequently require social reports to be prepared for individuals, as well as the completion of a personal means form prior to sentencing. However, with corporate defendants, there is generally no attempt made to investigate the financial background or assets, before imposing fines.

The case about fines for corporate crime is the subject of discussion in Smith and Hogan, *Criminal Law* (8th edn, 1996) Butterworths, which follows in part the case put by C M V Clarkson above in that the fine imposed is ultimately borne by the shareholders. If those who invested in the company had any real control over directors and therefore, over the management of the company, there might well be some justification. In reality it is generally recognised that shareholders have no such control over large, public companies. The case continues to advance that since the persons actually responsible for the offence may, in the great majority of cases, be convicted, is there any need to impose this additional penalty. This argument fails as the need for a 'corporate offence', for cases of gross negligence has arisen because of the difficulty of identifying individuals as being liable as the *brains* of the corporation who has undoubtedly authorised the offence. Corporate liability ensures that the offence will not go unpunished and that a fine proportionate to the gravity of the offence may be imposed, when it might be out of proportion to the means of the individuals concerned. The imposition of liability on the organisation gives all those directing it an interest in the prevention of illegalities, and they are in a position to prevent them, though the shareholders are not.

It is not only shareholders who see fines imposed for health and safety offences but also undertakings who provide a vital service to the public. One such example is the case of a health care trust, which was, fined £38,000 plus £17,000 costs. The trust admitted that it had failed to take the necessary steps to ensure the safe control of all stages of cardiac angiography procedures. As a consequence, a patient died after being injected with air instead of radio-opaque fluid during a routine cardiac angiography. The case highlights the need for the health care sector to manage health and safety at work properly, just like any other employer. The resulting investigation

showed that it was not a failure of the equipment itself, but a ~~f~~
of the management to implement a safe system of work to d
clinical judgement, which caused this tragic and avoidable dea..... ..t
passing sentence the judge identified that the case was important
because it raised issues not present in other cases concerning prosecutions of National Health Service trusts. The failure in this case
was the absence of a safe system of work to protect patients and
employees, which arose from the use of this equipment. The case
was heard in the magistrates' court but sent to the Crown Court for
sentencing where the level of fine is unlimited. The lawyer representing the NHS trust told the court that every pound that the
hospital is fined is a pound less spent on the care of our community.

Health and Safety at Work etc Act offences

8.2   The following table identifies the health and safety at work
offences and the penalties available to the magistrates' court and
the Crown Court. It must be noted that a case can be heard in the
magistrates' court and if after hearing all the evidence the magistrates consider that their powers in the form of fines or imprisonment are not sufficient they can send the case to the Crown Court
for sentencing. Prosecutions under the *HSWA 1974* may be brought
in respect of the following offences.

Offence	*Summary Conviction (magistrates' court)*	*On indictment (Crown Court)*
Failure to discharge a duty under *HSWA 1974, ss 2–6.*	£20,000	Unlimited fine.
Contravening *HSWA 1974, ss 7–9.*	£5,000	Unlimited fine.
Contravening health and safety regulations.	£5,000	Unlimited fine.
Contravening any requirement made by regulations relating to investigations or inquiries made by the Commission, etc under *HSWA 1974, s 14,* or obstructing anyone exercising his powers.	£5,000	–

Contravening any requirement under *HSWA 1974, s 20,* (powers of inspectors).	£5,000	–
Contravening any requirement under *HSWA 1974, s 25* (power of the inspector to seize and render harmless articles or substances likely to cause imminent danger).	£5,000	Unlimited fine.
Preventing a person appearing before an inspector or from answering questions under *HSWA 1974, s 20(2)* (examinations and investigations).	£5,000	–
Contravening a requirement or prohibition imposed by an Improvement Notice.	£20,000 and/or six months' imprisonment.	Unlimited fine and/or two years' imprisonment.
Contravening a requirement or prohibition imposed by a Prohibition Notice.	£20,000 and/or six months' imprisonment.	Unlimited fine and/or two years' imprisonment.
Intentionally obstructing an inspector.	£5,000	–
Contravening a notice served by the Commission under *HSWA 1974, s 27(1)* requiring information.	£5,000	Unlimited fine.

Using or disclosing information in contravention of *HSWA 1974, s 27(4)* (disclosure by the Crown or certain Government agencies of information to the HSC or HSE.	£5,000	Unlimited fine and/or two years' imprisonment.
Making a false or reckless statement in purported compliance with a statutory provision, or for the purpose of obtaining the issuance of a document under any statutory provision.	£5,000	Unlimited fine.
Intentionally making false entry in any register, book or other document required to be kept, or to making use of such entry, knowing it to be false.	£5,000	Unlimited fine.
With intent to deceive, using a document issued under a relevant statutory provision.	£5,000	Unlimited fine.
Pretending to be an inspector.	£5,000	–
Failing to comply with an order of the court under *HSWA 1974, s 42* (order to remedy).	£20 000 and/or six months' imprisonment.	Unlimited fine and/or two years' imprisonment.
Acting without a licence which is necessary under a relevant statutory provision.	£5,000	Unlimited fine and/or two years' imprisonment.

Contravening the terms of such a licence.	£5,000	Unlimited fine and/or two years' imprisonment.
Acquiring, using or possessing explosives contrary to the relevant provisions.	£5,000	Unlimited fine and/or two years' imprisonment.
Breach of regulations made for the purpose of *HSWA 1974, s 1(1)* of the *Offshore Safety Act 1992*.	£20,000	Unlimited fine and/or two years' imprisonment.

Large fines: cases

8.3   Undertakings found guilty of the offence of corporate killing will be subjected to unlimited fines. Fines will be in addition to the prosecution costs incurred and the costs associated with remedial requirements. The offence of corporate killing is to be equal to the current law of manslaughter which places it at a much higher level than offences under the *HSWA 1974* and health and safety regulations and therefore, the level of fines made for the more serious offence should be respectively higher. Fines for health and safety offences have seen an increase in recent years and a review is made of the cases where there were large fines and custodial sentences. Examples of cases where fines have been given are outlined below. It is not intended to be exhaustive, but provides an overview of the situation. The cases are in order of size of fine, and do not include costs unless identified as such. Some cases do not involve a fatality. The sources of information include the Health and Safety Executive Press Office, London, and the professional publications, The *Safety and Health Practitioner, Safety Management,* and *Health and Safety at Work.*

Heathrow Express railway link

8.4   On 15 February 1999, two companies were fined £1,700,000 following the collapse of three tunnels during the construction of the Heathrow Express railway link at Heathrow airport on 21 October 1994. No one was killed or injured in the collapse, which occurred at 1 am. Tunnelling was carried out with Balfour Beatty

Civil Engineering Ltd as the main contractor, using the New Austrian Tunnelling Method (NATM), on which Geoconsult ZT GmbH, an Austrian company, were consultants. Balfour Beatty pleaded guilty to charges under *HSWA 1974, ss 2 and 3* and was fined a total of £1,200,000, which was unapportioned between the two charges. Geoconsult pleaded not guilty to charges under *HSWA 1974, ss 2 and 3*. They were convicted and fined £500,000. The case was heard at the Old Bailey before Cresswell J, who took account of the *Howe* ruling of November 1998 *(R v F Howe & Sons (Engineering) Ltd [1999] 2 All ER 249* (see 8.75)), which laid down criteria for sentencing for serious breaches of health and safety law. As a result of the convictions Geoconsult subsequently sought leave to appeal against the conviction and the penalty. The outcome was that both appeals were rejected.

Port Ramsgate

8.5 On 28 February 1997, four companies were fined a total £1,700,000 following the death of six people and injuries to seven others when a section of an elevated ferry passenger walkway at Port Ramsgate, Kent, collapsed on 14 September 1994. Two Swedish companies who were main contractors did not appear at the Central Criminal Court trial, which began on 14 January 1997. They were tried and sentenced in their absence, not guilty pleas having been entered on their behalf at the court's direction. The charges alleged that all four companies involved in the project failed to conduct their undertakings in such a way as to ensure the safety of passengers using the walkway. In their absence Fartygsentreprenader AB (FEAB) a Swedish company, who built the walkway, were found guilty of a charge under the *HSWA 1974, s 3* and were fined £750,000. Fartygskonstruktioner AB (FKAB) a Swedish company, who designed the walkway, was also found guilty on a charge under *HSWA 1974, s 3* and fined £250,000. In addition to the fines, costs of £251,500 were awarded jointly against the two Swedish companies. Lloyd's Register of Shipping, who certified the walkway, pleaded guilty to a charge under the *HSWA 1974, s 3* and was fined £500,000 plus costs of £252,000. Port Ramsgate Ltd, who commissioned the walkway and had overall supervision of the project, pleaded not guilty to two charges under *HSWA 1974, s 3* and the *Docks Regulations 1988 (SI 1988/1655), Reg 7(1)*. They were found guilty on both charges and fined a total of £200,000. There is no breakdown of the fines made for each offence. An order for costs of £219,500 was made.

Great Western Trains

8.6   A record fine of £500,000 was made against an individual company, Great Western Trains Company Limited (GWT), at the Old Bailey on 27 July 1999 for a rail accident at Southall on 19 October 1997. Seven passengers were killed and 147 were taken to hospital when a high speed train operated by GWT went through a red signal and collided with an empty freight train operated by English, Welsh and Scottish Railway. The automatic warning system (AWS), which should have alerted the driver to his error, was not working. The train was fitted with automatic train protection, which would have halted the train when it passed the danger signal but the equipment was not switched on.

GWT pleaded guilty to contravening *HSWA 1974, s 3(1)* in that they failed to conduct an undertaking, namely the provision of transport by rail to members of the public, in such a way as to ensure that the public were not exposed to risks to their health and safety. The Crown Prosecution Service (CPS) had also charged the company with manslaughter but Mr Justice Scott-Baker ruled, on 27 July 1999, that a company cannot be prosecuted for gross negligence unless an individual is named. The CPS also charged the driver of the train, Mr Larry Harrison, with manslaughter and health and safety offences. These charges were dropped in June 1999, partly due to Mr Harrison's health.

BP Oil (Grangemouth) Refinery

8.7   On 21 March 1988 BP Oil (Grangemouth) Refinery Ltd was fined a total of £750,000 following three fatal accidents at their Grangemouth refinery in Scotland in 1987. A fine of £500,000 followed an incident on 22 March 1987 when a man died in an explosion in a production unit. A fine of £250,000 followed an incident on 13 March 1987 when two men died and two others received serious burns during work on the refinery flare system.

Friskies Petcare

8.8   Friskies Petcare (UK) Ltd (*R v Friskies Petcare (UK) Ltd [2000] 2 Cr App R(S) 401*) was fined £600,000 at Isleworth Crown Court after the electrocution of an employee in a meat silo at their factory at Southall, West London, which makes *Felix* catfood. Bryan Wilkins was repairing a metal ribbon stirrer at the bottom of the silo. He was arc welding in a confined, damp conductive environment in the silo when he was electrocuted while changing welding electrodes. There were two charges but a total fine was imposed, and not split between the two. The company pleaded guilty to *HSWA 1974, s 2(1)* for failing to ensure, so far as was reasonably practicable the safety of employees, including Bryan Wilkins, whilst arc welding in metal meat silos.

They also pleaded guilty to the *Management of Health and Safety at Work Regulations 1992 (SI 1992/2051), Reg 3* for failing to make a suitable and sufficient assessment of the risks their employees, (including Bryan Wilkins) were exposed to whilst arc welding in metal meat silos, for the purpose of identifying the measures needed to comply with the requirements, imposed by the relevant statutory provisions. The company appealed against the level of fine and the Court of Appeal subsequently reduced it to £250,000.

Balfour Beatty Rail Maintenance Ltd

8.9   On 22 March 1999 Balfour Beatty Rail Maintenance Ltd (BBRML) was fined £500,000 plus costs of £6,700 at Chelmsford Crown Court. The case followed the derailment of a freight train at Rivenhall, Essex where BBRML were working on the track. They pleaded guilty to a charge under the *HSWA 1974, s 3(1)* in that they failed to use a safe method of work, failed to take two vital pieces of equipment, and did not go back for them when they knew they did not have them. The gang was not properly monitored or supervised.

J Sainsbury plc

8.10   On 4 November 1998, J Sainsbury Plc was fined a total of £425,000 at Winchester Crown Court, after pleading guilty at Basingstoke magistrates' court on the 3 August 1998, to six charges. They were *HSWA 1974, s 2(1)*, the *Provision and Use of Work Equipment Regulations 1992 (SI 1992/2932), Reg 6(1),* and the *Management of Health and Safety at Work Regulations 1992 (SI 1992/2051), Regs 3(1), 3(4), 4(1), 6(1)*. An order was made for full prosecution costs of £75,000.

The prosecution, brought by Basingstoke and Deane Borough Council, followed the death of a worker crushed by a reach truck at the company's distribution depot in Houndmill, Basingstoke in

December 1996. An investigation by Environmental Health Officers (EHO's) found that a safety cut-out switch (to prevent trucks moving with no-one in the driving seat) had been disconnected. Switches were not working on 16 other reach trucks, over half the trucks of that type at the depot. Several had other serious defects.

Doncaster Council

8.11   Doncaster Metropolitan Borough Council was fined £400,000 in 2001 after being prosecuted for the death of an electrician. The electrician had been called to repair a heating unit in a false ceiling. He was electrocuted when he came into contact with exposed electrical wires. There was evidence that council managers had been aware of the danger for some time but failed to take action or notify the electrician. In addition to the fine there were costs awarded of £30,000.

London Underground

8.12   On 27 July 1999, at Isleworth Crown Court, London Underground Ltd were fined a total of £300,000 following the death of a passenger. Mrs Alice Thatcher fell between two cars of a Piccadilly Line train at Eastcote Underground Station on 31 December 1996. London Underground had not identified a 50-yard blind spot on the platform and this meant that Mrs Alice Thatcher could not be seen by the train driver.

London Underground Limited pleaded guilty and was fined £250,000 for contravening *HSWA 1974, s 3(1)* because it failed to ensure the safety of passengers by not using a method for the dispatch of trains which, ensured that drivers would know when it was safe to close the passenger train doors and move off. London Underground Limited also pleaded guilty and was fined £50,000 for contravening the *Railways (Safety Case) Regulations 1994 (SI 1994/237)* because it failed to ensure that the procedures and arrangements described in its Railway Safety Case were followed and failed to carry out a daily check of One Person Operation monitors as specified, in the London Underground Limited Reference Manual. This was the first prosecution taken under these Regulations.

BOC

8.13 On 2 August 1999, BOC were fined £300,000 at Kingston Crown Court, after an explosion at the company's special gases plant in Morden, South London, on 11 April 1997, killed an employee, Anthony Mulry. Mr Mulry had been filling gas cylinders with flammable oxidant mixtures. The company pleaded guilty to *HSWA 1974, 2(1)*. The judge identified that the company had a good safety record and had not short cut procedures. However, there had been a continuing dangerous state of affairs with the result that an employee had lost his life; and that the penalty had to reflect the means to pay. In addition to the fine an order was made for costs of £58,000.

BG Exploration and Production

8.14 On 10 February 2000, the offshore operator BG Exploration & Production Ltd, was fined £300,000 plus £198,596 prosecution costs at Kingston upon Hull Crown Court. The company had previously pleaded guilty before magistrates to six charges under: the *HSWA 1974*, the *Offshore Installations Prevention of Fire and Explosion, and Emergency Response Regulations 1995 (SI 1995/743)*, and *Reporting of Injuries, Diseases and Dangerous Occurrences Regulations 1995 (SI 1995/3163)*.

The case followed an incident in February 1998 when a large volume of natural gas was released from a leak in a pipework joint on the company's Rough 47/3B offshore gas platform. Fortunately, the gas did not ignite and there were no injuries but HSE's investigation identified management shortcomings. The focus was on the way in which the joint had been installed and how the incident was managed. In addition, the incident, a 'dangerous occurrence', was not reported to the HSE. This is the highest fine imposed to date on an offshore operator.

Nobel Explosives

8.15 On 11 April 1990 Nobel Explosives, an ICI subsidiary, were fined £250,000 at Peterborough Crown Court, following an incident on 22 March 1989 in which faultily packed detonators caused one of the firm's vans to blow up on the Fengate Industrial Estate, Peterborough. One fireman died, over 100 people were injured and a considerable amount of structural damage resulted.

British Rail

8.16   On 14 June 1991 British Rail were fined £250,000 at the Old Bailey following the Clapham Junction rail crash of 12 December 1988, in which 35 people, including the train driver, died and 69 were seriously injured.

Hickson & Welch

8.17   On 30 July 1993 chemical firm Hickson & Welch were fined £250,000 at Leeds Crown Court and ordered to pay costs of £150,000 following an explosion at their Castleford plant on 21 September 1992, in which five people died.

ARCO British

8.18   On 10 August 1993, offshore operators ARCO British Ltd were fined £250,000 by the High Court of Justiciary (sitting at Aberdeen) after pleading guilty to two charges following a blow-out, explosions and fire on the Ocean Odyssey drilling rig on 22 September 1988. Sixty-six members of the crew were successfully evacuated, but radio operator Timothy Williams died and the rig was destroyed. Rig owners ODECO Drilling (UK) Ltd (now Diamond Offshore) were also fined £25,000 after pleading guilty to three charges.

Nuclear Electric

8.19   On 14 September 1995 Nuclear Electric was fined £250,000 plus £138,000 costs at Mold Crown Court, after pleading guilty to four charges under the *HSWA 1974*. The charges related to an incident at Wylfa nuclear power station, Anglesey, on 31 July 1993, in which a parasol grab weight from a fuelling machine fell into a fuel channel in Reactor 1. It is the highest ever fine for the nuclear industry.

Royal Ordnance

8.20   On 26 February 1998, Royal Ordnance plc was fined £250,000 at the High Court of Justiciary (sitting in Glasgow) after pleading guilty to four charges, three under *HSWA 1974, s 2* and one under the *Management of Health and Safety at Work Regulations 1992 (SI*

1992/2051), Reg 3. The case followed a violent explosion and fire during extrusion of solid rocket fuel in a press at the company's explosives works at Bishopton, Renfrewshire, on 14 October 1995. Three workers were badly injured and heavy missiles were hurled up to a quarter of a mile.

St Regis Paper

8.21 On 23 May 1997 St Regis Paper Co Ltd of Taplow, Bucks, were fined £240,000 and ordered to pay £13,333 costs at Canterbury Crown Court. The company pleaded guilty to charges under *HSWA 1974,* the *Factories Act 1961,* the *Management of Health and Safety at Work Regulations 1992 (SI 1992/2051),* and *Provision and Use of Work Equipment Regulations (SI 1992/2932),* alleging machine guarding, risk assessment and electrical isolation failures. The charges followed two employee deaths, one in October 1995 and one in May 1996. There was a serious injury and a near miss for two other workers at a plant in Sittingbourne, Kent.

Colin Boswell

8.22 On 13 August 1999, Colin Boswell, an Isle of Wight farmer, was fined a total of £200,000, made up of £20,000 on each of eleven charges, at Portsmouth Crown Court, with nearly £17,000 costs. He pleaded guilty to charges related to pesticide misuse under the *Control of Substances Hazardous to Health Regulations* (SI 1999/437) and the *Management of Health and Safety at Work Regulations (SI 1999/3242).* Mr Boswell was also an adviser to MAFF.

Translink Joint Venture

8.23 On 26 November 1993 a total fine of £200,000 was made against the five companies making up the British half of the Channel Tunnel construction consortium, TML. Each company was fined £40,000 by Maidstone Crown Court after pleading guilty to a charge under *HSWA 1974, s 2* in respect of the death of employee David Griffiths, who was crushed between two trains in the Marine Service Tunnel on 6 October 1992. The total fine became the highest penalty for a construction case.

BP Chemicals

8.24   On 21 April 1994 BP Chemicals was fined £200,000 at Falkirk Sheriff Court after admitting failure to provide adequate means of escape for workers at its Grangemouth plant, following a fire in February 1992 in which one man died. BP was also ordered to pay £10,000 compensation to each of the three men seriously burned. The fire was on the site of a new £3 million chemical storage plant, where a storage sphere was being coated with polyurethane foam insulation. Fire broke out beneath four men on scaffolding and they were trapped inside thick plastic sheeting with only one set of ladders as an escape route. Eyewitnesses said the dead man fell from the ladder.

British Railways Board

8.25   On 7 October 1996 the British Railways Board was fined £200,000 after pleading guilty to two charges at Snaresbrook Crown Court. They were fined £100,000 for a charge under *HSWA 1974, s 2* and another £100,000 for a charge under *HSWA 1974, s 3*. They were ordered to pay £13,000 prosecution costs. The prosecution followed a collision at Wood Street between two trains at 5.30 am on 19 September 1995. There had been work overnight to replace a defective rail, but the work was not properly planned and the staff doing it were not properly trained. A passenger train ran into an empty stationary train from behind. There were no injuries.

Coflexip Stena Offshore

8.26   On 23 July 1997 Coflexip Stena Offshore Ltd were fined £200,000 at Norwich Crown Court, after pleading guilty to a charge under *HSWA 1974, s 2* and one under the *Diving Operations at Work Regulations 1981 (SI 1981/399)* (another charge under these Regulations was withdrawn). The case followed the death of a diver, Bradley Westell, who came into contact with a thruster on the diving support vessel *CSO Orelia* during cable-laying work for Shell off Norfolk in July 1995. Kenneth Roberts, a Stena diving supervisor, was acquitted of manslaughter but convicted of perverting the course of justice (by erasing part of a video recording of the operation)and imprisoned for one month. He also pleaded guilty to a charge of failing to take reasonable care for Mr Westell's safety under *HSWA 1974, s 7* and was fined £500.

Keltbray

8.27 On 7 September 1999, demolition company Keltbray Ltd were fined £200,000 at Southwark Crown Court after pleading guilty (at an earlier hearing) to a breach of the *Construction (Health, Safety and Welfare) Regulations 1996 (SI 1996/1592), Reg 6(3)(d)*. The case followed the deaths of two men after the floor they were working on collapsed in Gresham St, London EC2, on 31 January 1998. Judge David Elfer QC referred to *R v F Howe & Sons (Engineering) Ltd* (SEE 8.75) Costs of £8,037 awarded to HSE. The level of fine was appealed against but the Court of Appeal upheld the fine on 19 May 2000.

Mobil North Sea

8.28 On 2 March 1998, Mobil North Sea Ltd were fined £175,000 at Aberdeen Sheriff Court after pleading guilty to a charge under the *HSWA 1974, s 3(1)*. Co-defendants Cooper Cameron UK Ltd were fined an additional £45,000 after pleading guilty to a similar charge. The charges followed an incident on 10 August 1996 when a diver was killed when a high pressure cap blew off a Cameron subsea *Christmas tree* wellhead on Mobil's Ness field, connected to Beryl Bravo.

British Steel

8.29 In May 1999, British Steel was fined £175,000 after pleading guilty at Cardiff Crown Court following prosecution as a result of a fireball and explosion at its site in Llanwern South Wales on 16 January 1998. An explosion in a process vessel resulted in a 125-foot fireball reaching the roof where twelve contractors were installing a fume extraction system. Two contractors received very severe burns. The exact cause of the explosion is unknown, but was believed to be an LPG bottle included in the scrap in the process vessel. The company was charged under the *HSWA 1974, s 3(1)*. The company was ordered to pay costs of £14,544.

J Murphy and Sons

8.30 On 19 April 1993 J Murphy and Sons Ltd were fined £160,000 and ordered to pay costs of £28,000 at Knightsbridge Crown Court, London. The company pleaded guilty to two charges following the death of a subcontractor's employee electrocuted in the London Water Ring Main on 15 February 1991. The Court accepted not guilty pleas by director, James O'Callaghan. This was the second highest ever fine for a construction case.

Royal Ordnance plc

8.31   On 31 May 1994 Royal Ordnance plc was fined £150,000 at the High Court (sitting at Glasgow) after pleading guilty to four charges of breaching the *HSWA 1974*. This followed an explosion at the company's plant in Bishopton, Renfrewshire, on 29 July 1992 in which an employee received fatal burns.

Associated Octel

8.32   Associated Octel were fined £150,000 at Chester Crown Court on 2 February 1996 and ordered to pay costs of £142,600, following a major fire at the company's site at Ellesmere Port, Cheshire, on 1 February 1994. The company pleaded guilty to charges under *HSWA 1974, ss 2 and 3* the latter regarding hazards to non-employees, eg firefighters. The case was based upon the leak of chlorine which was attributed by the HSE to failure to assess the possibility of a leak with consequent lack of inspection and maintenance.

GATX Terminals

8.33   In February 1996, GATX Terminals of Avonmouth, Bristol, were fined a total of £150,000 for offences under the *HSWA 1974, ss 2(1) and 3(1)*. They were ordered to pay costs of £20,000. Fines of £75,000 were made on each of two counts of breaches of the *HSWA 1974*. The charges followed a fire at the docks on 4 August 1994 in which a senior operations controller died. Valves on a pipeline had not been closed following discharge of petroleum spirit from a ship to a bulk container, allowing vapour to escape. GATX disputed details in the HSE's report, but pleaded guilty to the charges.

Muir Construction

8.34   On 28 May 1996, Muir Construction Ltd of Inverkeithing were fined a total of £150,000. Fines of £75,000 at Dundee Sherriff Court were made on each of two charges under the *HSWA 1974, ss*

2 and 3. This followed the deaths of three sub-contracted steel fitters, who had been installing reinforcements for a concrete floor during construction of student accommodation at Dundee University when a four metre high wall collapsed on them. Muir Construction had built the wall but had failed to ensure that it was supported.

Cheetham Hill Construction

8.35   On 10 February 1997 Cheetham Hill Construction Ltd of Bury, Lancs, were fined £150,000 at Leeds Crown Court after pleading guilty to a breach of the *HSWA 1974, s 3(1)*. The case followed a labourer's death on 1 October 1995. He overturned a dumper whilst driving down a steep slope; there had been a similar incident (without injury) the previous day.

Trentham Leisure Ltd

8.36   On 27 October 1997 at Stafford Crown Court, Trentham Leisure Ltd, operators of Trentham Gardens leisure park, New-castle-under-Lyme, were fined £150,000 and ordered to pay costs of £6,680 costs after pleading guilty to a charge under *HSWA 1974.* The case followed the death of a seven-year-old boy on a go-kart track. The company had disregarded HSE advice on making an independent thorough examination of the track and making changes to the track layout that had created a gap in the barriers, through which the boy drove, striking an unprotected obstruction.

Neath Port Talbot

8.37   On 19 November 1997 at Cardiff Crown Court, Neath Port Talbot County Borough Council, were fined £150,000 and ordered to pay costs in excess of £43,000 after pleading guilty to a charge under the *HSWA 1974, s 2(1)*. The case followed the deaths of two council employees in a sewage pumping station at Crymlyn Burrows. The council had failed to ensure the safety of the employees when they were working in a confined space.

Hall and Co

8.38   On 16 February 1998, builders merchants Hall and Co were fined £150,000 at Chichester Crown Court (transferred from Chichester magistrates' court for sentencing in January). The case, taken by Chichester District Council, followed the death of a yardman at Hall's Westhampnett premises. The deceased was run over by a reversing lorry driven by another employee.

South East – Railtrack – Southern Track

8.39 On 8 September 1998, a 'global' fine of £150,000 was imposed on three defendants, South East Infrastructure Maintenance Company Ltd, Railtrack plc and Southern Track Renewals Company. This followed an incident at Bexley, Kent, on 4 February 1997, in which seven freight train wagons derailed at a bridge over Bexley High Street. Four members of the public, who were in or near the arches of the bridge, were injured. Each company pleaded guilty to a charge under the *HSWA 1974, s 3(1)*. An order for costs of £41,768 was made. Both the fines and the costs were split on a percentage basis with 55% for South East Infrastructure (fine £82,500; costs £22,972.40); 40% for Railtrack (fine £60,000; costs £16,707.20); and 5% for Southern Track Renewals (fine £7,500; costs £2,088.40).

Fashion Logistics

8.40 Fashion Logistics Ltd was fined £150,000 with £69,000 costs by Wood Green Crown Court for breaching health and safety regulations after a worker was crushed by a forklift truck in August 1996.

Ipswich Port Authority

8.41 On 13 June 1997 at Ipswich Crown Court, Ipswich Port Authority was fined £125,000 and ordered to pay £8,314.50 costs, after pleading guilty to three charges under the following two similar accidents (one a fatality on 12 August 1996) during the discharge of timber from a ship. The three fines were for £10,000, £100,000 and £15,000.

Translink

8.42 On 18 November 1991 Translink Joint Venture (TJV) were fined a total £125,000 at Maidstone Crown Court following the death of a Channel Tunnel workman who was crushed by a train. TJV comprises five companies, each being fined £25,000.

Kennedy Construction

8.43 On 29 October 1996 Kennedy Construction Group Ltd of Tyldesley, Manchester, were fined £125,000 at Worcester Crown Court. The fines comprised £65,000 under the *HSWA 1974, s 3(1)* and £60,000 under the *Electricity at Work Regulations 1989 (SI 1989/ 635), Reg 14(1)*. The company was ordered to pay costs of £10,000. A 24-year-old employee of one of the company's sub-contractors was killed after receiving an 11,000 volt shock when the mobile lighting boom he was helping to raise came into contact with overhead lines on the A449 near Claines, Worcester.

Scudder Ltd

8.44 On 15 November 1996 T E Scudder Ltd of Wembley, Middlesex, were fined £125,000 and ordered to pay costs of £20,255, at Leeds Crown Court. An employee died when a large section of the fourth floor of the Norwich Union building in Leeds collapsed on 16 May 1995.

Transco

8.45 On 19 February 1999 Transco were fined £120,000, and ordered to pay costs of £39,545, at Warrington Crown Court. Charges were brought under the *HSWA 1974, ss 2 and 3* following an explosion in April 1997, during work on a gas leak from a main at a disused gasworks in Runcorn, in which nine employees and a contractor were injured. The workers were replacing a corroded pipe, following reports of a leak. The prosecution case was that there was no effective safety management system, and the team, not having established the flammable gas zone, brought a source of ignition into it. There were numerous faults found and Transco instructions would have prevented the accident if followed.

Ringwood Highway Services etc

8.46 In February 2001, Ringwood Highway Services, Hewed Plant Hire and Phoenix Engineering Co Ltd were fined a total of £120,000. An employee was working with a reversing chipper spreader during surface dressing at roadworks in Cambridgeshire when an accident occurred resulting in an employee having a leg amputated.

Atlantic Drilling

8.47   On 29 April 1992 Atlantic Drilling Ltd were fined a total of £101,000 comprising fines £100,000 and £1,000 respectively on two charges at Aberdeen Sheriff Court following an incident in December 1990 on semi-submersible drilling rig *Ben Reoch*. An employee was killed when struck by a falling hose and two others were endangered. The company appealed and the higher fine was subsequently halved.

Nobels Explosives

8.48   On 29 March 1990, Nobels Explosives, a subsidiary of ICI, were fined £100,000 at Mold Crown Court, following an explosion at their Penrhyndeudraeth works in 1988 in which two employees were killed.

Tate and Lyle

8.49   On 30 November 1990, a fine of £250,000, imposed on Tate and Lyle at Sheriff Court, Greenock, on 5 March 1990, was reduced on appeal to £100,000. This followed an accident in a sugar silo in which a man was killed.

Shell UK

8.50   On 2 December 1991 Shell UK was fined £100,000. at Knutsford Crown Court after a blockage in a flare line prevented gas from being discharged safely at their Stanlow refinery near Ellesmere Port, Cheshire, in November 1990.

British Gas

8.51   On 18 March 1992 British Gas were fined £100,000 and ordered to pay costs of £75,000 at Liverpool Crown Court following an explosion during intentional discharge of gas at their plant at Partington, Urmston, near Manchester on 5 December 1989 in which two men were severely burned.

Shell UK

8.52   On 14 May 1992 Shell UK were fined £100,000 and ordered to pay costs of £10,341.33 at Chelmsford Crown Court following a leak on the detergent alkylate plant at the Shell Haven refinery site, Stanford le Hope, Essex, on 6 May 1991. Hazardous materials including hydrogen fluoride and benzene were released in a cloud. Thirty seven employees were treated on site and ten were found to have breathed in toxic substances.

Allied Colloids

8.53   On 29 January 1993 Allied Colloids Ltd were fined £100,000 and ordered to pay costs of £62,300 at Bradford Crown Court, after pleading guilty to three charges with two charges under the *HSWA 1974, s 2(1)* (two charges) and *s 3(1)* each resulting in a fine of £30,000 and £40,000. The prosecution followed a fire on 21 July 1992 at the company's chemical works at Low Moor, Bradford.

Rowen and Laing

8.54   On 23 July 1993, J N Rowen Ltd and John Laing Services were fined a total of £1000,000. Each company was fined £50,000, with Laing ordered to pay costs of £22,000 and Rowan ordered to pay £3,000. The two companies were prosecuted following the collapse of a tower crane across St James Garlickhythe Church and Thames Street, City of London, in September 1991.

MB Gas

8.55   On 1 July 1993, MB Gas was fined £100,000 at Knightsbridge Crown Court following an explosion at a bottled gas depot in Harlesden surrounded by terraced housing. Hammersmith and Fulham local authority assisted took the case. HSE assisted with the investigation.

Severn Trent Water

8.56   On 20 January 1995, Severn Trent Water was fined £100,000 at Leicester Crown Court. The fines comprised £100,000 under the *HSWA 1974, s 2(1)*. The prosecution followed the electrocution of a lorry driver, Kevin Sutton, when his tipper touched overhead cables in May 1994.

Firth Vickers Centrespinning

8.57   On 15 November 1996, Firth Vickers Centrespinning Ltd were fined £100,000 and ordered to pay costs of £6,600 at Sheffield Crown Court. The company pleaded guilty to charge under the *HSWA 1974, s 2(1)* after three employees were seriously burned, one with 40% burns when they were sprayed with two tonnes of molten metal, which escaped because of an unchecked defective guard.

Brown Lennox Engineering

8.58   On 26 June 1997 Brown Lennox Engineering of Pontypridd were fined £100,000 at Merthyr Tydfil Crown Court, after an accident in which one of its employees was crushed by a one-tonne steel girder in June 1996.

Brintons

8.59   On 18 December 1998 Brintons Ltd were fined £100,000 and ordered to pay costs of £2,170 at Worcester Crown Court after pleading guilty to a charge under the *Control of Asbestos at Work Regulations 1987 (SI 1987/2115), Reg 8(1)*. The company failed to prevent employees from exposure to brown asbestos at their Kidderminster factory between May 1996 and March 1998. Furthermore, the company had failed when buying the factory in December 1995 to act on a survey recommending asbestos sampling and had obtained no written assurances of freedom from asbestos from the previous owners (though they did get verbal assurance). The defendants appealed against the size of the fine which was dismissed on the 22 June 1999.

Dunlop Tyres

8.60   On 5 March 1999, Dunlop Tyres Ltd were fined £100,000 and ordered to pay costs of £2,855 having pleaded guilty to a charge under the *HSWA 1974, s 2* at Wolverhampton Crown Court. The prosecution resulted after a worker, Scott Dixon, died after being dragged into a machine at the company's Fort Dunlop site in March 1998. Case had been heard at West Bromwich magistates' court but was referred to the Crown Court for sentencing.

Scottish Adhesives

8.61 On 1 April 1999, The Scottish Adhesives Company Ltd, was fined a total of £100,000 at Glasgow Sheriff Court. This followed a fire in which two workers died at the company's Glasgow premises on 7 August 1996. The work involved handling flammable liquids in the manufacturing process. The precise source of the fire was not identified, but the investigation revealed deficiencies concerning the handling of highly flammable liquids and the control of ignition sources. The £100,000 fine had two components: £80,000 for a breach of the *HSWA 1974, s 2* and £20,000 for a breach of the *Management of Health and Safety at Work Regulations 1992 (SI 1992/ 2051), Reg 3* (the risk assessment provision). A director of the company, Colin Aldritt, was also fined £7,000 (£5,000 and £2,000) for the same breaches.

Tarmac

8.62 On 24 May 1999, Tarmac Heavy Building Materials UK Ltd of Snodland, Kent, who are road maintenance contractors, were fined £100,000 at Basildon Crown Court, and ordered to pay costs of £6,094.18p as a result of a prosecution under the *HSWA 1974, s 3*. The case was referred from Grays magistrates' court on 10 March 1999 for sentencing in the Crown Court. The prosecution was brought after a road worker, Mark Anthony Roberts, employed by subcontractor Bearsted Civil Engineering, and who came from near Maidstone, was struck by a reversing works lorry in a coned-off lane of the M25 at Junction 28 during night-time central reservation work. He died in hospital shortly after the incident.

Scottish Power

8.63 On 12 July 1999 Scottish Power was fined £100,000, following the electrocution of nine-year-old Joseph Lewsley, when cables carrying 6,300 volts passed through a tree he had climbed near Glasgow. The tree had not been inspected for four years; it should have been cut back clear of power lines.

Smurfit UK

8.64 On 22 June 2001 at Burnley Crown Court, Smurfit UK was fined £100,000 after the death of a 29-year-old paper maker on 26

January 2000. The deceased was killed while attempting to clean a paper machine, which was working at full speed with no guards fitted.

London Underground Ltd and Tilbury Douglas Construction Ltd

8.65   On 9 March 2001 London Underground Ltd and Tilbury Douglas Construction Ltd were fined a total of £95,000. The incident involved a crane jib, which fell through the roof of a house while the family slept. The crane collapsed causing the jib and hook block to come to rest in the roof of the house. The family had to undergo psychiatric treatment as a result of the incident.

Translink Joint Venture

8.66   On 28 April 1992 the five companies in Translink Joint Venture were fined a total of £90,000. This resulted in fines of £18,000 each following the death of William Cartman, a grouter, who was crushed by a machine in the Channel Tunnel in 1990. Costs of £35,000 were ordered to be shared between the five companies.

Floyd Construction

8.67   On 15 November 1991 Floyd Construction were fined £50,000 and ordered to pay costs of £15,000 at Middlesex Crown Court following the deaths of three workers overcome by toxic fumes while attempting to unblock a sewer at Watney Market, Tower Hamlets on 22 September 1990.

Translink Joint Venture

8.68   On 26 March 1990, the five partners in Translink Joint Venture were fined a total of £50,000 with each being fined £10,000 at Maidstone Crown Court following the death of a Channel Tunnel worker in February 1989.

Bartholomew and Rush

8.69   On 18 May 1990, A E Bartholomew and Rush & Tomkins were fined £25,000 each at Southampton Crown Court following the death of a man after the sides of a trench fell in.

Doncaster Council

8.70 On 26 July 1993, Doncaster Metropolitan Borough Council were fined £50,000 at Doncaster Crown Court following the death of a sports centre manager who was electrocuted when he touched an unearthed roof light fitting at Adwick Leisure Centre.

Caird Environmental

8.71 On 23 March 1992, Caird Environmental Ltd were fined £50,000 following the death of one worker and the serious injury of another caused by an explosion and fire while they were crushing a drum containing chromic acid.

British Rail

8.72 On 19 May 1993 British Rail were fined £50,000 following a collision between two trains when points were operated manually following a trackside fire. Twenty-five passengers were injured.

John Laing

8.73 On 17 October 1997, John Laing Services Ltd were fined £50,000 and ordered to pay costs of £5,022 at the Old Bailey after pleading guilty to one charge under the *HSWA 1974, s 3(1)* a fine of £30.000 and a charge under the *Construction (Lifting Operations) Regulations 1961 (SI 1961/1581), Reg 49* resulting in a fine of £20,000. The case followed an incident where 50 scaffold tubes fell onto the street at Poultry Lane, City of London in May 1996.

Level of fines

8.74 In an article, 'The Safety Debate – Corporate Killing', *Health and Safety Practitioner*, March 1999, D Bergman identifies that only one study has been undertaken in reviewing the level of fines given, balanced against the wealth of the company. The West Midlands Health and Safety Advice Centre obtained information on the annual profits of 65 of the 260 companies sentenced in the region between 1987 and 1993. The five companies with average profits of between £1–10,000 received an average fine of £750 per offence – 16% of their profits. Companies with profits of between £100–150,000 received fines of between £1,290 per offence – 0.5% of their profits. The five companies with profits of over £10 million received average fines of £1,185, equivalent to 0.002% of their profits.

The same concerns about the level of fines were discussed in 1996 by Frank Davies, the then Chairman of the Health and Safety Commission, who reviewed how magistrates' courts reacted to health and safety cases. The key issue was addressed in the opening paragraph where he stated:

> 'Fines for health and safety offences are too low. Employers who cause injury, or even death, get off lightly. These are views which we hear from members of the public as well as the media ... When prosecution and conviction follow, only the courts can decide penalties which send the right message: that risks to health and safety must be controlled ... Experience shows that the size of the fine has an important impact on preventative work with firms. If a court rewards with low fine the good fortune of an employer whose crime did not result in injury or death, other employers may believe they can neglect health and safety with impunity.'

('Avoiding Death and Danger', *The Magistrate*, April 1996).

The Howe Judgment

8.75   The status of fines for health and safety cases changed following the judgment of an appeal in the case of *R v F Howe & Sons (Engineering) Ltd [1999] 2 All ER 249* against a fine imposed by a court after a fatal accident. Repeated calls from the HSC and government ministers for higher fines to be imposed for health and safety offences appear to have been answered by a recent Court of Appeal ruling. The ruling concluded that fines for health and safety offences are too low and as a result is expected to lead to more health and safety offences being heard before the Crown Court, where judges can impose unlimited fines. Currently, the majority of health and safety cases are heard in the magistrates' courts, where the maximum fine that can be imposed for breaches of the *HSWA 1974* is £20,000. The Court of Appeal concluded that fines for health and safety offences must be large enough to bring home to those who manage a company, and their shareholders, the need for a safe environment for workers and the public. However, although it stated that fines should not be so large that they put the company at risk of bankruptcy or place the earnings of employees at risk, it said that there may be cases where the offences are so serious that the defendant ought not to be in business. Magistrates and judges should take into account any aggravating features when passing sentence in health and safety cases. These included whether there was a deliberate breach of health and safety legislation with a view to profit and if there was a failing to heed warnings and where death is the consequence of a criminal act, it should be regarded as an aggravating feature of the offence, and the penalty should reflect public disquiet at the unnecessary loss of life. The Court of Appeal has said that health and safety fines are too low. The judgment will help to ensure that the courts recognise the seriousness of health and safety crimes and punish the perpetrators appropriately.

The courts have a role to play in the legal process, both in the level of fines and whether a case should be transferred from the Magistrates' Court to the Crown Court. The former has limits on the level of fines that can be imposed, while the latter does not.

The Friskies judgment

8.76 When preparing a case for prosecution the regulating authorities carry out a 'Friskies' assessment to identify the aggravating and mitigating features of the defendant and submit the information as part of the prosecution bundle. This will provide the court with important information to aid them when determining the sentence. The case that brought about this change in procedure was *R v Friskies Petcare (UK) Ltd [2000] 2 Cr App R(S) 401*. The company was fined £600,000 at Isleworth Crown Court after the electrocution of an employee in a meat silo at their factory at Southall, West London. (see 8.8 for details of the case). The company pleaded guilty to *HSWA 1974, s 2* and the *Management of Health and Safety at Work Regulations 1992 (SI 1992/2051), Reg 3*. The company appealed against the level of fine.

The Court of Appeal (reviewed in *Health and Safety Bulletin*, December 2001, 304) heard *R v Friskies Petcare (UK) Ltd* in March 2000 and reduced the fine. This decision was made on the grounds that the trial judge had incorrectly included an 'aggravating' factor after he had erroneously found that the company had put profit before safety. It is considered that a deliberate breach of health and safety legislation with a view to profit seriously aggravates the offence. The court stated that: 'financial profit can often be made at

173

the expense of protecting employees and the public.' It was not disputed in court when the company claimed that there was no evidence of cost cutting for financial gain. The Court of Appeal's judgment reinforced the *Howe* sentencing criteria, (SEE 8.75 above) and noted that fines of £500,000 and above tend to be reserved for those cases where a major public disaster occurs. It can be anticipated that fines for corporate killing offences will be in the higher level. The court also provided guidance to the HSE and defendants about how they should prepare and present mitigating and aggravating factors to the trial court, which would allow all factors to be considered.

The Court of Appeal said:

> '... it found this case, "like so many cases", was one where no one consciously sits down and works out the expense of shutting a particular section down for a period of time against safety considerations. It is one of those difficult things where no attention is paid, no risk assessment is made and people get on with the job and do it. One of the failings that brings companies before the court is the fact they have not taken a proper risk assessment in cases of this nature.'

It was found that the Crown Court had made an error in finding the existence of the aggravating feature, 'profit', which meant that the fine of £600,000 took into account a factor that it should not have.

The Court found that the aggravating features were:

- The death of Mr Wilkins.

- The position of the switch for turning off the current, which was too inaccessible should anything go wrong.

- The fact that the breaches had been going on for some time;

- No employee had his or her attention drawn to HSE guidance on welding.

- The firm had conducted no assessment of the risk involved in repairing ribbon stirrers in situ.

- The incident represented a serious and obvious breach of duty.

It is worthy of note that it is often a matter of chance whether death or serious injury results from even a serious breach of health and safety legislation. Therefore, where death is the consequence of such a breach, the public regards it, as an aggravating feature of the offence and the penalty should reflect the unnecessary loss of life. In addition the Court of Appeal agreed with the judge in that the activities of the company fell a long way short of doing what was reasonable and practical.

The mitigating factors for the company were:

- A prompt admission and plea of guilty.

- A good health and safety record over the years.

- The steps it had taken since the incident to improve safety, all of which had been taken with the approval of, and confirmation by, the HSE and which now agreed that Friskies had 'a high level of commitment to safety'.

The Court of Appeal also took into account the financial position of the company, which it described as a very substantial business, with a considerable turnover, generating pre-tax profits at the relevant time of some £40 million. The court, reduced the fine from £600,000 to £250,000. However, it refused to allow Friskies costs from central funds.

Observers may consider that the company took steps after the incident to improve safety and submitted this as mitigation as opposed to adopting safety procedures before an incident. It may also be considered that the reduced fine was too low when balanced against the company's profit and original fine. Further, the offence was committed over a considerable period of time. It may also be argued that undertakings put profit at the top of their operating activities, and that it was no different in this case because it was only luck that there had not been an accident earlier.

The considerations above are important factors for legal debate but the Friskies judgment does focus the minds of the regulating authorities when investigating an incident and preparing the case for trial before the courts. This will be an equally important aspect when preparing a case for a corporate killing offence prosecution. This case should also serve as a warning to all undertakings to place health and safety at the top of the management agenda. The fine, prosecution costs and remedial action costs show that it would have been more financially effective to adopt safety management procedures in the first place.

Duties of directors and employees

8.77   There already exists within the *HSWA 1974* offences for individuals including directors, managers, employees and others. An offence under *HSWA 1974, s 36* occurs where there is the fault of another person while *HSWA 1974* s 37 is a corporate offence for directors, company secretaries and mangers. *HSWA 1974, s 7* is used for individuals. These three offences include a wide and diverse range of people who owe a duty of care to others with sanctions available when they fail in that duty.

Duties of directors, HSWA 1974, ss 36 and 37

8.78   Offences due to the actions of another person (*HSWA 1974, s 36*) occurs where the commission of an offence by any person is due to the act or wrongdoing of another person, that other person will be guilty of an offence. That person may be charged and convicted of an offence even though proceedings may not have been taken against the first person. If the Crown commits an offence, the Crown cannot be prosecuted, but if the offence occurred because of an act or wrongdoing by a person other than the Crown, then that person may be charged and convicted even though the Crown is immune.

HSWA 1974, s 37 offences by directors, managers and company secretaries occur where the offence is committed by a corporate body and is proved to have been committed with the consent or connivance of, or is attributable to any neglect on the part of any director, manager, company secretary or other similar officer of the corporate body, or person who was purporting to act in such a capacity. That person, as well as the corporate body will be guilty of the offence. A director consents to an offence when he is well aware of what is happening and agrees to it. He will also have connived to an offence when he is aware of what is happening but has not openly expressed encouragement, but allows the act to continue and does not say anything. He will be negligent if he has a duty to do something and fails to do it or is negligent as to how he does it. This section also includes persons who describe themselves as directors, managers, secretaries or similar officers who have been disqualified from holding office under the *Companies Act* and are equally liable. Therefore, anybody who acts in a management capacity could be held liable under *HSWA 1974, s 37*, no matter what title is used. If the corporate body is being managed by a *member*, such as may be found in a workers' co-operative, then the acts or wrongdoing of the individual, when acting in a managerial role are deemed to be within the scope of *section 37*. For a prosecution to succeed under *HSWA 1974, s 37* it has to be shown that an individual had responsibility to make management decisions and, be in a position of responsibility at the time.

HSWA 1974, ss 36 and 37: case profile

8.79 Between 1986/87 and 1997/98 there were 81 prosecutions under the *HSWA 1974, s 36* commenced (information's laid) resulting in 60 successful prosecutions (convictions).

Section 36	Information's Laid	Convictions	Total Fines
1986/87	13	9	£1,400
1987/88	11	9	£2,350
1988/89	5	5	£4,400
1989/90	10	10	£12,350
1990/91	12	8	£2,500
1991/92	9	6	£6,150
1992/93	5	3	£1,500

Between 1986/87 and 1997/98 there were 223 prosecutions under *HSWA 1974, s 37* commenced (information's laid) resulting in 118 successful prosecutions (convictions).

Section 37	Information's Laid	Convictions	Total Fines £	Average Fine per conviction
1986/87	45	5	2,000	£400
1987/88	6	4	750	£188
1988/89	8	6	3,700	£617
1989/90	23	18	31,150	£1,731
1990/91	6	4	1,000	£250
1991/92	10	7	6,250	£893

1992/93	34	23	20,425	£888
1993/94	13	6	3,940	£657
1994/95	13	8	12,450	£1,556
1995/96	21	12	63,750	£3,356
1996/97	35	19	63,750	£3,356
1997/98	9	6	13,250	£2,208

Details of the cases for each year, combined with successes, total fines and the average fine per conviction is shown in the tables above showing that the fines are generally low. They are fines against individuals as opposed to corporations. An individual's personal financial circumstances and ability to pay a fine are taken into consideration by the courts, as is the case with all criminal convictions.

Duties of employees, HSWA 1974, s 7

8.80 Employees can be prosecuted under *HSWA 1974, s 7* as they have a duty to take reasonable care for the health and safety of themselves and others who may be affected by their acts or omissions at work. This offence covers a wide range of issues such as a supervisor who supports an employee in undertaking an unsafe act, that supervisor could be prosecuted. An employee who through an act of horseplay or skylarking while at work, causes another to be injured, that employee could be prosecuted. Any employee who provided with safety equipment refuses to wear or use the equipment or abide by safety procedures could be liable for prosecution. In addition to the *HSWA 1974* the *Management of Health and Safety at Work Regulations 1999 (SI 1999/3242)* imposes additional duties on employees to report dangerous situations or shortcomings to the employer in matters of health and safety. It is often seen that the corporate body is prosecuted as having the ultimate general duty of care, with *HSWA 1974, s 7* charges against an individual for specific acts or omissions.

Harvestime Ltd, Fresha Bakeries etc: a Case

8.81 'Leicester Bakers Ordered to Pay £628,000 after Double Deaths in Oven', stated the headlines of a HSE Press release. Two directors and a manager at Harvestime Ltd, Fresha Bakeries were fined a total of £373,000 plus costs of £255,000 as a result of the death of two employees, at their factory in Leicester on 16 May 1998. The two men had been sent into a giant oven to retrieve a broken part, using a slow moving conveyor belt to enter the oven where the temperature was more that 100C and they died as a result.

Fresha Bakeries were prosecuted under *HSWA 1974, s 2* because they failed to provide a safe system of work. Harvestime were prosecuted under the same offence. Both companies were prosecuted under *HSWA 1974, s 3* for failing to ensure that persons in their employ were not exposed to danger. For these offences the companies were fined a total of £350,000.

Dennis Masters, the Chief Engineer and employee of Fresha Bakeries was prosecuted under *HSWA 1974, s 7* and fined £2,000. Brian Jones, an employee was prosecuted under *HSWA 1974, s 7* and fined £1,000. John Bridson, managing director of Harvestime Ltd and also managing director of Fresha Bakeries Ltd was prosecuted under *HSWA 1974, s 37* and fined £10,000 for each company. In total, John Bridston was fined £20,000. The costs were divided into £250,000 awarded against the companies and £5,000 against John Bridson.

Fines versus remedial action

8.82 Companies will often argue that to be delivered a heavy fine and costs will have a detrimental affect on the company shareholders and employees. An example is shown when a prosecution taken in against a company who pleaded not guilty at the initial hearings, opting for trial in the magistrates' court, later changed their plea to that of guilty. The case was presented to the magistrates and maximum fines were sought as well as full costs. There was no mitigation in respect to the offences but the case was put by the defence that if the company were fined the maximum, three members of staff would be made redundant that day so that the fines and costs could be paid. The magistrates, accepting that the case was serious identified that it was a high unemployment area and they could not impose fines to a level that would place people who were innocent to the offences and actions of the company out of work. Fines and costs were imposed on the company, but less than those sought. There is no legal rule that requires organisations to disclose its financial status through an accredited source of say a firm of accountants. They are only obliged to provide general figures and the same set of rules apply to directors, mangers and self-employed persons.

Celia Wells highlights the question of fines and the issue of others bearing the costs:

> 'British Rail was fined £250,000 and ordered to pay £55,000 prosecution costs for an admitted failure to ensure the safety of its employees and passengers following the Clapham rail collision in 1987. The judge was faced with an *acute problem* ... the fine could only be met either by increasing the burden on fare paying passengers or by reducing the finance available for improvement to the railway system.'

(Corporations and Criminal Responsibility, 1993).

Summay

This chapter has reviewed a sample of cases and fines imposed as well as examining individual offences, all of which come under the *HSWA 1974* and a number of Health and Safety Regulations. The variance in fines is obvious and the evidence shows that in some non-fatal accidents the fines were much higher than in some accidents that involved fatalities. Others may comment that some of the cases should have been prosecuted for manslaughter, but that is not being discussed here. However, it must be considered that in many of the cases the new corporate killing and possibly individual offences would be a very real option for the authorities.

9 The Legal Systems, Structures and Enforcement Agencies

This chapter considers the following:

- The European Union – EU directives.

- The *Human Rights Act 1988*.

- The legal system in England, Wales and Scotland.

- The role of the Health and Safety Commission and Health and Safety Executive and local authorities

- The role of the coroner, the police and the Crown Prosecution Service

- Deaths at work protocol.

- Accident investigation process.

- Employers Liability Insurance.

Introduction

9.1   The European Union is responsible for introducing directives, leaving each country to develop national legislation that fulfils the objectives behind health and safety regulation. While the European Court of Justice (ECJ) is the ultimate court for European jurisdiction, each nation's legal system provides the day-to-day judicial process. It is the responsibility of each country to have a legal system that will allow for accidents to be investigated and prosecutions initiated, enabling breaches of health and safety legislation to be enforced. The legal system in England and Wales differs from that of Scotland, but the regulating agencies enforce the same health and safety legislation. It will be seen that a number of regulating agencies are involved in the legal process and it is imperative that these agencies co-operate with each other. To aid this process the Health and Safety Executive (HSE), police and Crown Prosecution Service (CPS) have a protocol that allows for the evaluation of a case to ensure that appropriate enforcement is taken. The purpose of this chapter is to provide a broad overview of the legal structures and organisations that undertake the legal process and the enforcement options available.

The European Union

9.2   A significant change to health and safety legislation occurred as a result of the UK signing the Treaty of Rome in 1973 and the Maastricht Treaty in 1992, which binds the UK to European law. The European Union issue EU directives which provide a framework for occupational health and safety issues. The directives require member states to create legislation and guidance on the topics and to enforce compliance. The objective is that every member state, working from the same template, should produce legislation within that member state constitution that is broadly consistent with other member states. If there is a considerable disparity between member states' interpretation of the framework requirements, then the subsequent legislation and enforcement can create an socio-economic imbalance, which in turn can have a major impact on industry and business.

The Treaty of Rome

9.3   The *Treaty of Rome* was signed in 1957 by the six founding states, France, West Germany, Italy, Belgium, The Netherlands and Luxembourg. It was in 1973 that the UK, Ireland and Denmark signed. Greece joined in 1981, Spain and Portugal in 1992 with Austria, Finland and Sweden joining in 1995. The foundation of the Treaty is to create economic harmonisation. Within the context of health and safety matters if one country could economise on these issues it would be to the disadvantage of those countries that had addressed the issues. There is the added factor of the social dimension where there are positive steps being taken to increase the level of protection provided to workers from accidents and ill health at work. The following objectives were identified in *Article 118* of the *Treaty of Rome,* which stated that there was to be harmony in the laws relating to employment, labour law and working conditions, basic and advanced training and protection against occupational accidents and diseases. The outcome is that the effect of EU law on domestic law is increasing.

European health and safety law

9.4   As described above, the *Treaty of Rome* is the supreme law for all European member states with the supreme policy making body being the Council of Ministers, comprising a minister from each member state who attends each meeting. Support to the meetings is provided through the Committee of Permanent Representatives (COREPER). The European Commission has the task of initiating and drafting proposals for approval by the Council and mediates between states. It also monitors to ensure the EU rules are being observed and has the power to refer a member state to the ECJ if there are failings.

The European Parliament has Members of the European Parliament (MEP's) elected directly from each member state and can offer opinions on the Council of Ministers proposals by submitting questions and can as a sanction, dismiss the Commission on a vote of censure. The ECJ gives rulings on the interpretation of European law, either as a matter raised by the Commission, at the request of the courts of a member state or a claim brought by an individual of a member state. Based in Spain, a European Health and Safety Agency has been set up with the objectives of improving health and safety at work by imparting health and safety information and providing technical, scientific and economic information to member states.

EU directives

9.5   The system for adopting a directive under *Article 118A* of the *Treaty of Rome* is known as the co-operation procedure and must be adopted by the member states. The Commission submits proposals to the Council of Ministers. The European Parliament and the Economic and Social Committee are consulted for opinions to be offered. The Commission can amend the proposals, but are not obliged to do so. They are then submitted to the Labour and Social Affairs Council, a committee within the Council of Ministers. A review is undertaken and a majority vote option adopted. It is then reconsidered by the European Parliament with can approve the proposal, propose further amendments or reject them. If the outcome is the latter option then adoption is made by the Council of Ministers on a unanimous vote. Once a directive has been passed by the Council of Ministers it is binding on the member states and identifies the results that have to be achieved.

The European Court of Justice

9.6   Under the *European Communities Act 1972, s 3* decisions of the European Court of Justice (ECJ) are binding in matters of Community law, on all courts up to and including the House of Lords. The court sits in Luxembourg and is formed with 15 judges and nine advocate generals who are appointed for six years. The role of the court is to give rulings on interpretation of European law, from either a reference provided by the commission, a request from the courts of a member state or a claim brought by an individual person or corporation of a member state. Once the court has made a ruling the matter is returned to the member state courts to ensure compliance.

The Human Rights Act 1998

9.7   The *Human Rights Act 1998* is one of the most important developments in the English legal system in recent times. Many of our existing laws, practices and procedures are already compatible with the *European Convention on Human Rights*. The Convention seeks to establish a fair balance between the demands of the general interest of the community and the protection of human rights. The origins of the Convention evolved, as a result of the atrocities of the Second World War as a way of ensuring that such an event could not occur again.

The Act brings much of the Convention into domestic law. This means that the new legislation enables people to use the Convention in the UK courts as opposed to taking their case to the Court of Human Rights in Strasbourg.

The Convention comprises 18 Articles, which include the right to life, the right to a fair trial, no punishment without law and the right to liberty and security. It is a principal point that anyone charged with a criminal offence shall be presumed innocent until proved guilty according to the law. It follows that everyone is entitled to a fair public hearing within a reasonable time by an independent and impartial tribunal established by law and the judgment is pronounced publicly.

Acts of Parliament

9.8   Acts of Parliament form the basis of law in the UK and are the enabling Acts for developing more specific regulations. An example is the *HSWA 1974* that forms the foundation of health and safety legislation in the UK. A range of industry specific and more general regulations supports this Act.

An Act is introduced as a Bill into the Houses of Parliament. It receives a formal first reading where the House of Commons will hold a formal debate on the general concept of the proposed legislation. At this point a vote may be held on a proposal to give the Bill a second reading. If it is successful, the Bill is then sent to a committee where the content is considered in detail and amendments can be made. Having progressed to this stage, the Bill is produced in a report to the full House where amendments are considered. The final stage is the third reading of the Bill before it is passed to the House of Lords where a similar procedure is adopted. When both Houses have passed the Bill, it is presented to the Queen for Royal Assent, which is an automatic approval.

The House of Lords

9.9   The House of Lords is the highest court in the United Kingdom (SEE FIGURE 9.1). It comprises of Law Lords who are judges that have been promoted from the lower courts. The house will normally sit with five members whose judgment consists of speeches. Once a decision is made by the House of Lords on a point of law it will bind all lower courts until the House gives a different ruling, or until a decision is changed by an Act of Parliament. Precedence is given under the *European Communities Act 1972, s 3(1)* to decisions of the ECJ which are binding in matters of community law on all courts up to and including the House of Lords.

The legal process

9.10   There are two legal processes that affect health and safety which are criminal and civil law. While they are separate courts, the same case can be heard in both courts, which means that a civil case generally follows a successful criminal prosecution. For a case to be taken through the civil court there does not have to have been a criminal prosecution and it does not follow that where a company is found not guilty in criminal proceedings that there will not be any civil liability. In this respect the burden of proof differs with the criminal court requiring guilt *beyond reasonable doubt* while the civil court works on the *balance of probabilities*. A civil court cannot send anybody to prison or impose a fine or other punishment,

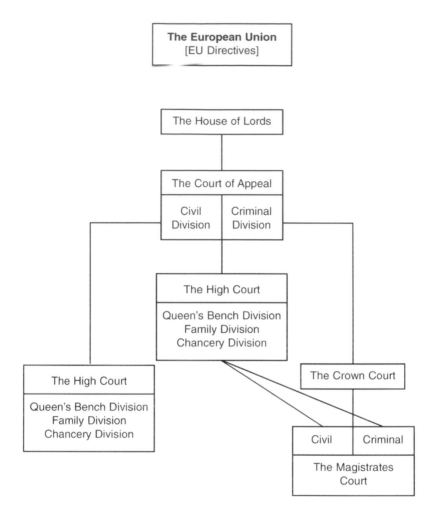

Figure 9.1: Hierarchy of the Courts

while a criminal court can. There are differences in the legal processes in England and Wales and those of Scotland, although the burden of proof and evidence is the same.

Criminal proceedings

9.11 Criminal offences are where there has been an offence against the state, which means in the case of health and safety offences, a breach of a statutory duty. The prosecution will be undertaken by the Crown which could be a Health and Safety

Inspector, a local authority Environmental Health Officer or a solicitor and barrister who may be appointed by these agencies to undertake the prosecution on their behalf. The case will be heard in a magistrates court before three lay magistrates or a district judge who sits alone, formerly titled a stipendiary magistrate. Fines in the lower court are limited to maximum levels. (SEE CHAPTER 8) For more serious offences the case can be sent to the Crown Court to be heard before a judge and jury. These offences are punishable by an unlimited fine and in some cases imprisonment is available. There is a right of appeal to a higher criminal court. The main focus of criminal prosecutions is the employer's liability of a duty of care and the prosecution would have to prove a failing or negligence beyond all reasonable doubt.

The Crown Court

9.12   The Crown Court hears indictable offences, which can only be heard in the higher court such as murder, manslaughter and rape as well as those cases of a serious nature where the prosecution or defendant elects to have the case, heard before a judge and jury. In the Crown Court, *HSWA 1974* offences are punishable by unlimited fine and there are eight offences that carry additional punishments of a term of imprisonment. There have been several instances where custodial and suspended prison sentences have been imposed. A *HSWA 1974* case heard in the magistrates' court can upon hearing all the evidence and with a guilty verdict, send the case to the Crown Court for sentence. An appeal against conviction and or sentence in the Crown Court is referred to the Court of Appeal.

The Crown Court sits with a single judge and a jury of twelve, selected from members of the public. England and Wales retains the formal dress code of wigs and gowns, both for the judge and the barristers who prosecute and defend cases. Both sides will present their case to the jury. The prosecution has the task of providing evidence that will prove their case beyond all reasonable doubt. The defence task is to counter that evidence and to put sufficient doubt in the jury's mind. At the end of the prosecution and defence case, the counsel for each side will sum up, highlighting salient points of the case that provide evidence for guilt or innocence. The judge then sums up the case to the jury and focuses on points of law, before sending them out to determine their verdict. The jury retires to a room equipped with copies of all the evidence, including any exhibits that can be taken into court. This will also include photographs, videotapes, drawings and statements. They remain in the room until they reach a verdict on which they all agree. When they reach that point they re-enter the court and the person appointed as foreman of the jury announces the verdict. If the jury cannot reach a unanimous verdict, a majority verdict may be accepted of ten to two for a guilty verdict. With a guilty verdict the judge will hear representations from the defendants as to the financial standing of the company before imposing a financial penalty, and if appropriate can commit individuals to prison.

The magistrates' court

9.13   There are three types of criminal offence:

- Cases that are summary only and heard in the magistrates' court.

- Cases that are indictable only and they will only be heard in the Crown Court.

- Cases that are triable either way and that includes most health and safety at work offences and can be heard either in the magistrates' court or the Crown Court.

The decision as to where the case is to be heard is made in the magistrates' court. This means that every health and safety at work criminal prosecution will be heard initially in the magistrates' court where having heard details of the case it is decided which court is the most appropriate. If the magistrates consider that the case is so serious that their powers of punishment are insufficient or it is a complex case then they can decline jurisdiction and send it to the Crown Court for trial. The prosecution may also make a strong argument as to the seriousness of the case and request that it is sent to the Crown Court for trial. The defendant may also seek trial by judge and jury in the Crown Court. Magistrates are not lawyers but are trained and assessed for competence to national standards. In the magistrates' court there may be a bench of three lay magistrates, with the Chairman sitting in the middle and is the only one who will speak in court. A court clerk who will be either a solicitor or barrister supports them. The clerk is not part of the decision-making process but advise the magistrates on matters of law. There may be a single justice who was formally known as a stipendiary magistrate, now called a district judge, who is a solicitor or barrister. They will also have a court clerk in the court. The magistrates may decide to hear a case, but having heard the evidence decide that the present levels of fines available to them are insufficient (SEE CHAPTER 8) and they can send the case to the Crown Court for sentencing.

Civil proceedings

The county court

9.14 Under civil law, employers have a duty to their employees to provide a reasonable standard of care. If a person is injured at work and considers that the employer has been at fault, then they can take the employer to court and sue for damages. This means that the focus of the civil court is to determine if there is a case for damages to be made and if so, the value of such compensation. Unlike the criminal court where the outcome of cases is determined beyond all reasonable doubt, the civil hearing is judged upon the balance of probabilities, which is a lower burden of proof. Cases are heard before a single judge with the provision for a trial involving a jury of eight persons. The vast majority of civil cases are settled out of court, where an offer of compensation is made to the claimant. There may be numerous offers and rejections before settlement and with claims that are dealt with outside of the court room, the claimant will also seek his legal costs. Often these settlements are made on the *steps of the court* where the defendants attempt to keep the level of compensation as low as possible. Even though an agreement can be reached over the level of compensation a corporation may not accept liability for the accident.

The Scottish legal system

9.15 In England and Wales an appointed health and safety inspector investigates an accident and prepares a prosecution report and the inspector or an appointed legal representative will take the case through the courts. In Scotland the inspector investigates the accident and prepares a report, which is submitted to the office of the procurator fiscal, who will then undertake an investigation and prepare a prosecution for trial in the sheriff's court.

There are no magistrates' courts in Scotland and so the sheriff's court combines the functions of the Crown and magistrates' courts in England and Wales. Criminal prosecutions may be tried in the sheriff's court, either on indictment before a sheriff and jury or on summary before a sheriff sitting alone. In Scotland there are no Coroner's courts and inquests as such are not held. *The Fatal Accident and Sudden Death (Scotland) Act 1976* requires that the procurator fiscal for a district will investigate the circumstances, and apply to the sheriff for the holding of an inquiry into a death. The death will be as a result of an accident in Scotland while the deceased was at work either as an employee or self employed. The only exception is that an enquiry does not need to be held in cases where criminal proceedings have been concluded against any person in respect of the death. Or if any accident in which the death, or the Lord Advocate is satisfied, that the circumstances of the death have been sufficiently established.

At the Fatal Accident Investigation (FAI) hearing before the sheriff, the procurator fiscal leads the evidence for the Crown. The conclusions of the inquiry will determine where and when the death and any accident resulting in death took place and the cause of death. The reasonable precautions if any in the system of working which contributed to the death or any accident resulting in the death and any other facts which are relevant to the circumstances of the death will also be investigated.

The Health and Safety Commission

9.16 The responsibility for health and safety within the government is with the Department of the Environment, Transport and Regions (DETR). The head of this department is the Secretary of State for Environment, Transport and the Regions, with a seat in the Cabinet, assisted by a number of junior ministers, one of whom will have been delegated responsibility for health, safety and welfare.

The *HSWA 1974* is the enabling Act for health and safety issues out of which the Health and Safety Commission (HSC) was formed with responsibility for the administration of the law on occupational health and safety. The corporate role of the HSC is to protect the health, safety and welfare of people at work, and to safeguard members of the public who may be exposed to risks from the way work is carried out. To undertake this work the HSC will propose new or update existing laws and standards, undertake research, as well as provide information and advice. The HSC comprises a Chairman, who is appointed by the Secretary of State, and not less than six and not more than nine members. The Secretary of State appoints members representing employers, employees, local authorities and others, as appropriate. One member represents the public interests. At the time of writing the HSC comprises ten members. In the process of the selection of members, the chairman must consult with various interested parties such as organisations representing employers, trade unions, local authorities and others representing health, safety and welfare. The HSC also appoints the Director General of the Health and Safety Executive (HSE). A prime role of the Commission is to make Regulations and provide consent for the issue of HSC Codes of Practice. The HSE and local authorities are the HSC's regulating authority and has among its duties the statutory responsibility for enforcing health and safety law. In addition local authorities enforce health and safety law in some kinds of workplaces such as distribution, retail, office, leisure and catering.

The Health and Safety Executive

9.17   The Health and Safety Executive (HSE) was established as a result of the introduction into law of the *HSWA 1974*. A Director General who is appointed by the HSC and approved by the Secretary of State heads it. The HSE's headquarters is in London with a major centre in Bootle, Merseyside and other regional offices located throughout the UK.

There are 14 directorates and other departments forming the basic corporate structure as illustrated in figure 9.2.

The HSE has to develop and introduce the policies of the Health and Safety Commission, and has policy units to undertake this work. Nearly half of the HSE's staff is in the Field Operations Directorate (FOD) and the Employment Medical Advisory Service (EMAS). Other key Directorates includes the Nuclear Safety Directorate, Hazardous Installations Directorate and the Railways Directorate. The diverse nature of the industries other than those identified above, that fall within the scope of the *HSWA 1974* means that there is a requirement for industrial specialisation's to support operational inspectors. This is achieved through National Interest Groups (NIG's) with specialisation's in metals and minerals; construction; services; agriculture and wood; fibres and polymers; engineering; utilities; customer services; safety issues and occupational health. The Health and Safety Laboratory pro-

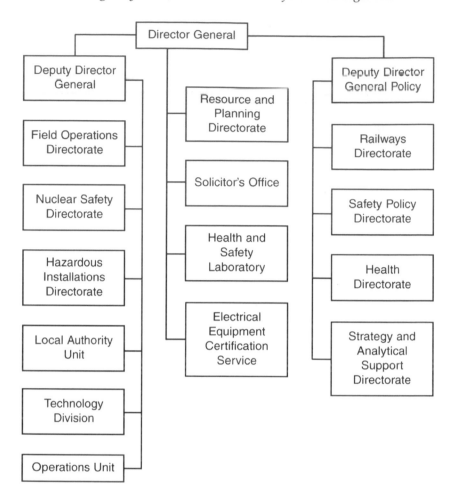

Figure 9.2: Corporate structure of the Health and Safety Executive

vides valuable technical and specialist support to investigations, but it is the Operational Inspectors who are in the front line providing advice, undertaking inspections, investigating accidents and incidents as well as carrying out enforcement actions.

Local Authority Environmental Health Departments

9.18 Local authorities have responsibilities for the enforcement of health and safety in certain activities, and are located within either District or Borough Councils in England or Wales or Islands or District Councils in Scotland.

There are situations of potential overlap between the HSE and local authorities and there are qualified divisions in types of organisations, industry and activities. There is a link between the HSE and local authority's through the Local Authority Unit. The unit is located at the HSE headquarters in London, and there are local authority liaison officers within the HSE regional offices. This is to ensure co-operation and support to local authority's and provide a go-between in cases of potential overlap. The local authority officials have a variety of titles such as Enforcement Officers however, the most common title is the Environment Health Officer (EHO) and will generally be a member of the Chartered Institute of Environmental Health (CIEH). The EHO has a wide range of duties including food safety, hygiene as well as health and safety. The powers of EHO's are the same as those of an HSE inspector.

A local authority is able to transfer authority to the HSE and the HSE transfer authority to a local authority. There has to be agreement by both parties and will generally only be done if the primary activity being carried out at premises is one for which the local authority does not have the appropriate expertise available. The other option is that a transfer will generally only apply if there is a substantial change of activity from one normally enforced by the local authority to one enforced by the HSE. There is no option for self-inspection by an authority, and so the HSE will inspect local authority controlled premises and the local authority will inspect HSE premises.

The police

9.19 In the event of a death at work or caused by a workplace activity the police have to be notified and will begin an investigation. They will take possession of any relevant documentation and equipment and will take statements from witnesses. At this point in time the police will be gathering evidence as to cause of death on behalf of the coroner. The HSE or the local Environmental Health department will also have to be notified and they will co-operate with the police in undertaking a joint investigation. The police will look for evidence of an unlawful act such as negligence, violence or arson that caused the death and advise the coroner of their findings. The health and safety inspectors will seek to identify the cause of the accident and if health and safety legislation has been breached. Once the police determine that there is no unlawful action or the level of negligence was not sufficient to consider manslaughter then they will cease their investigation. It will be left to the HSE or Local Authority to undertake a full investigation under the *HSWA 1974* and associated Regulations. If in the course of the investigation the HSE or local authority discover evidence that identifies that there may have been an action of such a serious nature that there may be a case of gross negligence, then the case can be referred back to the police. The HSE or local authority will co-operate with the investigation as they have workplace and safety management systems knowledge and expertise, which the police do not. The Protocol for Liaison (SEE 9.29) is described in detail and provides additional information. If after an initial review the police consider that there is evidence, they will notify the Coroner who will postpone the inquest and the Crown Prosecution Service will be notified of the police findings. A review of the evidence will be undertaken and if the CPS is satisfied that there is a case for further investigation then they will direct the police to investigate. The HSE or local authority inspectors will work with the police in the investigation. An investigation report is submitted to the CPS who then decides whether there is a case to answer or not. If there is a case to answer, the CPS will initiate the prosecution, if not the case is transferred back to the HSE or local authority for those bodies to proceed with appropriate action and the police take no further action.

Crown Prosecution Service

9.20   The Crown Prosecution Service (CPS) is a government department, which prosecutes people in England and Wales who have been charged by the police with a criminal offence. They are completely independent of the police although they work closely with them.

The head of the CPS at the time of writing is David Calvert-Smith QC, the Director of Public prosecutions (DPP). The DPP is super-intended by the Attorney General who is the Minister responsible to parliament for the conduct of most criminal prosecutions.

The role of the CPS involves four main functions:

- Advising the police on possible prosecutions.

- Reviewing prosecutions started by the police to ensure that the right defendants are prosecuted on the right charges.

- Preparing cases for court.

- Prosecuting cases at the magistrates' court and instructing counsel to prosecute in the Crown Court and higher courts.

Once the police have investigated a crime they pass the papers to a crown prosecutor. The case will be examined to decide whether or not to go ahead with the case. The prosecutor's decision is based on the tests set out in the code for crown prosecutors.

The tests are focused upon two principal points:

1   Is there enough evidence.

2   Is it in the *public interest* to prosecute.

A case has to pass these tests before progress can be made to continue to a prosecution. The prosecutor also has to determine if there is sufficient evidence to provide a *realistic prospect of conviction*. If there is not sufficient evidence then the prosecutor can refer the case back to the police to re-examine the evidence again. If there is still insufficient evidence then the case will not progress to court.

Even with enough evidence the prosecutor will consider if it is *in the public interest* to proceed. This will include the seriousness of the offence, the interests of the victim's family and friends and, the need to send a *message* to industry/business.

When the prosecutor considers that there is sufficient evidence and it is in the *public interest* the case continues to prosecution in court. Throughout this process HSE inspectors will have an advisory role and in some cases the CPS may include *HSWA 1974* or Regulation charges in addition to manslaughter charges.

Coroners

9.21   The coroner is generally a lawyer who is responsible for investigating deaths that occur in a number of situations. Among those that may be relevant are where the cause of death is not known or is uncertain, the death was violent or unnatural or occurred under suspicious circumstances. Another consideration is where a doctor during the last illness did not attend the deceased or the doctor treating the deceased had not seen him or her either after death or within 14 days before death. The coroner may arrange for a post mortem examination of the body. The consent of the relatives is not needed, but they are entitled to be represented at the examination by a doctor. In certain circumstances the coroner can direct the death to be further investigated, and can revert the case to the CPS for a police investigation.

The *Coroners Rules 1984 (SI/1984/552), r 57* states that the coroner is required to supply to any properly interested person, on application and on payment of the prescribed fee, a copy of any depositions taken at any inquest, of any report of a post mortem examination or special examination, of any notes of evidence, or any document put in evidence at an inquest. The coroner may also permit such a person to inspect such documents free of charge.

Prior to the inquest most dealings are with the coroner's officers, who may be former or serving police officers who investigate on behalf of the coroner. In workplace accidents the coroner will obtain a report from the inspector on the who, how, where and when, of the case. The inspector can be called to give evidence and if there is equipment involved an expert may be called to give evidence to assist the court. The coroner will hold an inquest and where the death was caused by an accident, poisoning or disease will normally appoint a jury.

It was held in *R v Poplar Coroner, ex p Chaudry, (1992) Times, 20 October*, that the coroner's task is to consider whether there is reason to suspect that the death occurred, in, 'circumstances the continuance or possible recurrence of which is prejudicial to the health and safety of the public'. If it appears that there are such circumstances then a jury must sit.

It is not the role of the coroner's court to apportion blame and the way individual coroners go about their investigations and conduct their inquests varies widely, as there is no formal structured format. Having heard the evidence a verdict is returned. The common verdicts are of accidental death or death by misadventure, which are materially the same. If a verdict of unlawful killing were reached then the coroner would refer the case to the police for further investigation. The coroner may under the *Coroner's Rules 1984 (SI 1984/552), r 43* announce at the inquest that he is reporting the matter to the HSE with recommendations for action to prevent the recurrence of similar fatalities. A report is then forwarded to the HSE for action.

Enforcement actions

9.22 The enforcing authorities have a number of enforcement options available to them and have the support of the law to ensure that they are complied with. The options include Improvement Notice, Prohibition Notice and prosecution. It is a policy of health and safety inspectors to ensure compliance with health and safety legislation by giving advice and using persuasion rather than resorting to the courts. The majority of prosecutions are taken in the magistrates' court where there is a maximum fine limit of £20,000 for each offence and if found guilty there will be prosecution costs to pay as well as the person's legal costs for going to court. Pleading guilty reduces court costs and reduces the size of the fine. More serious cases will be sent to the Crown Court for trial where fines are unlimited and costs increase to making it an expensive process. Imprisonment is also a possibility if found guilty.

Improvement Notice

9.23 An inspector can issue an Improvement Notice if they are of the opinion that a person is contravening a statutory provision, or in other words, there is a breach of the *HSWA 1974*, or Regulations and that the person has contravened one or more provisions, and is likely to repeat the contravention. If an inspector issues an Improvement Notice, it either has to be complied with or there can be an appeal. At the time of issuing a notice, the recipient will be informed of the appeal procedure, which is a formal process. The appeal is held before an Industrial tribunal who will hear and consider the inspector's reasons for the notice and the objections of the person who is appealing before making a ruling. This does mean the recipient will have to prepare a reasoned objection as to why they should not have to comply with the notice. The process is generally informal compared with the courtroom environment situation. Once an appeal is made, the actions required by the Improvement Notice are suspended until the appeal is heard. If there is no appeal then the person has to comply with the requirements specified in the notice.

An example of the appeals process is shown in the Industrial tribunal for the case *Belhaven Brewery Co Ltd v A McLean (HM Inspector of Factories) [1975] IRLR 370*. It involved Belhaven Brewery Co Ltd who was served with an Improvement Notice requiring that a safety screen with an interlocking device be fitted around a keg-ging plant. The interlocking device would cut off the power and compressed air supply to the plant when a screen door was opened. As was its right, the company appealed against the notice, arguing that a far cheaper safety screen could be fitted, which would still meet statutory requirements. Further, the company argued that the staff were sufficiently intelligent to ensure that the screen was kept in place whilst the machinery was operating and there would be a high level of management supervision. The case against the company was based upon the judgement of Mr McClean of HM Inspectorate of Factories. The inspector disagreed and maintained that irrespective of the staff's level of intelligence and the degree of supervision, only a system with an interlocking device could be secure and comply with the relevant legislation. The Industrial tribunal considered that failure to fit a system with an interlocking device would be a contravention of the *Factories Act 1961*. Further, it was considered reasonably practicable for the company to fit the interlocking device. The reason for this view was because the risk associated with not fitting the device was not insignificant in relation to the sacrifice involved in fitting it. The tribunal held that the Improvement Notice was to stand without modification and to be complied with.

The case clearly shows that a suitable safety device was available that integrated a fail safe system and that even though the work-force may be intelligent and there may be management supervision the two factors were not sufficient to provide a suitable safeguard to equal that of the interlocked guard.

Prohibition Notice

9.24   If an inspector is of the opinion that activities are being carried out or likely to be carried out which would mean there is risk of serious injury to any person, then the inspector can stop the activity by issuing a Prohibition Notice which has immediate effect. The inspector will provide details as to what has to be done to comply with the notice. In the case of a Prohibition Notice the inspector has only to be in the opinion that there is a risk of serious personal injury. The notice can be appealed against and placed before an Industrial tribunal and the effects of the notice are sus-pended until after the hearing. It must be borne in mind that if an Inspector has issued a notice and stopped an activity because of safety issues, there will be grounds for that action so there needs to be caution in pursuing an appeal. If a person appeals and continues with the action in dispute and there is an accident there could be more serious action taken against the organisation or individual.

An example of the appeals process is shown in the High Court, Queen's Bench Division appeal involving *Readmans Ltd and Another v Leeds City Council (1992) Unreported*. The company Readmans were a cash and carry store using shopping trolleys which had a seat for babies or toddlers. There were a number of incidents in which it was alleged that trolleys had tipped forward due to the weight of children carried in them. As a result, Leeds City Environmental Health Inspector served a Prohibition Notice stating that the use of the trolleys to carry children involved *a risk of serious personal injury* and contravened the *HSWA 1974, s 3*. Readmans appealed to an industrial tribunal, which held that the company had not put forward any convincing evidence as to why the Prohibition Notice should be lifted.

The judge held that the tribunal had misdirected itself by not considering the correct burden of proof. He determined that it was for the inspector to establish, on the balance of probabilities, that there was a risk of serious personal injury and to make out a *prima facie* case that there had been a breach of the *HSWA 1974*. If this was established, the burden then shifted to Readmans to show, again on a balance of probabilities, that they had ensured, so far as was reasonably practicable, that visitors to Readman's cash and carry were not exposed to those risks. In this regard, the judge stated that Readmans:

> 'Do not have to guarantee absolute safety, if such a thing is achievable, nor do they have to show that they have done what is practicable, that is to say, all that is physically possible. What they would have to establish is that they have done what is reasonably practicable to ensure that such risks as exist are avoided.'

The burden of proof rests with the company to establish that all reasonably practicable steps have been taken in the circumstances. In this case, evidence was presented concerning the facts that no other local authorities had moved to impose Prohibition Notices on the relevant trolleys, even though the trolleys were in wide use. Whilst such evidence may assist the company in certain circumstances, it is unlikely that a failure of one local authority to enforce relevant laws would demonstrate that no risk exists or that all reasonable practicable steps have been taken.

Appeals to industrial tribunal

9.25   When a notice is issued there will important information on the reverse or as a separate page and the recipient will be advised of their right of appeal to an industrial tribunal and given an explanatory leaflet for appellants and respondents: *Appeals to Industrial Tribunals Concerning Improvement or Prohibition Notices under the Health and Safety at Work etc Act 1974.* The leaflet: ITL 19 explains the appeal procedure and how to lodge an appeal, where and within what period an appeal may be brought, that an appeal may be brought on any grounds, and that action required by a notice is suspended while an appeal is pending. The procedures and rights outlined above provide ways for those making the appeal to have their views heard if they are not happy with the inspector's action. If these procedures have not been followed, the appellant can take up the matter with the inspector's line manager.

Prosecutions

9.26   In England and Wales the decision to proceed with a prosecution case is a matter for the enforcing authority. There are also public interest factors to be considered that are described by the Director of Public Prosecutions in the *Code for Crown Prosecutors*. No prosecutions may proceed unless the prosecutor finds there is sufficient evidence to provide a realistic prospect of conviction, and decides that prosecution would be in the public interest. The HSC considers that there is a public interest factor if any of the following issues apply:

- Death was a result of a breach of the legislation.

- The gravity of an alleged offence, taken together with the seriousness of any actual or potential harm, or the general record and approach of the offender warrants it.

- There has been a reckless disregard of health and safety requirements.

- There have been repeated breaches which give rise to significant risks, or persistent and significant poor compliance.

- Work has been carried out without or in serious non-compliance with an appropriate licence or safety case.

- A duty holder's standard of managing health and safety is found to be far below what is required by health and safety law and to be giving rise to significant risks.

- There has been a failure to comply with an improvement or prohibition notice; or there has been a repetition of a breach that was subject to a formal caution.

- False information has been supplied wilfully, or there has been an intent to deceive, in relation to a matter which gives rise to significant risk.

- Inspectors have been intentionally obstructed in the lawful course of their duties.

Consideration of whether it is in the public interest to prosecute will also be considered where:

- It is appropriate in the circumstances as a way to draw general attention to the need for compliance with the law and the maintenance of standards required by law, and conviction may deter others from similar failures to comply with the law.

- A breach which gives rise to significant risk has continued despite relevant warnings from employees, or their representatives, or from others affected by a work activity.

Scotland

9.27 In Scotland it is the procurator fiscal who decides whether to bring a prosecution. The same standards apply in respect to there being sufficient evidence and that prosecution is in the public interest.

Prosecution of Individuals

9.28 The Enforcement Policy Statement of the Health and Safety Executive, HSC 15, January 2002 identifies that individuals can and are prosecuted for health and safety offences. This can include directors, managers and supervisory staff where they have played a role in a breach, or the offence was committed with their consent or connivance or they have been negligent by their actions. Charges can be made under *HSWA 1974* or health and safety regulations.

There is also the option for the courts to disqualify directors under the *Company Directors Disqualification Act 1986*.

Protocol for liaison

9.29   As part of the evolving process of ensuring effective investigations and legal processes of accidents involving a death at work, a joint protocol was established by the HSE, the Association of Chief Police Officers (ACPO) and the CPS. The protocol is effective in England and Wales and where the HSE is the enforcing authority for health and safety legislation. The objective of the protocol is to draw the three organisations together where there has been a death at work to determine if there is evidence that there may be a case for individual or corporate manslaughter. When the Protocol is reviewed and updated it will include a fourth signatory with the inclusion of local authorities through their involvement with workplace fatal accidents.

The three signatories to the protocol have different roles and responsibilities where there has been a work-related death (see above).

The key points of the Protocol are:

- The HSE, police and CPS will establish effective mechanisms for liaison.

- The HSE will investigate under the *HSWA 1974* and pass information suggesting possible manslaughter offences to the police or CPS.

- The police will conduct an investigation where there is an indication of possible manslaughter.

- The decision concerning prosecution will be made based on a sound investigation of the circumstances surrounding work-related deaths. The CPS, HSE and police will make it without undue delay.

The protocol has been signed up to and is public information.

The investigation process

9.30   In the event of a death at work the police are notified as are the HSE. A police detective of supervisory rank should attend the scene. At this point the liaison between the police and HSE will commence with a joint investigation. That initial investigation will identify whether there is a need for police involvement or whether it is an HSE investigation. If the police decide that a charge of manslaughter or other serious offences cannot be justified, the investigation and forthcoming prosecution will be undertaken by the HSE. Should the police in liaison with the HSE decide that there might be a case to answer, then they will investigate for gross negligence or recklessness by either a company or an individual. In this situation the HSE will provide technical support to the police and continue to investigate for offences under *HSWA 1974*.

When the investigations are completed a report is produced and sent to the CPS with recommendations for prosecution for manslaughter or other serious offences. The final decision of whether to prosecute and with what charges will be made by the HSE, police and CPS in consultation. Where there are additional offences under the *HSWA 1974* the HSE and CPS will consider the initiation of joint proceedings.

To ensure that the protocol is working and effective, a two-tier management system has been established. The first is where the HSE, police and CPS have formed a national liaison committee, which meets at least once a year and deals with high level issues. The second tier involves local liaison offices from each of the three groups and they meet on a regular basis to discus the day to day working of the protocol.

Bereaved families

9.31   An inspector from the HSE or local authority investigating a fatal accident provides advice and information to bereaved families and has a leaflet that explains what the HSE does following a fatal accident. This information is separate from that which may be given if there is an investigation for more serious incidents and the police are the lead authority. Others may be involved such as the coroner's office, solicitor or other advice organisation.

The initial purpose of the investigation is to prevent similar accidents in the future and to determine if any health and safety laws have been breached. At this point if the HSE or local authority officer considers that there is evidence of a serious individual offence then the police will be notified and they will take the lead in the investigation for the individual offences.

Some investigations are straightforward and progress can be made within a reasonable time. Others are more complex and the decision as to whether to prosecute may be delayed until after the inquest. The inspector will speak to the family and keep them informed about progress. The amount of detail about the case that can be given throughout this period may be limited because if a prosecution is to follow, the case cannot be discussed and the inspector is not allowed to answer questions. During this period the case is 'subjucidy' which precludes information being used or discussed prior to the case reaching court.

Accident investigation

9.32   As the result of an accident in connection with work, the HSE or local authority can undertake an investigation. Priority will be given to fatal and serious accidents and will be dependant upon the availability of resources. The HSE or local authority will investigate to determine the cause and if there were breaches of health and safety legislation. If during their investigation the HSE or local authority discover evidence that could make an individual culpable of a more serious offence, the case can be referred back to the police. This will include cases of individual reckless killing and or perverting the course of justice. In the event of an accident it is expected that an undertaking will carry out its own investigation so as to identify the cause and introduce appropriate measures to ensure that it does not reoccur.

The authorities will collect evidence that will form the basis of a prosecution case if such an option is adopted. Evidence consists of witness statements, documentation, physical evidence and evidence of the previous character of the organisation and/or individuals.

Inspectors have the power to take possession of any article or substance in premises, which appears to have caused or be likely to cause danger to health and safety. The owner of the item is given a Taking into Possession Notice identifying the item and stating that the object has been taken under *HSWA 1974, s 20(2)(i)* powers. If the item cannot be moved the inspector can still take possession and will require that nobody touches or tampers with it, as it could be evidence for a prosecution. The powers under *HSWA 1974, s 20* extends to premises, or any part of them that they are left undisturbed for as long as is reasonably necessary for the purposes of an investigation. A notice to this effect can be issued if there is any doubt that there might not be compliance. As part of the investigation an inspector can require any documents to be produced which may be relevant to the investigation. To fulfil the above procedures an inspector can take a police officer to the premises to enter and take possession of the items.

Witness statements

9.33 Witness statements are taken from those who have first hand knowledge of what occurred, and have seen or been part of the accident. Information obtained will aid determination of the sequence of events and the witness's ability to judge the risks and avoid the risks. This may be in the form of training, instruction and supervision. Management will also be interviewed because of their background knowledge of the systems of work that were in place and any control measures in place to ensure safety. Those being interviewed will be treated with courtesy and the interview should be conducted where possible in a private room but if that is not possible, then a quiet private area should be sought. The inspector will explain why a statement is being taken and how it could be used in due course. All statements should be written and signed in ink, and any alterations should be identified, crossed out and initiated by the person being interviewed. There are safeguards for the witness who cannot be intimidated by the inspector to alter or withdraw evidence through bribery, threats or improper pressure.

Voluntary statement

9.34 An investigation requires the gathering of witness evidence and this can include obtaining voluntary witness statements. When obtaining a voluntary statement an inspector would not invoke the *HSWA 1974 s 20* powers and would simply ask the witness to provide information, which is written down, signed and dated. The witness is under no obligation to make the statement however, if the Inspectors deem the evidence important to the investigation the *HSWA 1974, s 20* power could be used if the witness will not provide a statement. With a voluntary statement there are no warnings or cautions made.

Involuntary statement

9.35   Under the *HSWA 1974, s 20(2)(j)* an inspector can compel a person to answer questions. That person is required to sign a declaration of the truth of those answers, but the answers will not be admissible against that person or their spouse. Inspectors may not refer to their *HSWA 1974, s 20* powers so as not being seen to be repressive or authoritarian, unless challenged. All witnesses are entitled to have another person present at the interview however, that person cannot become involved in the discussions between the witness and the inspector or influence what is being said. It is intended to be a comfort factor for the witness. If the inspector does not wish the other person to be present they can invoke their *HSWA 1974, s 20* powers to exclude the person while still requiring the witness to make a statement. The witness can request a copy of their statement however, if a defence solicitor requests a copy it will only be provided if the witness gives written and signed authority for it to be made available. The statement is sent to the witness leaving it to them to forward to their legal representative. A witness may have legal representation provided by the organisation and is against the statement being forwarded to that person who may well pass it on to the organisation. In some circumstances a witness may have another person present to assist if there is a case of witnesses with a visual or hearing impediment, readings difficulties or non-English speaking witnesses.

Because it is a written statement the inspector will talk through what information is sought and make notes. The statement is then written on a form LP7 and continuation form LP8 preferably using the witness's own words, reflecting what was actually said. If during the interview the witness gives evidence that could incriminate them, the inspector will terminate the interview and caution the witness. To continue gathering evidence from a witness in this situation will require the statement to be taken under the *Police and Criminal Evidence Act 1984* (PACE) rules.

PACE statement

9.36   A statement is taken from anybody who could be prosecuted and that can include directors or other officers of a company. Questioning will be done under the *Police and Criminal Evidence Act 1984, s 67(9)* which places a duty on persons other than police officers who are charged with the duty of investigating offences or charging offenders to have regard to any relevant provisions of the Code of Practice. The interviews are tape-recorded and the person to be interviewed is advised to have a solicitor accompany them. As this interview is voluntary, the person being interviewed can leave at any time and do not have to answer the questions.

Unlike the police, the HSE or local authority inspectors do not have powers of arrest. In the interview there will be two members of the investigating team, a PACE tape recording machine and a selection of tapes that are sealed in cellophane wrapping. When the witness and their solicitor are in the room and seated, the procedure will be explained to them and one of the investigators will unwrap two tapes and place them in the machine. Both tapes record at the same time so that there are two identical tapes. One tape is called the *master tape* and as soon as it is taken out of the machine it is sealed in its container in a manner that does not allow access to the tape. The seal is signed by the person being interviewed and is held at the investigating inspector's offices. The tape remains sealed and can only be opened in court should there be a dispute over the content on the other tape. The other tape is the *working tape* and is retained by the inspectors who will have it transcribed into a typed transcript. A typist will identify each person speaking and what they say. On long interviews this can amount to many pages and it is from this interview that the investigators and legal team will extract any appropriate evidence.

At the commencement of an interview the machine is switched on and a noise emits indicating that it is working. When the noise stops every person in the room will identify themselves and a caution is issued to the person being interviewed in the following terms:

> 'You do not have to say anything. But it may harm your defence if you do not mention when questioned something which you later rely on in court. Anything you do say may be given in evidence.'

Minor deviations are permissible, provided that the sense of the caution is preserved. If the person being interviewed is unclear of what has been said the investigator can explain what the caution means. Once the caution is given the person is advised that they are not under arrest or obliged to remain at the interview and may seek legal advice if no solicitor is present.

The interview will continue with questions being asked and answers sought, until the investigators have sufficient information, whereupon they will end the interview. Both tapes are removed and sealed. On a long interview there may be a number of tapes. The comfort of the person being interviewed is taken into consideration and comfort breaks, refreshments and private access to legal advice is available. The person being interviewed is entitled to a copy of the tapes for which there is a charge for reproduction. A form LP 74 is provided which gives details of how and where to apply for copies of the tape.

Employers' Liability Insurance

9.37   Since 1975 the HSE been the enforcing authority for the *Employers' Liability (Compulsory Insurance) Act 1969* otherwise referred to as the ELCI Act, under an agency agreement between the Department of the Environment and the HSC The field of responsibility includes premises allocated to Local Authority's for HSWA enforcement as well as premises normally inspected by the HSE.

Under the ELCI Act employers are obliged to:

- Issue against liability for injury or disease to an employee arising out of and in the course of their employment in Great Britain.

- Display the certificate of insurance at their places of business.

- Produce the certificate or send a copy when required to do so by an authorised inspector.

- Send the certificate or copy in response to a Notice served on behalf of the HSE.

- Permit an authorised inspector to inspect his policy or copy provided that reasonable notice has been given.

With certain specified exceptions, an employer carrying on business in Great Britain is required to insure against liability for injury or disease to any employee, arising out of and in the course of their employment in Great Britain, in that business. This does not give an automatic right to damages. For an employee to qualify there must be evidence that the injury or disease was due to some fault on the part of the employer. Cases where injury was due to the negligence of a fellow employee acting in the course of their employment would be covered, but negligence of a third party, eg an independent contractor, would not be covered.

Changes in employment practices have resulted in problems for the insurance industry. Smaller companies employ a much higher proportion of the workforce and subcontracting has become much more common. This has resulted in employees of numerous employers working on a single site. This has made it more difficult for insurer's to assess risks and potential serious outcomes.

The principle of using the insurance industry to penalise bad performance and reward good performance in companies' health and safety practices was initially thought to be sound. Linking risk and insurance premiums, the principle being that those companies implementing high standards present a lower risk, and should accordingly be charged lower premiums for their employers' liability insurance.

The overriding difficulty concerns the competitive nature of the insurance market in the UK, which mitigates against the introduction of financial incentives. In short, if a company finds its insurance premiums raised as a result of poor health and safety performance it can simply approach a different insurance company, which is often willing to undercut the original quote.

There are a number of other factors upon which insurance premiums are based which distort the creation of a more direct link between premiums and health and safety practices. Premiums are determined according to size of business; historic insurance claims record, and sector. Changes in these factors often have a greater impact on premiums than any health and safety issues.

The Association of British Insurers argue that insurance premiums are too insignificant a proportion of running costs for the vast majority of companies and that: 'it is therefore possible that it would cost more (for the company) to change business practice than that change would be worth in premium reductions'

The evidence from the insurance industry is that this is not an effective tool in the UK, in the context of the existing legislation. The conclusion was therefore that in practice it is very difficult to create an explicit link between insurance premiums and health and safety practices and that, as a result, the ability of the insurance industry to effect a change is limited, except perhaps for high risk, highly capitalised firms where the cost of an accident may be high and may indeed influence premiums.

Summary

This chapter has reviewed the legal systems, structures and enforcement agencies with the aim of providing an overview of the legal process in the event of a fatal accident. The law relating to health and safety is an evolving process and there will be changes that will affect undertakings and individuals, particularly those with management responsibilities. This will be particularly important as corporate killing cases are processed through the courts, creating case law from tried cases. Of equal importance will be the outcomes resulting from cases of reckless killing, killing by gross carelessness and killing where the intention is to cause less serious injury. The focus is on the management of health and safety within an undertaking, which is the subject of CHAPTER 10.

10 The Management of Health and Safety

This chapter considers the following:

- Senior management duties and responsibilities.

- Corporate governance.

- Management of risk.

- Safety management systems.

- HS(G) 65 and BSI: SMS.

- Duties on directors and individuals.

- Enterprises and undertakings.

Introduction

10.1   The corporate killing and individual offences are focused upon the management of health and safety, and any failure that evolves from an act or omission by individuals or within the corporate structure itself. The structure encompasses the main board directors, executives or others identified as being in control of the organisation, the so-called *controlling mind.* It follows that every company should have a safety management system, which should be an integrated part of the company's day-to-day activities. To enable management to encompass this function within its activities, a seamless system to ensure the safety and health of all its employees must be equal to all other business functions such as finance, manufacturing and marketing.

It is recognised that companies not only vary in size and complexity, but also vary by industry and even by constitution. This means that there will be varying hazards that can affect those employed as well as those who are not employed, such as contractors or members of the public. It is therefore, the responsibility of those at boardroom level that set the policy and standards of the

211

organisation to create a safe working environment. This is achieved in part by identifying the hazards, controlling the risks and monitoring the effectiveness of their control procedures.

This book will not provide the definitive answer to safety management systems as there are numerous excellent publications and papers on the subject. The objective of this chapter is to show that the responsibility for health and safety lies in the boardroom or its equivalent, and there are case histories to support this. If there is a defence or mitigation for an offence of corporate killing it must be having proper management systems in place and acceptance of and compliance with those systems.

Modern business operations

10.2   In recent years modern business structures have undergone major changes. Companies have reduced staff numbers through downsizing and many of the functions previously done in house are now outsourced. This means that much of the work bought in involves specialist contractors, small contractors or self-employed persons. The HSE had defined this phenomenon as:

> 'The process of restructuring or other initiatives carried out by an organisation to enable contractors to be used to replace and augment directly employed staff in performing functions.'

In addition to contractors being employed, many organisations have introduced partnering and alliancing arrangements, which means that the overall responsibility of managing health and safety has to be shared. This may not be the case with a contract where the client may impose health and safety issues. The main body of outsourced contractors are with agency workers, consultants and peripatetic or mobile workers, many of which work from home. These individuals or organisations often do not have the benefit of in-house health and safety advice and rely to a degree on the client for appropriate support.

Outsoucing and health and safety

10.3   Outsourcing may lead to less supervision by people knowledgeable of the hazards of the plant. Contractors may not have access to comprehensive health and safety advice or training and may be under more stress because of the uncertainty of future work. Commercial pressures or no corporate memory may be allowed to outweigh health and safety issues and sometimes the riskier work is outsourced. On the other hand business re-organisation may lead to more efficient working and better health and safety management. Also clients may be able to adopt good health and safety practice from specialist contractors.

Information available shows outsourcing increases health and safety risks and although accident rates are generally falling, they are higher for contractor's staff than direct employees. There is consensus that contractors have a greater exposure to risk. Accident statistics also tend to show that small firms have higher accident rates than large firms and that many small firms work as contractors. However, it is not clear whether the higher rates are due to a small firm not having the health and safety resources available to employees in larger firms or whether it is a result of working as a contractor.

Unsafe working practices damage both the client and contractor's reputation although the public will usually associate it with the client's site. Clients are well advised to ensure that their contractors have a good health and safety record and good practice is to have preferred contractor lists. A number of points emerge as good practice in the selection and use of contractors to ensure risks are properly controlled:

- A risk assessment is carried out on the activity to be outsourced.

- A suitable contractor is selected.

- The contractor is given adequate information about the job, site-specific risks, rules and emergency arrangements and the contractor understands what health and safety standards are expected.

- The client identifies the person to act on his behalf to liaise with the contractor, especially about any variations to the work proposed by the contractor.

- The arrangements for providing health and safety assurance are agreed between the client and the contractor, including the level of supervision and control to be exercised by the client, the level of monitoring to be carried out by the contractor, and the reporting arrangements on health and safety matters.

- The effectiveness of the safety management arrangements is reviewed at intervals and after completion.

- There is agreement between client and contractor about the selection use and control of any sub-contractors.

- The client and contractor ensure there is co-operation and co-ordination between their employees and with any other contractor that the client has employed.

- The contractor advises the client of any risks that his work may cause to the client's employees or the public.

Client-contractor responsibilities

10.4   One of the crucial questions is what is the balance of responsibility between the client and contractor. In any client-contractor relationship both parties will always have some duties under health and safety legislation. A client cannot pass on all the responsibility to a contractor to ensure the work is carried out safely, but the extents of the responsibilities on each party will depend on the circumstances. Particular attention needs to be paid to situations where there are contractual chains to ensure that health and safety responsibilities are not blurred.

Factors which increase the client's responsibilities are:

- The client's work in the area of the contracted job continues and may affect the safety of contractor's staff.

- The client's undertaking has particular or peculiar risks, that the contractor may not be aware of.

- The client has specific rules and requirements for health and safety.

- The work being carried out by the contractor was previously done by the client's own employees.

- The work is frequently re-tendered and given to different contractors.

- The risk from the contractor's activities to the client's employees, and/or public is high.

- The degree of health and safety knowledge and expertise of the client.

- Where the client appoints an employee to exercise some influence over the day to day running of the contract.

Factors which increase the contractor's responsibilities:

- The client has no work or permanent employees in the location of the work.

- There are no risks to the contractor's employees from the client's assets.

- The risks from the contractor's work are only to the contractor's employees.

- The work is specialist in nature and therefore the contractor has the greater knowledge and expertise; and where the client does not exercise any control over the contractor's design, arrangements or day-to-day running, such as in turnkey projects.

- Whether different types of management arrangement such as partnering or alliancing affects health and safety culture and performance. Also whether corporate memory on health and safety issues is being eroded and how clients ensure they have sufficient staff with the right skills to manage contractor's work. This will extend where a contractor employs sub-contractors to carry out some or all of the work, both the client and the main contractor retain some health and safety responsibilities.

Whenever a client outsources work the health and safety responsibilities of each party must be clear and good safety management systems need to be in place. Recent court cases have shown that the client will always retain some duties in respect of the health and safety of his employees, contractor's employees and the public.

Topek (Bur) Ltd v HM Advocate

10.5   The criminal law aspects of the relationship between contractors, subcontractors and employees in the context of health and safety legislation were considered in *Topek (Bur) Ltd v HM Advocate* *1998 SCCR 352.*

In this case, Topek Ltd installed a platform for a subcontractor. The company failed to instruct the subcontractor's employees in its use and also failed to ensure that work would be suspended in severe wind conditions. An employee of the subcontractor was killed when the platform overturned in high winds.

Topek Ltd was convicted under the *HSWA 1974, s 3* for failing to ensure the health and safety of non-employees. The company was fined £20,000, which amounted to half of the company's profits, and although the company appealed against the penalty, it was dismissed. The court decided that it was an important feature of health and safety legislation that the principal contractor assumed responsibility for subcontractors and it was not appropriate for Topek Ltd to claim that it had relied on the subcontractor. The level of the fine had been assessed having taken into account Topek Ltd's profits and had not been arbitrarily arrived at.

R v Octel Company Ltd

10.6 Another case that clearly shows that responsibility for health and safety where contractors are concerned is a shared responsibility is that of *R v Associated Octel Company Ltd [1996] 4 All ER 846.* The company engaged an independent specialist contractor to repair the lining of a tank within their chemical plant. An employee of the contractor was badly burned when a broken light bulb ignited acetone vapor being used by the employee to clean the tank lining prior to repair. The contractor was convicted under the *HSWA 1974, s 2* and Octel were charged and convicted at the Crown Court for breach of the *HSWA 1974, s 3.*

Octel appealed to the Court of Appeal on the grounds that since a competent independent contractor did the work, they were conducting the undertaking and not Octel. Octel would only have a duty under the Act if they exercised control over the contractor's work. The Court of Appeal dismissed the case, stating that undertaking meant enterprise or business and that the cleaning, repair and maintenance of plant, machinery and buildings, necessary for carrying on business was part of the conduct of the undertaking whether or not such work was carried out by employees or by independent contractors. Octel appealed to the House of Lords.

The House of Lords affirmed the lower court's decision and dismissed the appeal. Whether a work activity is part of the conduct of an employer's undertaking, is a question of fact. It does not depend on whether the employer engages employees or independent contractors to carry out that work or whether control is exercised over the activity. If the work itself is part of the undertaking, a duty is owed under the *HSWA 1974, s 3* to ensure that it is done without risk – subject to *reasonable practicability*. The place where the activity takes place will, in the normal case, be an important determining factor.

Corporate memory

10.7   Trevor Kletz identified some interesting points in his article in the *Safety and Health Practitioner*, December 1996, when he identifies that overall, accident statistics show that smaller organisations have higher accident rates than larger organisations, but it is not known if the reason is that smaller organisations do not have the resources to adopt health and safety procedures, or whether being a contractor implies that it is a matter for the client and not them. A client that has a comprehensive and effective health and safety management system can impart much of that knowledge and culture to those contracted in whatever form. In any situation a client must ensure that all contractors are protected from risks whilst working on its premises or site under its control. Equally, the contractors must not take any form of action that could place the client's employees at risk, which means that both clients and contractors have duties of care to each other as well as the public. Kletz makes some valuable points about corporate memory:

'The following actions can help us remember the lessons of the past. If we have paid the high price of an accident we should at least turn it into a learning experience:

Include in every instruction, code and standard, a note on the reason it was introduced and accounts of accidents which would not have occurred if it been followed;

Describe old accidents as well as recent ones in safety bulletins and newsletters and discuss them at safety meetings: *giving the message once is not enough;*

Follow up at regular intervals to see that the recommendations made after accidents are being followed, in design as well as operation;

Remember that the first step down the road to the next accident occurs when someone turns a blind eye to a missing blind;

Never remove equipment before you know why it was installed. Never abandon a procedure before you know why it was adopted;

Include important accidents of the past in the training of undergraduates and company employees;

Before experienced people retire, get them to write down their know-how, especially the information that younger and less experienced people are not aware of;

Devise better retrieval systems so that we can find, more easily than at present, details of past accidents, in your own and other companies, and recommendations made afterwards;

...'

Management structures within organisations

10.8   S Field and N Jorg, in their paper, 'Corporate liability and manslaughter: should we be going Dutch?' *1991 Crim LR 157*, highlighted some very important issues in respect to management within organisations.

'This bifurcation of the corporate structure limits the potential effectiveness of legal controls in several ways. First, Wells has recently pointed out that one effect of this identification doctrine is that the more diffuse the company structure, the more it devolves power to semi-autonomous managers, the easier it will be to avoid liability.

This is of particular importance given the increasing tendency of many organisations specifically to decentralise safety services. It is clearly in the interest of shrewd and unscrupulous management to do so. Braithwaite's study, Corporate Crime in the Pharmaceutical Industry pointed out the way that companies sought to abrogate responsibility for the quality of their safety research by using contract laboratories, where the effects of fierce competition over price on the standard of safety checks could be said to be responsibility of the laboratory itself. If corporations perceive themselves to be at risk of prosecution for corporate manslaughter, an analogous process of decentralisation within the corporation might be developed to evade liability.'

The limits of criminal liability constructed by the identification doctrine do not reflect properly the limits of the moral responsibility of the corporation itself. This cannot be limited to responsibility for the acts of high-ranking officials such as company directors.

Priorities in hierarchical organisations like corporations are set predominantly from above. It is these priorities that determine the social context within which a corporation's shop floor workers and the like made decisions about working practices. A climate of safety or unsafety may permeate the entire organisation but be created at the highest level. Thus, if criminal law is to reflect this moral responsibility, in appropriate cases legal responsibility ought to extend to acts done by the *hands* of a corporation.

There are a number of key issues that apply to all undertakings and are imperative for the culture of any undertaking to eliminate if possible, any harm to any person.

- Health and safety must be adopted as part of the undertakings business plan.

- Leadership is the key, and that must come from the board-room.

- Systems that are compatible and understandable must be adopted.

- Everybody in the undertaking must know and understand the health and safety standards senior management require.

- Senior management must communicate with those in the undertaking to obtain feedback.

- Contractors, part-time and agency staff must be integrated into the system.

- Ownership of safety, health and environment includes everybody from the top to bottom of the undertaking.

Corporate governance

10.9   During the 1980's Polly Peck, British Commonwealth, BCCI and Robert Maxwell's Mirror Group News International were victims of poorly managed business practices that led to failure of those companies. Amid the concern of such failures, the Cadbury Committee was established by the UK Stock Exchange. The membership of the committee included representatives from the senior level of British industry. Their task was to develop a code of practice that would provide guidance in defining and applying internal controls to limit the risks of financial loss whatever the cause. While the effects of serious accidents were not specified, there would be losses and the consequences would be financial as well as management failure.

The Cadbury committee report

10.10   The committee produced a report in 1992 and a code of best practice (*The Financial Aspects of Corporate Governance*, December 1992). The recommendations of the code were not mandatory, but all UK quoted companies, listed on the UK stock exchange, must now clearly state whether or not the code has been followed, and if it has not, then they must explain why. The report focused on corporate governance by identifying that there was a need for a clearly accepted division of responsibilities at the head of a company. The objective was to ensure a balance of power and authority, such that no individual had unfettered power of decision.

The foundation of the report was on the role of directors, both in their boardroom function and as individuals. It identified a need to introduce thorough reporting and control measures. Risk management was not identified as an official duty for directors however, there is a requirement for board members to include a formal statement confirming compliance with the code, which raises the profile of risk management overall.

A key objective of the code was to make directors and non-executive directors aware of the need for boardroom confirmation that their companies are protected from major losses resulting from inappropriate working practices. A problem that was identified in obtaining full support from the boardroom was that it was generally considered that risk management was linked to insurance. This was a situation that had to be addressed, as boardroom members could not absolve their responsibilities to a third party *safety net*.

There are three key points for risk management: identification, evaluation and control, which encompass all aspects of corporate activities and that, includes safety management. Hazards need to be identified and controlled with an audit system to identify compliance, all as an integrated part of a safety management system. The code should place full responsibility for health and safety within a corporation at boardroom level, where directors, who are the pinnacle of the corporate safety culture, provide leadership of the organisation.

Turnball guidance

10.11 Following the Cadbury report and code the *Combined Code of the Committee on Corporate Governance* was published in 1999 by the Institute of Chartered Accountants. It was applied to listed companies on the London Stock Exchange of which there are some 2,700 companies. The code focuses on corporate governance which, whilst centered upon the financial aspects of an organisation, is linked to corporate losses in the wider context. That includes health and safety, a major risk factor for all organisations and where there is a need for boardroom control.

The document is (known as the 'Turnbull Guidance' named after the chairman of the committee Nigel Turnbull), provides a structure for assessing the effectiveness of a company's risk and control process which encompasses health and safety as a key factor in the management process.

The guidance identifies risk assessment as a boardroom issue and determines that the company should have clear objectives and make sure that they have been communicated to employees so as to provide effective direction on the identification and assessment of risk. This should ensure that significant internal and external health and safety risks are identified and assessed, and that there is knowledge by management and others within the company as to what risks are acceptable to the board.

Control is a key factor within management and that requires the board to have clear strategies for dealing with the significant risks that have been identified. This is established within the company's culture, code of conduct, human resource, operating procedures and policies that support the overall business objectives including risk management. Senior management has to demonstrate, through its actions as well as its policies, the necessary commitment to ensure competence and integrity so as to develop a culture of trust within the company. The control element needs to ensure that responsibilities and accountability are clearly defined and that decisions are made and actions taken by the appropriate people and in a diverse organisation, effectively co-ordinated.

Boardroom members must communicate to their employees what is expected of them and define in detail the scope of their freedom to act and make decisions. This would include internal and out-sourced activities regarding health and safety. The management must ensure that the people in the company as well as its providers of outsourced services have the competence to fulfil the company's objectives in supporting the management of the organisation's health and safety risks. Because risks within an organisation are subject to constant change there need to be controls in place that can reflect new or changing risks, or operational deficiencies.

Information and communication are vital to any organisation and it is important that management and the board members receive timely, relevant and reliable reports on health and safety issues that could affect the business objectives. The sources should evolve from both inside and outside the organisation providing information that allows for decision-making and management review of health and safety. There will also need to be periodic reporting procedures, including half-yearly and annual reporting where matters relating to health and safety are on the agenda. This should identify that there are effective communication channels that will allow individuals to report suspected breaches of laws, regulations or concerns in respect to health and safety.

To ensure compliance there is a requirement to have systems structured within the organisation's overall business operations, that are accessed by senior management, to monitor the effectiveness of the policies, processes and activities related to health and safety. These processes are required to review the company's ability to re-evaluate risks and make suitable amendments as an effective response to changes. That in turn requires there to be a system to monitor any follow-up procedures so to ensure that the appropriate changes or actions are carried out in response to changes identified through risk management. The systems will allow the board or board committees to ensure the effectiveness of the ongoing processes of risk and control matters, which should include identifying any significant health and safety issues and the degree of risk. To complete the control process there needs to be specific arrangements for management to report to the board on health and safety risk and control matters.

The statement 'good governance is good business' is the foundation of corporate governance, encompassing the management of financial and operating risks within an organisation. An important ingredient within the organisations operations is health and safety and as such must occupy an equal place within an organisations' activity.

Senior management responsibilities

10.12 With the introduction of corporate killing and the individual offences the adoption of a corporate governance structure for any sized organisation must be considered as being a valuable if not vital tool available to management. As part of an organisations corporate health and safety management system the HSC introduced a guidance document: *Directors Responsibilities for Health and Safety* for board members of all types of organisations. The objective of the guidance is to ensure that risk to employees and those not employed are properly managed. The focus is on company directors to establish effective management of health and safety risks with the emphasis on the following key issues:

- Maximise the well being and productivity of all people working for an organisation.

- Stop people getting injured, ill or killed through work activities.

- Improve the organisation's reputation in the eyes of customers, competitors, suppliers, other stakeholders and the wider community.

- Avoid damaging effects on turnover and profitability.

- Encourage better relationships with contractors and more effective contracted activities.

- Minimise the likelihood of prosecution and consequent penalties.

It is important to note that while the guidance uses the term *director* to indicate a member of the board, the guidance applies to other undertakings that do not have to have a director to comply with the law. Therefore, the guidance must be deemed to apply to trust executives, trustees, partners etc.

The guidance is not compulsory and undertakings are free to take other action, but if they follow the guidance they will generally be doing enough to comply with the law, and in the legal sense the guidance can be used to illustrate good practice.

There are five action points which identify that the board needs to accept formally and publicly its collective role in providing health and safety leadership for their organisation. The board needs to ensure that all of their decisions reflect its health and safety intentions, as described in the health and safety policy statement. It needs to recognise its role in engaging the active participation of workers in providing health and safety and needs to ensure that it is kept informed of and alert to, relevant health and safety risk management issues. The HSC recommends that boards appoint one of their number to be the health and safety director.

It is the last action that has provoked most comments and concerns as many directors and organisations see the appointed director as being the 'scapegoat' for the boardroom when things go wrong. There is no intention for there to be an individual exposed for the failings of the board, providing that the individual who has responsibility for health and safety has not been negligent. The director appointed, and the HSC would ideally like to see the chairman, chief executive or the head of an undertaking appointed to that role, to ensure that there is in place an effective and positive system for health and safety.

Safe system of work

10.13 The term 'safe system of work' is broad based and includes the precautions that have to be made to account for the safety of the workers at all times, and that includes having sufficient persons to do the job, and that those persons are competent to undertake the work tasks. In addition it extends to those not employed who have to be safeguarded against harm caused by the activities of the undertaking.

The definition of a 'safe system of work' is most effectively dealt with by the examination of cases that have progressed through the appeals system. While it is not definitive, it does provide the details of what the management failed to do, the actions of the employee and the legal determination.

General Cleaning Contractors Ltd v Christmas

10.14 A leading case for safe systems of work is that of the appeal to the House of Lords in 1952 of *General Cleaning Contractors Ltd v Christmas [1952] 2 All ER 1110*. This is the case of a window cleaner employed by General Cleaning Contractors Ltd who was cleaning the outside of the windows of a club. There were no fittings to which he could attach a safety belt so he stood on the sill of the window, a method commonly used by his colleges. A defective sash window fell on his hand, causing him to let go and fall. He was awarded damages against both the employer and the occupier of the premises. However, the decision against the occupier was reversed on appeal because the defective window was not an unusual danger of which the occupier was bound to warn the window cleaner.

The employer appealed to the House of Lords. The House of Lords ruled that where the practice of ignoring an obvious danger had developed, it was not reasonable to expect the individual employee to take the initiative in devising a system of work against the danger. This is regardless of the fact that other systems of work were not practical. General Cleaning Contractors Ltd were still obliged to consider the situation, to take reasonable steps to provide a system that would be reasonably safe having regard to the dangers inherent in the operation and to ensure that its employees were instructed on how to prevent accidents in their work, including providing the implements. The employer had not done so and had not discharged its duty to the employee and therefore, the appeal was dismissed.

This is a case that explains the relationship between the duty of care owed by employers and the obligations on workmen to take reasonable care for their own safety. Those at work are not in the position of employers when taking decisions.

It is the responsibility of the employer to take the initiative in devising and using precautions and the workman is not expected to do so himself. If a man is doing work as specified and expected by his employer and there has been a failure to take adequate precautions, then the blame should not rest on the man. The main issue is whether the employer has taken responsibility with reasonable care to provide a safe system of work for the employees. Where a practice of ignoring an obvious danger has developed then it is not the workman's responsibility to devise a system to overcome it. As to the decision as to what is reasonable, the employer must take into account the conduct and long established practices in the trade.

Lord Oaksey who highlighted the key issues in the case said:

> 'It is the duty of an employer to give such general safety instructions as a reasonably careful employer who has considered the problem presented by the work would give his workmen.'

Lord Oaksey continued to state:

> 'It is well known to employers ... that their workpeople are very frequently, if not habitually, careless about risks which their work may involve. It is ... for that very reason that the common law demands that employers should take reasonable care to lay down a reasonably safe system of work. Employers are not exempted from this duty by the fact that their men are experienced and might, if they were in the position of an employer, be able to lay down a reasonably safe system of work themselves. Workmen are not in a position of employers. Their duties are not performed in the calm atmosphere of a boardroom with the advice of experts. They have to make their decisions on narrow sills and other places of danger and in circumstances where dangers are obscured by repetition.'

Lord Reid said in the same case:

> 'Where the practice of ignoring an obvious danger has grown up I do not think that it is reasonable to expect an individual workman to take the initiative in devising and using precautions. It is the duty of the employer to consider the situation, to devise a suitable system, to instruct his men what they must do and to supply any implements that may be required.'

The general consensus of the legal ruling and commentators is that the definition of what is a safe system of work is being broad and open to interpretation. It is therefore a matter of fact and will be a matter for a judge and jury to determine. It does however, place the duty for the development of a safe system of work with the employer. It further places the duty on the employer to inform the employees of what is required.

Paris v Stepney Borough

10.15   Another case, which is unusual because it involves a member of staff who had a partial disability and as a result of failure in the management of health and safety, the employee, was completely disabled. The case was the House of Lords appeal in 1951 of *Paris v Stepney Borough Council [1951] 1 All ER 42.* It was a case where a one-eyed garage worker become completely blind after a chip of metal entered his good eye. It was not usual practice for Stepney Borough Council to provide protective goggles to its employees working in garages on the maintenance and repair of vehicles and so no protective equipment had been given to Mr Paris.

After the accident he claimed damages from his employer, alleging negligence. The claim was successful in the High Court but the Court of Appeal reversed the decision. Mr Paris then appealed to the House of Lords who held that where an employer is aware that an employee has a disability which although does not increase the risk of an accident occurring but does increase the risk of serious injury, special precautions should be taken if the employer is to fulfil its duty to take reasonable care for the safety of its employee. The condition of Mr Paris's eyes, the employers knowledge of his condition, the likelihood of an accident occurring and the gravity of the consequences should an accident occur were all to be considered in determining whether the employer took reasonable steps to protect its employee's safety. It was determined that Stepney Borough Council owed a special duty of care to Mr Paris and had been negligent in failing to supply goggles to him, even though such equipment was not given to other employees.

In the same case Lord Morton stated:

'There are occupations in which the possibility of an accident occurring to a workman is extremely remote, while there are other occupations in which there is a constant risk of accident. Similarly, there are occupations in which if an accident occurs, it is likely to be of trivial nature, whilst there are other occupations in which ... the result ... may well be fatal ... there has to be in each case a gradually ascending scale between the two extremes ... the more serious the damage which will happen if an accident occurs, the more thorough are the precautions which an employer must take.'

Morris v West Hartlepool Steam Navigation Co Ltd

10.16 Lord Reid further clarifies the duty of the employer in 1956 who in the case of *Morris v West Hartlepool Steam Navigation Co Ltd [1956] 1 All ER 385* said:

'It is the duty of an employer in considering whether some precautions should be taken against foreseeable risk, to weigh, on the one hand, the magnitude of the risk, the likelihood of an

accident occurring and the possible seriousness of the consequences if an accident does happen, and, on the other hand,
the difficulty and expense and any other disadvantage of taking
precaution.'

A high standard of care must be taken when the employer knows
that there are particular risks, and where the employer knows of
risks of which others are ignorant and his conduct should be
judged upon the employers knowledge of the risks.

Nilsson v Redditch

10.17   This example of an employer's duty to provide a safe system
of work based upon widespread custom and practice balanced
against unreasonable cost is in the Court of Appeal case of *Nilsson v
Redditch Borough Council (1994) Unreported*. Redditch Borough
Council employed Nilsson as a dustman, where black plastic bags
were used for rubbish collection. The accident happened when Mr
Nilsson was swinging a bag up into the collection lorry and was
nicked on the leg by a piece of glass that had worked its way
through the bag. The incident caused him to slip and fall, injuring
his shoulder. He argued that the council was negligent for failing to
provide a safe system of work and it was in the proceedings that
Mr Nilsson raised the issue of the use of wheelie bins as an alternative.

The question was, to identify whether the employers had taken
reasonable steps to provide a system that was reasonably safe,
having regard to the dangers necessarily inherent in its operation.
The court was required to consider the extent to which the system
used was widespread or of long-standing. If it was found to be
both, then Mr Nilsson would have a heavy burden to establish a
breach of duty of care. Where a claimant raises the point that an
alternative system of work should have been adopted, that alternative must be judged comparatively, taking into account issues of
practicability and commercial viability as well as safety.

The Court of Appeal held that Mr Nilsson had not been able to
show that the bin bag was unsafe. It was found to be a system of
widespread use across the country, and therefore, provided evidence that the system was reasonably safe. Judge Waite considered
that there had not been enough evidence adduced to enable a
proper comparison of the competing bin bag and wheelie-bin

systems in respect to practicability, commercial viability, safety and extent of use elsewhere. This case identifies the importance of a system being commonplace and generally accepted as a system which is safe. The rubbish system was used throughout the country and to replace the system would have cost a lot of money.

Stokes v Guest, Keen and Nettlefold (Bolts and Nuts) Ltd

10.18 Another important case involving the requirement for proper safe systems of work was the case heard in the High Court, Birmingham Assizes in 1968 of *Stokes v Guest, Keen and Nettlefold (Bolts and Nuts) Ltd [1968] 1 WLR 1776*. Mr Stokes died from scrotal cancer and it was established on the balance of probabilities, that this was induced by contact with mineral oils during the course of his employment as a toolsetter and that his work played a part in the development of cancer. An action was brought by Mrs Stokes who alleged negligence and breach of duty by the company to provide a safe system of work. It was contended the company knew or should have known that contact with mineral oils could lead to a risk of cancer and should have warned Mr Stokes of the dangers of the material, instructed him on safe working practices, provided protective measures and conducted periodical medical examinations. Even though the company had employed a medical officer since 1941, no warnings or information were provided about the potential risks of mineral oils. No medical examinations were conducted, despite recommendations to the contrary since that date and a Factory Inspectorate leaflet on the dangers of scrotal cancer in 1960. The medical officer considered that medical examinations were unnecessary because of the low incidence of the disease.

The High Court held that an employer must meet the standards of a reasonable and prudent employer and follows recognised and general practice. The practice must have been followed for a substantial period in similar circumstances without mishap unless in the light of common sense or newer knowledge it is clearly bad. Where there is developing knowledge concerning the safety of workers, however, a reasonable and prudent employer should keep reasonably abreast of it and not to be slow to apply the new knowledge. If the employer had a more than average knowledge of the risks, more than average precautions should be taken. When determining what action to take, the risk of injury occurring and its consequences should be weighed against the effectiveness, expense and inconvenience of that action. Where the employer falls below the standards to be expected of a reasonable and prudent employer, it has been negligent. In situations where a task requiring a special skill is delegated to an employee such as a medical officer, the individuals performance should be judged by the standards relating to that skill to the extent of his abilities. However, more general principles should be used to judge the non-medical aspects of the medical officer's work, such as advice concerning economic and administrative considerations. Applying these tests, the High Court held that the company's medical officer was negligent in failing to conduct medical examinations of employees at risk of developing scrotal cancer and failing to issue a notice drawing attention to that risk, and the company was vicariously liable for that negligence.

Employers who are responsible for health and safety of their employees, should keep up to date with developing knowledge in the various fields of potential illness that their employees may be exposed to as a result of their work. A subjective element was imported into the test to be applied to employers, in that when determining the liability of the employer, it is necessary to take into account the amount of knowledge and awareness of developments in the law that the employer actually has. Where an employer has a greater than average knowledge of the risks, he should put into place precautions which reflects this greater level knowledge.

In the case Swanwick said:

> '... the overall test is still the conduct of the reasonable and prudent employer, taking positive thought for the safety of his workers in the light of what he knows or ought to know; where there is a recognised and general practice which has been followed for a substantial period in similar circumstances without mishap, he is entitled to follow it, unless in the light of common sense or newer knowledge it is clearly bad; but, where there is developing knowledge, he must keep reasonably abreast of it and not be too slow to apply it; and where he has in fact greater than average knowledge of the risks, he may be thereby obliged to take more than average or standard precautions. He must weigh up the risks in terms of the likelihood of injury occurring and the potential consequences if it does; and he must balance against this the probable effectiveness of the precautions that can be taken to meet it and the expense and inconvenience they

involve. If he is found to have fallen below the standard to be properly expected of a reasonable and prudent employer in these respects, he is negligent.'

Ward v T E Hopkins and Sons Ltd

10.19 The focus has been on the employers requirement to provide a safe system of work but there are situations where there is some failing on behalf of the employee such as in the Court of Appeal case of *Ward v T E Hopkins & Sons Ltd [1959] 3 All ER 225*. This was the case of Mr Ward who was employed by a building company on a job that required him to empty a well of water. He and another workman and a director of the company built a platform down inside the well, from which they were using a petrol driven pump to remove the water. After an hour and a half usage, the pump was stopped where a haze of fumes was visible involving carbon monoxide. In the evening the director returned to the site and noticed the haze and the smell of fumes. The following morning he instructed Mr Ward and the other workman to go to the site but not to enter the well until he arrived. The two men arrived and ignoring the instruction entered the well, where they were overcome by the fumes. A doctor was summoned and although warned about the fumes, went down into the well to rescue the two men. Fumes overcame him and the rope that had been tied around him fouled on a pipe and he could not be pulled up. The outcome was that Mr Ward; the other workman and the doctor all died. The Court of Appeal held that in respect of the death of Mr Ward, the company had been negligent and had adopted a dangerous system of work. Even though the director had warned Mr Ward not to go down into the well, he had not been sufficiently clear about the danger involved and so did not discharge the company's duty. The fault was not entirely with the company and it was found that there was some contributory negligence on the part of Mr Ward.

These examples provided some of the test cases that have progressed through the courts and offer some detail to show the failings within management to ensure health and safety.

Management of health and safety

10.20 The *Management of Health and Safety at Work Regulations 1992 (SI 1992/2051)* was implemented as a result of the *EC Directive 89/*

391 EEC on the introduction of measures to encourage improvements in the safety and health of workers at work. The original Regulations were revoked and replaced with the *Management of Health and Safety Regulations 1999 (SI 1999/3242)*. These Regulations extend that requirement to all employers (and the self-employed) and to all workplaces covered by the *HSWA 1974* from the simplest office to the most hazardous process.

The first step is to recognise the hazards and risks that are found in a particular work environment, which leads the employer to identify hazards and ensure that there are arrangements, in place to combat the risk. These arrangements should include the effective planning, organisation, control, monitoring and review of the preventive and protective measures. There is a requirement for employers to undertake health surveillance, which means having regard to the risks to their health and safety that are identified by the assessment. The employer has a duty to obtain health and safety assistance by appointing one or more competent persons to assist with health and safety issues within the undertaking. That person shall be regarded as competent where he has sufficient training and experience or knowledge and other qualities to enable him properly to assist. It is also a duty for the employer to provide procedures to manage serious and imminent danger and for danger areas. These can include a written emergency action plan and a procedure for identifying foreseeable events that need to be covered. Employers have to provide information to employees that is relevant, understandable and achievable for:

(a)   any risks to their health and safety identified by the assessment and;

(b)   the preventive and protective control measures.

Estimates attribute up to 80% of accidents to human factors with human error being an element in many major incidents. In the past placing blame for incidents on human error was seen as a viable explanation and beyond the control of an undertakings management. This is not acceptable and the human element needs to be managed in the same way and with the same seriousness as technical and systems failures.

The management of health and safety must review the types and causes of human failures and develop ways of reducing them. Management needs to develop better design of tasks, equipment and procedures. Critical issues for many undertakings are operational issues that include shift work and the potential implications, communications with shift workers, employee's perception of risk, their behaviour and the need for a positive safety culture.

Management will need to examine:

- *The job*: which encompasses what people are being asked to do, such as workload, task, environment, controls and procedures.

- *The individual*: the person doing the job, their competence, skills, personality and attitudes.

- *The organisation*: the health and safety resources, the corporate culture, works systems and communications.

All undertakings will have three principal elements that encompass the management of health and safety. The elements are:

- Liveware – people.

- Software – systems of work.

- Hardware – plant and equipment.

All of these elements have to interface and be considered in the management process. A failure in any one of the elements could be the cause of an accident. The chart in figure 10.1 below profiles how the three elements flow into the undertaking, which extends its

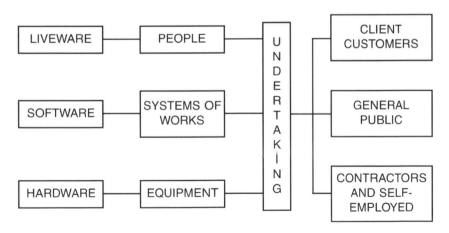

Figure 10.1: Three principal elements of health and safety management

management of health and safety to a range of customers. The liveware–people element includes a diverse range of individuals who may be direct employees, members of the public, contractors, sub-contractors, self employed and home workers. All of these individuals have to interface into the undertaking and must be competent to undertake the tasks they are assigned. The software–systems of work element, includes issues such as the management of risks, operational procedures, emergency planning and management control and supervision. The hardware element includes all plant, machinery, equipment and vehicles. These are the elements of an undertaking that will need to extend its management system of health and safety to its clients, customers as well as those who are contracted into the organisation to carry out work.

Management of risk

10.21 Every undertaking has different circumstances surrounding its hazard risk activities. A large undertaking may expose its employees and those not employed to minimum risk, while a small undertaking may have a high hazard activity with the subsequent high-level risks. Therefore, all undertakings require safety management systems that are developed specifically to meet the undertakings needs, all based upon a number of basic principles.

A key factor is the requirement for management to develop a system that is not only ownership which shows commitment, but also knowledge, and it is the knowledge of a particular industry and organisation that is important. T Kletz identifies the significance of an effective system in an article in *The Safety and Health Practitioner, December 1996*, when he states:

'In a typical factory it is often hard to find anyone who has been there for more than ten years. After a while people move, taking their memories with them, and the lessons learnt after an accident are forgotten ... The present enthusiasm for down sizing makes the problem worse; we can manage without the advice and experience when everything seems to be going well, until we fall into the hole in the road that no one knew was there, except old Joe who retired early.'

He further identifies a good example for management to learn from the past such as with the Aberfan disaster in 1966. The village in South Wales was the scene of a colliery tip slide that engulfed part of the village with the result that 144 people were killed most of whom were children. The underlying cause of the disaster was that the tip had been located over a stream on sloping ground. This is a classic management failure highlighted through an extract of the official report, which states:

'... forty years before it occurred, we have the basic cause of the Aberfan disaster recognised and warned against. But, as we shall see, it was a warning which went largely unheeded ... Tip slides are not new phenomena. Although not frequent, they have happened throughout the world and particularly in South Wales for many years, and they have given rise to an extensive body of literature available long before the disaster ... In 1939 there was a tip slide at Cilfynydd in South Wales ... Its speed and destructive effect were comparable with the disaster at Aberfan, but fortunately no school, house or person lay in its path ... It could not fail to have alerted the minds of all reasonably prudent personnel employed in the industry of the dangers lurking in coal tips ... the lesson if ever learnt, was soon forgotten ... In 1944 another tip at Aberfan slid 500-600 feet. Apparently, no one troubled to investigate why it had slipped, but a completely adequate explanation was to hand ... it covered 400 feet of a totally unculverted stream ... Why was there this general neglect? Human nature being what it is, we think the answer to this question lies in the fact that ... there is no previous case of loss of life due to tip stability.'

In addition to the lack of management knowledge in respect to accidents both large and small, involving employers and those not employed there are cases where management do not accept responsibility for accidents and the issue is identified by Denis Smith, *The Health and Safety Practitioner*, February 1998 who states:

'Despite the presentation of data which shows that health and safety makes financial as well as moral sense, there are still clear barriers to making the necessary step change. The first is that managers show a clear reluctance to blame themselves for accidents, despite research that shows the importance of latent managerial error in accident generation. Why then would managers be willing to accept many of the non-intangible costs associated with accidents such as, opportunity costs, loss of reputation and the like? While they are more likely to acknowledge the more tangible costs of damage, compensation, loss of production, loss of product and raw materials, it is unlikely that they will accept that the management function has been instrumental in creating these costs – indeed, the search for scapegoats serves to legitimise management actions. Secondly, many organisations have shown clear reluctance to change their procedures and systems in the wake of accidents occurring elsewhere because they believe that it couldn't happen to them.'

The commentary continues to state:

'... management plays a central role in the process of failure by providing the environmental and cultural conditions in which operator error occurs. Management, after all, is responsible for the development of standard operating procedures and is an important element in the development of a safety culture. It is also important to note that many managerial decisions have a long latency period before their implications are known, thus embedding an error cost within the system. Such strategic decisions can obviously play a major role in system safety.'

This is clearly a poignant statement, especially when reviewing a subject such as corporate killing. Disregard and non-acceptance of management failure will expose an organisation not only to accidents but also to charges under the proposed offence.

Risk assessment

10.22 The *Management of Health and Safety at Work Regulations 1999 (SI 1999/3242), Reg 3* state:

'(1) Every employer shall make a suitable and sufficient assessment of –

(a) the risks to the health and safety of his employees to which they are exposed whilst they are at work; and

(b) the risks to the health and safety of persons not in his employment arising out of or in connection with the conduct by him of his undertaking ... '

Because of the importance of risk assessment in undertakings the Health and Safety Executive produced a guidance, *Five Steps to Risk Assessment* which contains information on good practices which while not compulsory are of help to management in understanding what is required and how to set about undertaking risk assessments. The leaflet contains a blank risk assessment form that can be adopted by most businesses and industries, focusing on types of hazards, who might be harmed, is the risk adequately controlled and what further action is necessary to control the risks. The success of the guidance gave rise to an updated version produced in 1999 with the same title which retains the same message, setting the basis for employers and self employed to assess the risks in the workplace with the aim of ensuring that there are sufficient precautions taken to make sure that no-one gets hurt. It explains that accidents and ill health can affect a business, through lost output, machinery damage, increased insurance costs or court action. *The Management of Health and Safety at Work Regulations 1999 (SI 1999/ 3242)* states that there is a legal requirement to assess risks in the workplace. The fact that risk assessment is enshrined in law means that risks have to be assessed and controlled. Failures that cause deaths at work could show a management failure to heed advise and adopt safe practices. This in turn would be an evidential factor in potential corporate killing prosecutions.

Employers have to identify the capabilities and competencies of its staff and provide training where necessary with the emphasis on health and safety. This can be achieved by providing adequate health and safety training when staff are recruited and when they are exposed to new or increased risks.

Organisations differ in size, location, type and management structure, and they will involve a range of hazards from very low to very high, providing a wide range of risks that have to be managed. It follows that the law pertaining to health and safety can also be complex and may not be readily understood by management, they may consider that their role is much wider than health and safety law. The senior management of many undertakings will argue that it is not financially viable to employ a competent health and safety professional. However, that does not preclude utilising the services of a health and safety consultant, providing that person is competent as a corporate member of the Institution of Safety and Health (IOSH) and most importantly, is a Registered Safety Practitioner with IOSH, where competence can be verified.

Employees also have duties when at work and that means that every employee has to use any machinery or equipment in accordance with any training in the use of the equipment. The employee is required to inform his employer or any other employee if there is any work situation where it is considered that there could be a serious and immediate danger to health and safety. Having done all of this the employer has to investigate the situation and act appropriately, as it is the employer who has the ultimate responsibility for health and safety in the undertaking.

HS(G) 65: Safety management system

10.23 In order that directors, senior management as well as those involved in health and safety management within a corporation have information available to them, a practical guide: *Successful Health and Safety Management HS(G) 65* has been produced by the HSE. The key elements of this guidance apply to any organisation, from multinationals to small enterprises, and comprise, policy, organisation, planning, and measurement of performance, auditing and reviewing performance and are outlined in figure 10.2.

By adopting this system the directors and management have to establish a corporate policy with regard to health and safety, so as to ensure that all employees are motivated and involved in the organisations vision, values and beliefs. This means that senior management has to provide leadership in the development of a positive health and safety culture.

Planning is an important part of an organisations system as it is aimed at identifying hazards and minimising or removing risks. This has placed the onus on the management of an organisation that creates the risk, to control the risks and this is undertaken by risk assessments. The objective is to develop safe methods and procedures for working as part of a corporate health and safety culture.

The management having undertaken the risk evaluation and mitigation process need to ensure that what has been adopted is effective. This is achieved by the measuring of performance, which will identify strengths and weaknesses within the system. By analysis of the information, management can maintain effective control of the corporation's activities in respect to safety and health.

Management can monitor progress of the corporate safety system, through feedback from all levels of the work force, either through union officials, safety representatives or others appointed as spokespersons, and if necessary, individuals who raise specific concerns. While this can be effective in theory, what happens in

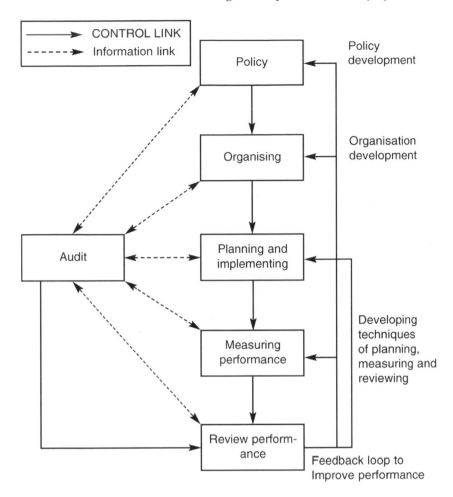

Figure 10.2: Successful health and safety management HS(G) 65 model

practice may provide a different story and therefore the system needs to be audited, preferably by an independent source, who can identify positive and negative outcomes. There should be access to every level of the corporation's work force, including the chief executive or managing director, so that the safety management system is seen to be transparent within the organisation, and part of its culture.

The HS(G) 65 model provides a sound basis for the management of safety and can be used to evaluate failures in an undertakings activities. The example chosen is that of the sinking of the *Herald of*

Free Enterprise. The incident has been examined in some detail earlier (SEE 2.12) and is a prime example of a management failure that led to a major disaster. The key elements of HS(G) 65 can be used to highlight some of the failures within premises/place, procedures, people, planning, risk assessment, communication, control, competence, monitoring and audit. The example given in figure 10.3 is not a complete review of the case, but provides easily identifiable evidence of senior management's failings. There was lack of knowledge of what was occurring within the organisation, and more damming, was where it was known what was being done, condoned the activities. The example used proactively by an undertaking can readily identify failings within the system, individuals and those in control.

British Standards Institution

10.24 An alternative, which corporations have adopted, is the *British Standards Institution Guide to Occupational Health and Safety Management Systems – BS: 8800: 1996* is designed to base health and safety management on the BS EN ISO 1400, the environmental systems standard to identify common areas in the overall management system. The *BS EN ISO 140001 Occupational Health and Safety Management System* comprises a number of key elements (SEE FIGURE 10.4). The focus of the adoption of the elements depends upon the size of the organisation and type of activities that are undertaken. This is based upon the hazards that are created or encountered by the corporation for those employed and those not employed, but who could be affected by those hazards.

Companies adopting the BS EN ISO 140001 approach for their safety management system will require the management to review the companies current status in respect to health and safety. This initial review should determine the scope and adequacy of any system in place and identify a base line on which to develop an effective system, with a method of measuring progress.

The development of the occupational health and safety policy requires the organisation's senior management to define, record and endorse the policy. The policy should quantify the management's commitment as being an important part of the company's culture. This places the burden with the senior management, which should be endorsed by the chief executive or managing director.

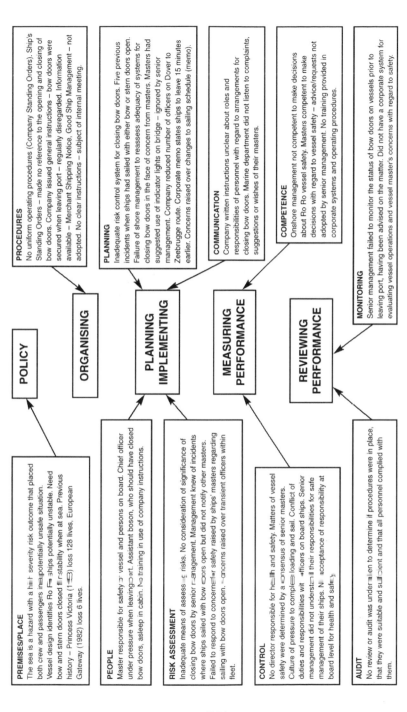

PREMISES/PLACE

The sea is a hazard with a high severity risk outcome that placed both crew and passengers in a potentially unsafe situation. Vessel design identifies Ro Ro ships potentially unstable. Need bow and stern doors closed for stability when at sea. Previous history – Princess Victoria (1953) loss 128 lives, European Gateway (1982) loss 6 lives.

PROCEDURES

No uniform operating procedures (Company Standing Orders). Ship's Standing Orders – made no reference to the opening and closing of bow doors. Company issued general instructions – bow doors were secured when leaving port – regularly disregarded. Information available – Merchant Shipping Notice, Good Ship Management – not adopted. No clear instructions – subject of internal meeting.

PLANNING

Inadequate risk control system for closing bow doors. Five previous incidents when ships had sailed with either bow or stern doors open. Failure of shore management to reassess adequacy of systems for closing bow doors in the face of concern from masters. Masters had suggested use of indicator lights on bridge – ignored by senior management. Company reduced number of officers on Dover to Zeebrugge route. Corporate memo states ships to leave 15 minutes earlier. Concerns raised over changes to sailing schedule (memo).

COMMUNICATION

Company written instructions unclear about roles and responsibilities of personnel with regard to arrangements for closing bow doors. Marine department did not listen to complaints, suggestions or wishes of their masters.

COMPETENCE

Onshore management not competent to make decisions about Ro Ro vessel safety. Masters competent to make decisions with regard to vessel safety – advice/requests not adopted by senior management. No training provided in corporate systems and operating procedures.

MONITORING

Senior management failed to monitor the status of bow doors on vessels prior to leaving port, having been advised on the matter. Did not have a corporate system for evaluating vessel operations and vessel master's concerns with regard to safety.

POLICY

ORGANISING

PLANNING IMPLEMENTING

MEASURING PERFORMANCE

REVIEWING PERFORMANCE

PEOPLE

Master responsible for safety of vessel and persons on board. Chief officer under pressure when leaving port. Assistant boson, who should have closed bow doors, asleep in cabin. No training in use of company instructions.

RISK ASSESSMENT

Inadequate means of assessing risks. No consideration of significance of closing bow doors by senior management. Management knew of incidents where ships sailed with bow doors open but did not notify other masters. Failed to respond to concerns for safety raised by ships' masters regarding sailing with bow doors open. Concerns raised over transient officers within fleet.

CONTROL

No director responsible for health and safety. Matters of vessel safety were determined by a consensus of senior masters. Culture of pressure to complete loading and sail. Conflict of duties and responsibilities with officers on board ships. Senior management did not understand their responsibilities for safe management of their ships. No acceptance of responsibility at board level for health and safety.

AUDIT

No review or audit was undertaken to determine if procedures were in place, that they were suitable and sufficient and that all personnel complied with them.

Figure 10.3: Linking corporate and systems failures with the HS (G) model

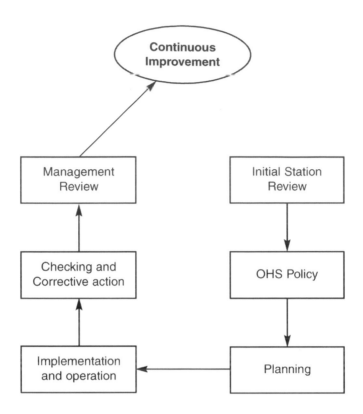

Figure 10.4: BSI Safety Management System

Planning is identified as being a critical part of company policy and this includes health and safety requirements. To achieve this, management should set the performance standards, identify who is responsible and monitor progress.

The responsibility for health and safety lies with senior management, at boardroom level. Therefore, the implementation of an occupational health and safety management system should be allocated to a board member, who has the authority to ensure its effectiveness within the company. To ensure that the occupational health and safety management system is effective, the performance outcomes need to be measured. This requires the system to be checked and supported by an effective method of introducing corrective action.

Senior management can introduce a management system, but they must ensure that the criteria they have set down in the policy and any subsequent changes made to that policy is being followed. This requires a senior management review of the policy, its effectiveness throughout the organisation and implementing any changes for continual improvement.

The proposed new law of corporate killing encompasses undertakings such as schools, hospitals, trusts, partnerships, and the self employed as well as incorporated and unincorporated organisations. There is a need for senior management however titled to understand the changes that there will be if the new offences of corporate killing and the individual offences are bought in. The implications for senior management with corporate killing are far reaching because instead of the manslaughter element, it is now a case of management failure and, it will be the degree of that failure that will determine the corporate and individual charges that could be laid.

Senior management at boardroom, or its equivalent in an undertaking will need to focus on its responsibilities. This clearly places the ownership of health and safety at the highest level of management in every organisation. It is therefore, imperative that health and safety is adopted as an integral part of day-to-day activities and culture. This means that management will need to show that they take suitable and sufficient steps, to manage health and safety in the same way that they manage other aspects of the business. This is the situation no matter what the size of an undertaking and it is a matter for those who create the risks to manage the risks. While having management systems in place is no guarantee that criminal sanctions will not be imposed, a court will take the level of positive health and safety management into consideration.

The evidence is clear, the number of manslaughter at work cases that have progressed through the courts have been few. There is strong evidence to indicate that there will be a substantial increase in the number of prosecutions, for both the corporate killing and individual offences if the draft *Involuntary Manslaughter Bill* comes into force.

Appendix

The draft Involuntary Homicide Bill

Create new offences of reckless killing, killing by gross carelessness and corporate killing to replace the offence of manslaughter in cases where death is caused without the intention of causing death or serious injury.

1 Reckless Killing

(1) A person who by his conduct causes the death of another is guilty of reckless killing if –

    (a) he is aware of a risk that his conduct will cause death or serious injury; and

    (b) it is unreasonable for him to take that risk having regard to the circumstances as he knows or believes them to be.

(2) A person guilty of reckless killing is liable on conviction on indictment to imprisonment for life.

2 Killing by gross carelessness

(1) A person who by his conduct causes the death of another is guilty of killing by gross carelessness if –

    (a) a risk that his conduct will cause death or serious injury would be obvious to a reasonable person in his position;

    (b) he is capable of appreciating that risk at the material time; and

    (c) either –

        (i) his conduct falls far below what can reasonably be expected of him in the circumstances; or

        (ii) he intends by his conduct to cause some injury or is aware of, and unreasonably takes, the risk that it may do so.

(2) There shall be attributed to the person referred to in subsection (1)(a) above –

(a) knowledge of any relevant facts which the accused is shown to have at the material time; and

(b) any skill or experience professed by him.

(3) In determining for the purpose of subsection (1)(c)(i) above what can reasonably be expected of the accused regard shall be had to the circumstances of which he can be expected to be aware, to any circumstances shown to be within his knowledge and to any other matter relevant for assessing his conduct at the material time.

(4) Subsection (1)(c)(ii) above applied only if the conduct causing, or intended to cause, the injury constitutes an offence.

(5) A person guilty of killing by gross carelessness is liable on conviction on indictment to imprisonment for a term not exceeding 10 years.

3 Omissions causing death

A person is not guilty of an offence under sections 1 or 2 above by reason of an omission unless the omission is in breach of a duty at common law.

4 Corporate killing

(1) A corporation is guilty of corporate killing if –

(a) a management failure by the corporation is the cause or one of the causes of a person's death; and

(b) that failure constitutes conduct falling far below what can reasonably be expected of the corporation in the circumstances.

(2) For the purposes of subsection (1) above –

(a) there is a management failure by a corporation if the way in which its activities are managed or organised fails to ensure the health and safety of persons employed in or affected by those activities; and

(b) such a failure may be regarded as a cause of a person's death notwithstanding that the immediate cause is the act or omission of an individual.

(3) A corporation guilty of an offence under this section is liable on conviction on indictment to a fine.

(4) No individual shall be convicted of aiding, abetting, counselling or procuring an offence under this section but without prejudice to an individual being guilty of any other offence in respect of the death in question.

(5) This section does not preclude a corporation being guilty of an offence under section 1 or 2 above.

(6) This section applied if the injury resulting in death is sustained in England and Wales or –

    (a) within the seaward limits of the territorial sea adjacent to the United Kingdom;

    (b) on a British ship or vessel;

    (c) on a British-controlled aircraft as defined in section 92 of the Civil Aviation Act 1982; or

    (d) in any place to which an Order in Council under section 22(1) of the Oil and Gas (Enterprise) Act 1982 applies (criminal jurisdiction in relation to offshore activities).

(7) For the purposes of subsection (6)(b) and (c) above an injury sustained on a ship, vessel or aircraft shall be treated as including an injury sustained by a person who is then no longer on board, and who sustains the injury, in consequence of the wrecking of, or of some other mishap affecting, the ship, vessel or aircraft.

(8) In this section 'a corporation' does not include a corporation sole but includes any body corporate wherever incorporated.

5 Remdial orders against convicted corporation

(1) A court before which a corporation is convicted of corporate killing may, subject to subsection (2) below, order the corporation to take such steps, within such time, as the order specifies for remedying the failure in question and any matter which appears to the court to have resulted from the failure and been the cause or one of the causes of the death.

(2) No such order shall be made except on an application by the prosecution specifying the terms of the proposed order; and the order, if any, made by the court shall be on such terms

(whether those proposed or others) as the court considers appropriate having regard to any representations made, and any evidence adduced, in relation to that matter by the prosecution or on behalf of the corporation.

(3) In subsection (2) above references to the prosecution include references to the Health and Safety Executive and to any other body or person designated for the purposes of that subsection by the Secretary of State either generally or in relation to the case in question.

(4) The time specified by an order under subsection (1) above may be extended or further extended by order of the court on an application made before the end of that time or extended time, as the case may be.

(5) A corporation which fails to comply with an order under this section is guilty of an offence and liable –

   (a) on conviction on indictment, to a fine;

   (b) on summary conviction, to a fine not exceeding £20,000.

(6) Where an order is made against a corporation under this section it shall not be liable under any of the provisions mentioned in subsection (7) below by reason of anything which the order requires it to remedy in so far as it continues during the time specified by the order or any further time allowed under subsection (4) above.

(7) The provisions referred to in subsection (6) above are –

   (a) sections 1, 2 and 4 above;

   (b) the provisions of Part I of the Health and Safety at Work etc Act 1974;

   (c) the provision of any regulations made under section 53(1) of the Act.

   (d) the exiting statutory provisions as defined in section 53(1) of that Act.

6 Alternative verdicts

(1) On an indictment for murder a person found not guilty of murder may be found guilty of reckless killing or killing by gross carelessness.

(2) On an indictment for reckless killing a person found not guilty of that offence may be found guilty of killing by gross carelessness.

(3) On an indictment for reckless killing, killing by gross carelessness or corporate killing a person found not guilty of that offence may be found guilty of an offence under section 2 or 3 or the Health and Safety at Work etc Act 1974.

(4) Subsections (2) and (3) above are without prejudice to section 6(3) of the Criminal Law Act 1967 (alternative verdicts).

7 Abolition of involuntary manslaughter

The offence of manslaughter is abolished except for –

(a) the cases for which provision is made by sections 2(3) and 4 of the Homicide Act 1957 (cases which would be murder but for diminished responsibility or a suicide pact); and

(b) cases which would be murder but for provocation.

8 Supplementary provisions

(1) In this Act 'injury' means –

    (a) physical injury, including pain, unconsciousness or other impairment of a person's physical condition; or

    (b) impairment of a person's mental health.

(2) This Act has effect subject to any enactment or rule of law providing a defence, or providing lawful authority, justification or excuse for an act or omission.

(3) This Act has effect subject to the rules relating to the effect of intoxication on criminal liability.

9 Consequential amendments

The enactments mentioned in the Schedule to this Act are amended in accordance with that Schedule.

10 Commencement and saving

(1) This Act comes into force at the end of the period of two months beginning with the day on which it is passed.

(2)   This Act does not apply in relation to anything done or omitted before it comes into force.

11 Short title and extent

(1)   This Act may be cited as the Involuntary Homicide Act 1995.

(2)   The amendments in the Schedule to this Act have the same extent as the enactments to which they relate but, subject to that, this Act extends to England and Wales only.

Schedule.

Text not included.

Table of Cases

Table of Statutes

Bills

Table of Statutory Instruments

Index

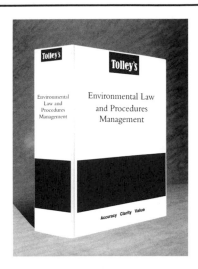